Daily Strength

Daily Strength

One Year of Experiencing the Psalms

Victor M. Parachin

Liguori
LIGUORI, MISSOURI

Published by Liguori Publications
Liguori, Missouri
http://www.liguori.org

ISBN 0-89243-677-8
Library of Congress Catalog Card Number: 94-73016

Printed in the United States of America
03 02 01 00 99 7 6 5 4 3

Psalm 149

Praise the LORD!

Sing a new song to the LORD;
praise him in the assembly of
his faithful people!

Be glad Israel,
because of your Creator;
rejoice, people of Zion,
because of your king!

Praise his name with dancing;
play drums and harps
in praise of him.

The LORD takes pleasure
in his people;
he honors the humble with victory.

Let God's people rejoice in their triumph
and sing joyfully all night long.

Let them shout aloud as they praise God,
with their sharp swords in their hands
to defeat the nations and to punish the peoples
to bind their kings in chains,
their leaders in chains of iron;
to punish the nations as God
has commanded.

This is the victory of God's people.

Praise the LORD!

INTRODUCTION

A mother and father became alarmed when their infant son, Aaron, stopped gaining weight. Their concern was greatly heightened when his hair began to fall out. Desperately, they sought medical help. After seeing a succession of prominent physicians, they were informed that their son had an extremely rare illness called progeria, or rapid aging. The father and mother were told that Aaron would never grow much beyond three feet in height, would have no hair on his head or body, and would look like an old man while still a child. His life expectancy was limited to the early teenage years.

In fact, Aaron died two days after his fourteenth birthday. Based on that devastating experience, Aaron's father, Rabbi Harold Kushner, wrote a best-selling book, *When Bad Things Happen to Good People.* Rabbi Kushner says that since his son's death in 1977, he has not known a day in which he did not think about Aaron and feel his absence powerfully. Yet Rabbi Kushner adds that faith in God has "given me the strength to bear his loss without being broken by it, to remember but to be able to enjoy life."

In the midst of facing the troubles, trials, and tragedies of life's chances and challenges, men and women throughout the ages have turned to the Psalms for comfort, guidance, and daily strength.

The purpose of this book is to give you, the reader, an opportunity to experience the Psalms in your daily life for an entire year. Day by day, you will find information and inspiration based on a text from the Psalms. I hope that each reader will find this book of meditations from the Psalms a powerful source of daily strength.

VICTOR M. PARACHIN, M. DIV.

This is the day that the LORD has made;
let us rejoice and be glad in it.
Psalm 118:24
(New Revised Standard Version)

Celebrating Life

In 1979 a man was booked on a flight from Chicago to Los Angeles, where he was scheduled to deliver a speech. Delayed by last-minute business details, he raced to Chicago's O'Hare International Airport. As he ran through the terminal toward the departure, the man was dismayed to see the gate agent locking the door and the mobile ramp being pulled away from the plane. In desperation, he begged, pleaded, and argued with the gate agent, hoping to persuade her to stop the plane. His plane taxied away without him despite his protests.

The man stormed away from the gate area and went back to the ticket counter to register a formal complaint. As he stood in line at the counter twenty minutes later, he heard the devastating news that the plane had crashed on takeoff. An engine had broken loose and had fallen back onto the runway. The hydraulic lines and control cables had been severed, and there was nothing the pilots could do to control the aircraft. There were no survivors.

The man who missed the flight was best-selling author and popular motivational speaker Denis Waitley. Upon hearing of the plane crash, Waitley left the ticket line, booked a room at a hotel, and knelt beside his bed in prayer. Waitley still has his unvalidated ticket for Flight 191. It is tacked on the bulletin board in his home office as a reminder that just being alive is a fabulous gift.

As a new year begins, let today's text be a reminder that each day is a gift from God. It must be used wisely, approached with joy, and celebrated in the heart.

Thought for the Day

I laugh and shout for life is good,
though my feet are set in silent ways.
Helen Keller

So they are punished by their own evil
and are hurt by their own violence.
Psalm 7:16

How to Have a Happy New Year

Some people are their own worst enemies. They are the source of their own misery because they

- talk about themselves constantly
- demand to be appreciated
- are jealous and envious of others
- insist on being number one
- expect agreement with their views
- never forgive or forget a hurt
- do as little as possible for others
- see themselves as the center of the universe

As a new year dawns, let us resolve to be the people of God as described in Isaiah 57:15—"humble and repentant"—and in the apostle Paul's Letter to the Colossians: "You are the people of God…clothe yourselves with compassion, kindness, humility, gentleness, and patience" (3:12). Being the people of God means

- being the host, not the guest, in life
- seeking to comfort rather than be comforted
- seeing Christ in every person we meet
- living rather than demanding

The way to ensure a happy new year all year long is to act on the teaching of Jesus: "Whoever wants to be first must place himself last of all and be the servant of all" (Mark 9:35).

Thought for the Day

Dost thou wish to enjoy the first rank?
First concede that place to another.
Saint John Chrysostom

How wonderful it is, how pleasant,
for God's people to live together in harmony!
Psalm 133:1

The Golden Rule Around the World

The start of a new year is an ideal time to make a deeper commitment to live by the golden rule. Here are various ways the golden rule is expressed by people of faith around the world.

Christianity: Do for others what you want them to do for you (Matthew 7:12).

Judaism: What is hateful to you, do not do your fellow men. That is the entire Law; all the rest is commentary (*Talmud*, Shabbat, 31a).

Brahmanism: This is the sum of duty: Do not unto others which would cause you pain if done to you (*Mahabharata*, 5, 1517).

Buddhism: Hurt not others in ways that you yourself would find hurtful (*Udana-Varga*, 5, 18).

Confucianism: Surely it is the maxim of loving kindness: Do not unto others that you would not have them do unto you (*Analects*, 15, 23).

Taoism: Regard your neighbor's gain as your own gain, and your neighbor's loss as your own loss (*Tai Shang Kan Ying Pien*).

Zoroastrianism: That nature alone is god which refrains from doing unto another whatsoever is not good for itself (*Dadistan-i-dinik*, 94, 5).

Islam: No one of your is a believer until he desire for his brother that which he desires for himself (*Sunnah*).

-------- *Prayer for the Day* --------

Loving God,
If there is to be love in the world,
it must start with me;
if there is to be harmony in the world,
it must start with me;
if there is to be peace in the world,
it must start with me.
Let me be filled with your love,
your harmony, your peace.
VMP

He knows what we are made of;
he remembers that we are dust.
Psalm 103:14

God Knows How Much We Can Handle

Anyone who has ever done cleaning knows that dust must be handled carefully, even delicately. If not, it easily breaks up and scatters. In this text, the writer reminds us that God relates to people gently and tenderly. God handles us delicately. He knows that we are soft, fragile, vulnerable, easily broken, much like a dust ball.

Consider Sherri, who was devastated by the death of her seventeen-year-old daughter. Her daughter was born with Down syndrome and never left home. She brought Sherri great joy, and the two were very close. After the girl's death, Sherri could not come to terms with the loss and was on the verge of a complete physical and emotional breakdown.

Although Sherri did not receive instant relief, many kind, compassionate people entered her life, people who listened tenderly and loved unconditionally. Today Sherri says, "I do not have a doubt in my mind that God saved me through these people. Had he not sent them along I would have spent the rest of my life in a mental hospital."

When we are discouraged and feeling deeply the pressures of life, we must remind ourselves that God knows how much we can handle. Our creator "knows what we are made of" and "remembers that we are dust." Always remember, with God behind you, you can face whatever is ahead of you.

Thought for the Day

The heart is a small vessel,
but all things are contained in it; God is there,
the angels are there, and there is also life and the Kingdom,
the heavenly cities and the treasures of grace.

Saint Makarios

Evil men testify against me
and accuse me of crimes I know nothing about.
Psalm 35:11

The Cost of Commitment

With the collapse of the Berlin Wall and the Iron Curtain, people of Eastern Europe are experiencing greater religious freedom. Recently, Pope John Paul II ordained the following bishops for Albania:

- Franco Illia, seventy-four, who spent twenty years in prison, accused of being a Vatican spy
- Robert Ashta, seventy-four, who was forced to give up ministry as a priest and made to work for eleven years as a construction laborer
- Zef Simoni, sixty-four, who spent twelve years in jail

Clearly, commitment can be costly. Whenever we read of persecuted Christians, we should first thank God for the religious freedom that we enjoy. Then we ought to do a quick inventory of our own Christian lives, asking, "Does my faith cost me anything?" If the answer is "No," we should engage in an examination of conscience. If keeping the faith is too easy, it can mean we are not acting on it in any deep and profound manner. Here are some ways to examine your conscience:

- Is God the most important person in my life?
- Am I faithful in my public witness to that relationship?
- Do I put my faith into practice daily?
- Do I remain silent in the face of injustice?
- Am I working at creating a kinder, gentler world?

While no Christian should deliberately seek out persecution, the presence of opposition is often the sign that something is right and not wrong about our faith. The psalmist reminds us that people who live by their faith convictions have always experienced resistance and persecution. As we begin the new year, let us resolve to live a life for God that makes a difference. Let us remember to trust God for the strength to deal with whatever may come as a result of that commitment.

Thought for the Day

Nothing is more to be feared than too long a peace. You are deceived if you think that Christians can live without persecution.

Saint Jerome

I believe I shall see the goodness of the LORD.
Psalm 27:13
(New Revised Standard Version)

Leaning Our Whole Weight on God

During the nineteenth century, John Paton, a Presbyterian, was sent as a missionary to Vanuatu, a island group in the Southern Pacific under joint British and French administration. Since the people there had no Bible in their language, Paton began to translate Scripture. During the course of his work, he discovered there was no national equivalent for the word *believe*. For days he researched and struggled to find a term or phrase to convey the word *believe*.

A solution presented itself one day when a national came into his office worn out from a hard day's physical labor. The man flung himself on a chair, stretched out, and rested his legs on another chair. Lying full-length on two chairs, the man told Paton it felt good to lean his whole weight on those chairs. When Paton heard the man say "lean my whole weight on," he knew he had discovered the right term for the English word *believe*.

There is great truth in that lesson. To believe in God is to lean our whole weight upon him. It means trusting confidently and completely that God will come through for us. As a spiritual exercise this week, try John Paton's discovery for yourself. Find a verse of Scripture that contains the word *believe*. Then substitute "lean your whole weight on God." One example is Mark 5:36: "Don't be afraid, only [lean your whole weight on God.]"

Thought for the Day

The only way to make rapid progress
on the path of divine love
is to remain very little
and to put all our trust in Almighty God.
This is what I have done.
Saint Thérèse of Lisieux

"Give thanks to the LORD,
because he is good;
his love is eternal!"
Psalm 107:1

You Can't Outgive God

Sister Antonia Brenner is a remarkable nun with a unique ministry. She lives voluntarily with inmates at La Mesa Penitentiary in Tijuana, Mexico. She shares the following experience to illustrate that we can't outgive God:

Sister Brenner was exhausted at the end of a long, hard day, when a woman who had just visited her husband in prison stopped to see her. "I was tired and had only fifteen dollars. I thought to myself, *Here goes my money*," she recalls.

Of course, the woman needed money. She explained to Sister Brenner that because her husband was in prison, she had nothing to feed her children and no money with which to buy groceries. Sister Brenner handed her ten dollars. "Just then, my Lord spoke clearly to me," she says. "Is this the way to give away what's mine?"

"I'm sorry, Lord," she said and called the woman back. Asking more questions about the woman's family circumstances, Sister Brenner gave her the remaining five dollars and sincerely invited her to come back if she ever needed help again.

Returning to her room in the prison, Sister Brenner felt resentful that she gave away her last fifteen dollars. As she was about to enter her room, someone told her that a man was there to see her. When she walked up to the man, he said, "I just wanted to say hello and give you a hug." As he embraced Sister Brenner, he put something in her hand. It was a hundred-dollar bill. Immediately, her resentment toward God gave way, first to humility and then to a deep and profound appreciation.

As the new year emerges, let us remember to be generous with those who are less fortunate, keeping in mind that we can't outgive God.

Thought for the Day

A generous action has its own reward.

William Walsh

The LORD is with me, I will not be afraid.
Psalm 118:6

How to Cope With Fear

As I sat at my computer writing, I could see three tree cutters removing a large old oak tree on my neighbor's property. I was impressed with the way the three men removed that large tree in less than an hour.

First, a man climbed the tree and began to cut off all the branches. When only the shaft of the tree remained, he cut it down in four-foot sections. Then he cut the trunk off close to the ground. Finally, the remaining stump was pulverized. A casual passerby would never know that a large tree had stood there an hour earlier.

God helps us cope with and eliminate fear in the same way the tree cutters removed that tree. We begin by snipping away the small fears first. Then we can attack the larger ones by removing them in sections, step by step.

As we go after our fears, we need to remind ourselves of God's presence in our lives. It can help to repeat the psalmist's declaration: "The Lord is with me, I will not be afraid." God is ready to strengthen us and guide us in controlling and eliminating our fears.

Thought for the Day

I have learned more from having recourse
to divine grace than from the telescope.

Galileo

They grow stronger as they go.
Psalm 84:7

Getting Stronger Day by Day

One of the most common themes running throughout the Psalms is strength. The writers declare that God provides strength for the tasks and trials of life. Today's text is a profound one, reminding Christians that we can go through life from strength to strength, not merely watching our energies and creativities depleted with the years.

A good example is John Wesley, an Anglican priest who established Methodism in the eighteenth century. During his lifetime, Wesley preached forty-two thousand sermons. On average, he preached three sermons per day. Riding horseback, he averaged forty-five hundred miles each year, often riding up to sixty and seventy miles a day. In addition, he wrote and edited scores of books and booklets.

When he was eighty-three, John Wesley wrote in his diary, "I am a wonder to myself. I am never tired, either with preaching, writing, or traveling."

Closeness to God is a source of spiritual and physical strength. So whenever we feel worn out by life's burdens, let us recall the words of today's psalm: "They grow stronger as they go." And let us turn to God for renewal of the body and the spirit.

Thought for the Day

My secret is quite simple: I pray.
Mother Teresa of Calcutta

Give thanks to the LORD,
proclaim his greatness.
Psalm 105:1

Thanksgiving Is a State of Mind

One of the most profound lessons in thanksgiving comes through a young handicapped child who told her pastor, "When I can't sleep, I play with the stars." Although young, her life was filled with pain and trauma. At her birth, a host of physical abnormalities were discovered. One of those was a severe curvature of the spine.

As a result, she lived in a Phelp's box, a device that resembled a shallow coffin. Earlier in this century, children with a curvature of the spine were placed into a Phelp's box and strapped in as flat as possible. The only part of the body that could be moved was the head. It was not only physically confining but extremely painful as well.

When the pastor visited the little girl, he commented how nice it was that her box was by the window. She replied, "In this position, I can only look up. On those nights when I can't sleep, I play with the stars." Intrigued with the child's game, the pastor asked, "How can you play with the stars?"

Her reply reveals a depth of wisdom far beyond her young age and an insight that would be rare even in an adult: "I pick out the brightest star I can find and I say, 'That's Mommy. And I thank God.' I pick out another bright one and say, 'That's Daddy. And I thank God.' I find a twinkling one for my brother, my puppy, my wheelchair. And I thank God."

For a few moments the child continued on and on. Nothing seemed forgotten or overlooked. Finally, she concluded with this simple and profound observation: "But there aren't enough stars to go around!"

When it comes to thanksgiving, people divide themselves into two groups. There are those who count the stars and those who don't. Today the psalm writer reminds us that thanksgiving is not merely a holiday or the one time each year when people count their blessings; it is a state of mind. Today we are challenged to be the people who maintain the attitude of gratitude daily.

Thought for the Day

Cultivate the thankful spirit.
It will be to you a perpetual feast.
John R. MacDuff

My soul will feast and be satisfied.
Psalm 63:5

See What Remains, Not What Is Gone

Some people deprive themselves of satisfaction and joy because they focus on only what they have lost or never had. The issue of their lives is one of perspective: they see a cup half empty and not half full.

Yet consider a man who has had more than his share of suffering. He married a charming, intelligent woman and they became the proud parents of a tall son and a beautiful daughter.

When the man's wife was in her thirties, she was stricken with multiple sclerosis and spent the remainder of her life in a wheelchair. It was a difficult situation, but they made the most of it. No one ever heard them complain.

The man was with his wife when she could no longer battle her disease. Shortly after his wife's death, his son died from a sudden heart attack at age forty-six. Two years later, the man attended his daughter's funeral. She died from a stroke at forty-four.

All those losses caused the man to suffer, weep, and grieve deeply. Yet he never gave up on life. Now he is very old and spends his days and nights in a nursing-home bed. One source of his great joy comes through his grandsons, who visit him regularly. For all the older man has lost, he takes delight in what he still has: grandchildren and many warm, wonderful memories.

For our "soul to feast and be satisfied," we need to focus more on what is left and less on what is gone.

Thought for the Day

Birds sing after a storm;
why shouldn't people feel as free
to delight in whatever remains to them?
Rose Kennedy

I praise you, for I am fearfully and wonderfully made.
Psalm 139:14
(New Revised Standard Version)

Created With Great Potential

God has created us greater and stronger and more creative than we often believe ourselves to be. Inherent within us is the ability to expand our physical, spiritual, and mental boundaries. Consider the following barnyard facts:

A hundred years ago, a cow was viewed as outstanding if she produced six hundred pounds of milk in one year. Yet in 1972 one cow produced over forty-four thousand pounds of milk in one year—more than seventy times the national average of one hundred years earlier.

Another example is the farmer's hen. Whereas wild birds lay a mere six eggs per year, hens have been cultivated to lay as many as three hundred sixty-five eggs—one hen can lay one egg each day of the year.

Just as animals have a natural capacity to expand, so do human beings. Just when we feel we have no more strength to get through another day, the strength we need emerges.

Just when we believe that we have no more energy to deal with the pain and disappointments of life, more energy flows from us. Just when we feel most indecisive and uncertain, greater decision-making powers and certainty of purpose arise within us.

When we feel discouraged about some aspect of our lives let us remember that we have been "fearfully and wonderfully made."

-------- *Thought for the Day* --------

Almighty God has crowded miracles into you.
Why not let them come forth and live?
Dr. Norman Vincent Peale

You crowned him with glory and honor.
Psalm 8:5

The Person We See Is the Person We Will Be

A legend tells of a prince who suffered from a spinal problem; he could only walk with his back arched and his face looking down. This caused him great physical pain and emotional despair.

Finally, he went to a great sculptor and asked him to carve a statue that would portray him without a spinal deformity. Working rapidly, the sculptor soon created a magnificent likeness of the prince tall and straight.

"Shall I place it in front of the palace gate for all to see?" asked the sculptor.

"No," answered the prince. "I want it placed in my private garden, where only I can see it."

Once the statue was in place, the prince spent part of each day observing it, dreaming of the man he might have been if his back were straight. As time passed, people in his kingdom noticed a change in the prince. He was standing a little taller and straighter. A physical change was definitely taking place. As the prince visualized himself with a straight back, he began to rise up to the image in his mind.

Today's psalm declares that we occupy an important and unique place in God's creation, a position of "glory and honor." This is an especially important psalm for those suffering from low self-image and low self-esteem. Such negative perceptions can be minimized and reduced when we see ourselves the way God does. In the eyes of our Creator, we are worthy of honor, respect, and love. To shed feelings of inferiority, we need to hold that mental picture before us. Then, like the legendary prince, we will grow into the image. The person we see is the person we will be.

Thought for the Day

Numberless are the world's wonders,
but none more wonderful than man.
Sophocles

Happy are those who are concerned for the poor.
Psalm 41:1

The Joy of Helping Others

In her mid thirties, Kim Foley is a makeup artist who leads an exciting and glamorous life working with film and television stars. Although she had a fulfilling career and was happily married with two bright, healthy children, Kim felt a void in her life.

All that changed when her children's pediatrician suggested that Kim volunteer her skills to help children with facial disfigurements. As a makeup artist, she had created all sorts of grotesque wounds for the film industry. Why not use the same skills to cover up real scars?

With that seed planted, the pediatrician directed Kim to a nearby children's hospital. The first child she visited was a burn victim who shrank away from Kim because his face was so severely scarred. He was embarrassed because he thought he looked like a monster. Gaining the child's confidence, Kim coaxed the boy to allowed her to exercise her skills on his face.

"When I finished, he was so excited, he jumped around the clinic laughing," Kim says. "I've been doing reconstructive cosmetics ever since."

And the void she felt has been filled with the joy of helping others.

Kim is a living example of the ancient writer's observation: "Happy are those who are concerned for the poor." In this new year, let us evaluate our talents and time. Then let us consider using them to help others. It will bring us joy.

Thought for the Day

If someone comes to you asking for help,
do not say in refusal, "Trust in God. God will help."
Rather, act as if there were no god,
and no one to help except you.
Hasidic Teaching

I waited patiently for the LORD's help;
then he listened to me and heard my cry.
Psalm 40:1

Every Life Is Filled With Sunrises and Sunsets

We need to remind ourselves of two realities:

- *Life provides us with minimal protection.* Bad things do happen to good people. Tragedy can strike with random force. The road is not always smooth and easy. The skies above are not always bright and blue. There are times when living is a steep, upward climb.
- *God provides us with maximum support.* In all of the trials and traumas of life, God is present to provide help and hope, strength and support, love and loyalty.

During difficult times, we need to reclaim the witness of Scripture and the promises of God that darkness gives way to light, despair to hope, sadness to joy, and ultimately, death gives way to life.

Today the psalmist also reminds us to exercise patience in the face of suffering. No crisis is permanent. God can and will transform hurt into healing and pain into peace.

Thought for the Day

When our days become dreary with low-hovering clouds
and our nights become darker than a thousand midnights,
let us remember that there is a great benign power in the universe
whose name is God and who is able to make a way
out of no way, and transform dark yesterdays
into bright tomorrows.

Dr. Martin Luther King, Jr.

LORD, place a guard at my mouth,
a sentry at the door of my lips.
Psalm 141:3

Using Wise Words

Today let us consider the fact that our words can heal or hurt, injure or inspire, bring peace or pain. Here are five important sentences that we would do well to include in our conversations daily. Their frequent use will ensure that our words are helpful, not hurtful, in our relationships.

I love you. People around us need to know they are loved and valued.

I thank you. Let us express appreciation for the many kindnesses and services we receive daily.

I am sorry. Whenever our words or actions cause confusion or hurt, let us quickly acknowledge the wrong and make an apology.

I forgive you. Likewise, when someone wrongs us and extends an apology, we must be quick to forgive. No one is perfect.

I understand you. Conveying this shows we have made an effort to walk in the shoes of another person. Trying to see events from another person's perspective will keep us from making harsh, hasty judgments about them.

Thought for the Day

Speech is a mirror of the soul:
as a man speaks, so is he.
Publilius Syrus

Tears may flow in the night,
but joy comes in the morning.
Psalm 30:5

Growth From Suffering

Paul Tournier, a prominent Swiss psychologist and Christian author, grew up an orphan. His father died when he was an infant, his mother when he was six. As a result, Tournier and his sister grew up without the security and stability of a loving mother and father. The home life that many of us sometimes take for granted was never a part of Tournier's childhood.

Yet he writes with great insight and deep compassion about the struggles common to all people. His books convey a profound understanding about issues of love and acceptance, loneliness and despair.

Tournier's life is one example of the truth that good can come from our personal tragedies. When we face struggle and suffering, trauma and trial, let us take comfort in the fact that positive effects can result from them. In times of distress, we must remind ourselves that God can do wonders with the pieces of a broken heart if given all the pieces. That is the meaning of the words: "Tears may flow in the night, but joy comes in the morning." In the New Testament, Paul expressed the same thought this way: "We know that in all things God works for good... (Romans 8:28).

Thought for the Day

Tears are the showers that fertilize the world.
Owen Meredith

I will always thank the L*ORD;*
I will never stop praising him.
Psalm 34:1

Making an Attitude Adjustment

There are two types of people in our world. One group fills their thoughts and conversations with D-words. They think and talk constantly about discouragement, difficulty, disease, disaster, decay, disorder, danger, defeat, discord, dread, destitution, desolation, distress, disappointment, disarray, and disapproval. This group finds no reason for celebrating life.

The other group fills their thoughts and conversations with P-words. They think and talk constantly about prosperity, power, progress, promotion, persistence, purpose, potential, production, proficiency, perseverance, patience, and prayer. This group finds life filled with unlimited possibilities and, therefore, many reasons to celebrate.

The writer of today's verse from Psalm 34 is definitely a "P" person: "I will always thank the Lord; I will never stop praising him."

Today let us consider which group we resemble and identify with more closely. If we discover that we are more like the "D" people, then today is a good day to make an attitude adjustment. Let us ask God to help us see and enjoy more of life's possibilities.

Thought for the Day

People see only what they are prepared to see.
Ralph Waldo Emerson

Listen to me, LORD, and answer me,
for I am helpless and weak.
Psalm 86:1

Bringing Our Distress to God

"Is anybody listening? Is anybody listening? Please somebody help me!" came the plea via an airplane radio. The cry was from a desperate woman whose pilot-husband had died suddenly of a heart attack while at the controls of their tiny aircraft.

Although the woman had flown often with her husband, she knew nothing about piloting the aircraft. By her own admission, she had never even closed the door of the tiny plane before. Now she was thirty-five hundred feet above the ground, soaring through the air with no idea how to keep the plane aloft or, even more importantly, how to bring it down for a landing.

Her first thought was to press the button on the plane microphone and pray that someone would pick up her desperate message: "Is anybody listening? Is anybody listening?"

Fortunately, and perhaps miraculously, someone was listening. A seasoned pilot heard her and calmly guided her step by step to a perfect landing.

In today's psalm, the writer expresses a similar desperation. It is always appropriate to bring our cares to God. We must remember that our distress is a forcible reason for being heard by God who is merciful, compassionate, and loving.

Thought for the Day

Usually prayer is a question of
groaning rather than speaking,
tears rather than words.
For He sets our tears in His sight,
and our groaning is not hidden from Him
who made all things by His word.
Saint Augustine

God gives great victories....
Psalm 18:50

Some Important "Why Nots?"

The Bible clearly and consistently reminds us that God is on our side in the battles of life. Today's Psalm simply and straightforwardly declares that "God gives great victories."

When facing a difficult and perhaps despairing challenge, ask yourself these important "why nots?"

- Why not ask God to strengthen me for the task?
- Why not invite God to help me turn an obstacle into and an opportunity?
- Why not petition God to transform adversity into advantage?
- Why not implore God to help me turn my pain into a vehicle for understanding and helping others?
- Why not beg God to empower me to change a tragedy into a glorious triumph?
- Why not ask God to help me forget what was and move on to what can be?

There are times when we will not know why certain things happen to us. The key is to cease dwelling on the "whys?" and focus upon the "why nots?" When we do that, we will experience God's great victories in our lives.

.... *Thought for the Day* ....

Out of suffering have emerged the strongest of souls;
the most massive characters are seamed with scars.

Edwin Hubbel Chapin

Give me wisdom and knowledge....
Psalm 119:66

Responding, Not Reacting to Pain

Approaching fifty years of age, Mary has had more than her share of suffering: a serious automobile accident in college, seven miscarriages, a seizure disorder that has led to six concussions, a cracked spine that was corrected by spinal fusion.

For the last twelve years, Mary has lived with a debilitating, mysterious neuromuscular disease that impairs her ability to walk and induces nausea, fatigue, and skin rashes. The medical community has been unable to diagnose her condition. Yet far from becoming a bitter woman, Mary has committed herself to helping others.

Despite her physical limitations, she travels and speaks before groups, conveying a message of faith, hope, help, and love to others who are suffering. "I have learned how to live with conflict, pain, self-doubt, frustration, despair, and unanswered questions," she says. "It has not been easy. But I have been strengthened by choosing to make adversity a challenge for personal growth and change."

Whenever we face suffering, we can offer the prayer of today's psalm: "Give me wisdom and knowledge." Through that prayer, we ask for the wisdom to respond positively to pain rather than react negatively. In that prayer, we also ask to let the pain teach and instruct us. Then, like Mary, we can experience growth through suffering. Like Mary, we can become better, not bitter, because of our trials.

Thought for the Day

Each problem has hidden in it
an opportunity so powerful
that it literally dwarfs the problem.
Joseph Sugarman

He is the God who makes me strong.
Psalm 18:32

Operating From a Position of Strength

Being a Christian means we are not to live as timid, hesitant, fearful, or weak people. "He is the God who makes me strong" ought to be permanently etched in our minds and souls. As Christians, we are to operate always from a position of strength. And we can do this when we bring to mind these five facts:

- *The fact of God's presence*. Sometimes we falter and feel lonely because we lack the assurance of God's presence. Yet the Bible repeatedly says that God will never forsake us. (See Hebrews 13:5.)
- *The fact of God's power.* "I have strength to face all conditions by the power that Christ gives me," declares Paul (Philippians 4:13). What was true for Paul in the first century is true for us in these times as well.
- *The fact of God's promise*. Let us remember God's promises to help carry our burdens and to provide hope in the face of despair and light for our path.
- *The fact of God's protection*. Although we cannot escape life's trials completely, God guarantees our ultimate safety. We are in God's hands and live in God's world.
- *The fact of God's purpose*. Some people go through life with little or no purpose, merely existing from day to day. Our purpose is to bring glory to God through our lives. Thus we have a great and noble task: to help others and bear witness to God's great love for all people.

Thought for the Day

When God is our strength,
it is strength indeed.
When our strength is our own,
it is only weakness.
Saint Augustine

He is the God who…
makes my pathway safe.
Psalm 18:32

Trusting in God's Safety

In a remote region of Hawaii, amid the orange and ironwood trees, is a statue depicting Christ leaning from the cross to embrace Saint Francis of Assisi. The inscription reads: "In memory of Reverend Mother Marianne, born January 23, 1838, died August 9, 1918." Marianne Cope was a Franciscan Sister who responded to God's call to serve the people of Hawaii suffering with Hansen's disease, commonly called leprosy.

At that time, those with Hansen's disease were quarantined to a small, secluded, filthy facility. Although it was called a hospital, the patients received no medical care.

Working eighteen hours a day and lacking masks or rubber gloves, Mother Marianne and her Sisters began their life mission of helping and aiding lepers. Some of the younger Sisters hesitated at first, fearing contagion. However, Mother Marianne, while insisting upon aprons and well-scrubbed hands, boldly reassured the Sisters that God would protect them. She declared that no Franciscan Sister would contract Hansen's disease.

As it happened, throughout a century of service, not one Sister contracted Hansen's disease, despite the position of physicians that the disease could be contracted through physical contact.

Whenever we are doing God's will and work in our lives, he makes our pathway safe. With that assurance, we can engage in our daily tasks with peace and joy.

Thought for the Day

If God sends us on stony paths,
he will provide us with strong shoes.
Alexander Maclaren

Turn away from evil and do good.
Psalm 34:14

Providing a Transfusion of Love

According to Scripture, it is never sufficient to merely abstain from hurtful actions; that alone does not produce women and men who are responsive to the suffering of others. Instead, Scripture calls us to "turn away from evil and do good." There are ample occasions when people are hurting and bleeding and need a transfusion of love.

Here are some ways we can become more sensitive to and aware of hurting people:

- *Be alert*. We can train our eyes and minds to notice the most subtle pain and anxiety in another man, woman, or child. We can then act accordingly.
- *Be available*. As soon as we learn that someone is hurting, we can respond with our presence or prayers. This will let that person know that someone cares. It will ease the anxiety and soften the pain.
- *Be approachable*. We can maintain a lifestyle that is open and inviting. Then people in pain will come to us, sharing their hurt and shedding their tears.
- *Be acceptable*. It is impossible to help another effectively if our heart is filled with negative thoughts. The adage to love the sinner but dislike the sin is based on a valid distinction.

Thought for the Day

No one has a right to sit down and feel hopeless.
There's too much work to do.
Dorothy Day

In my distress I called to the LORD;
he answered me....
Psalm 118:5

When Prayer Changes the Pray-er

Shortly before bedtime, a little boy lost one of his favorite marbles—a large, colorful one. After searching for it unsuccessfully, the boy approached his father in tears, saying, "Can I pray and ask God to help me find my marble?" The father agreed, and they both closed their eyes for prayer.

With all of the innocence and great faith of a child, the boy prayed, "Dear God, please, please help me find my favorite marble."

The next day, the father was afraid to ask his son if he had found the marble. He was concerned that the boy's sincere faith would be hurt if, after praying, he could not locate the marble. Nevertheless, the father gently asked, "Did you find the marble, Son?"

"No," replied the boy, "but God made me not want to care about it anymore."

Today's psalm simply states, "In my distress I called to the Lord; he answered me...." The fact is that God has more ways to answer our prayers than simply saying yes and granting our wish. Like the little boy, there may be times when we pray about an issue and then simply come to a place of peace about it.

Thought for the Day

God is perfect love and perfect wisdom.
We do not pray in order to change his will
but to bring our wills into harmony with his.

William Temple

...in his pride he thinks that God doesn't matter.
Psalm 10:4

Cultivating Healthy Humility

A humble person is not someone with low self-esteem. Rather, humble people are those who understand profoundly that the ultimate source of their gifts and talents is God.

Samuel Morse, inventor of the telegraph, was a truly humble person. He was asked if he ever became completely confused and lost in the course of his many experiments.

"More than once," Morse replied candidly. "And whenever I could not see my way clearly, I knelt down and prayed to God for light and understanding."

Then the great inventor added, "When flattering honors came to me from America and Europe on account of my invention, I never felt I deserved them. I had made a valuable application of electricity, not because I was superior to other men, but solely because God, who meant it for mankind, must reveal it to someone, and was pleased to reveal it to me."

The first message to be sent via telegraph between the cities of Washington and Baltimore in May 1844 was dispatched by Morse himself. Not surprisingly, his message was "What hath God wrought?" In more modern language, Morse simply and humbly declared, "Look what God has done!"

An important aspect of spiritual maturity and emotional health is the ability to exercise humility and acknowledge God's gifts within us.

Thought for the Day

The way to be humble is not to stoop
until you are smaller than yourself
but to stand at your real height
against some higher nature
that will show you how small your greatness is.
Phillips Brooks

Happy is the person who is generous....
Psalm 112:5

The Joy of Generosity

A man tells of a memorable incident that took place two decades earlier when he was a college student working in a sporting-goods store. A seven-year-old boy would visit the store two or three times a week. His purpose was to see and handle a baseball glove that he desperately wanted to buy.

Week after week, the boy would visit the store, put on the glove, pound his fist into the pocket a few times, and then very carefully place it back on the shelf and depart.

The man telling the story relates how he and the owner were impressed by the young man's dedication. He not only came in regularly but selected the most expensive glove in the store. It would take the boy months if not years to save enough money for the purchase.

One day, the boy came into the store with an enormous smile. He carried with him a small box stuffed with single dollar bills and coins. Eagerly the boy announced that he wanted to buy the glove. The owner brought the baseball glove to the cash register while the boy counted out a box full of nickels, quarters, dimes, and dollar bills. His savings came to exactly $19.98.

However, the glove cost $79.98 not including tax. The owner looked at the price tag; sure enough, the seven was slightly smudged, just enough that an eager and hopeful seven-year-old thought it was a one. With consummate grace and generosity, the store owner looked at his young customer and declared, "Yes. Exactly $19.98." And wrapping up the glove, he gave it to the boy.

Today's psalm correctly notes that a generous person will be a happy one. Generosity brings joy for several reasons. There is the pleasure of seeing the delight a generous action produces in another person. There is the satisfaction of knowing that a generous action softens some of life's harsher realities. There is the spiritual gratification of knowing that a generous action pleases God.

Thought for the Day

A gift of fragrance
always clings to the hands
that give roses.
Chinese Proverb

Light shines in the darkness...
for those who are merciful, kind, and just.
Psalm 112:4

Penetrating Darkness With Kindness

Hasidic Rabbis tell the story of a man who had two sons. Upon the man's death, the sons inherited the fertile farm. Rather than divide it in half, the two chose to farm the land together and split the harvest. They did this for years. Then one brother married and had seven children. The other brother never married.

One year, the single man thought to himself, *My brother has eight other mouths to feed. It is not right that we split the harvest equally, for he has greater needs than I. I will give him some of my grain.* So the single brother took three bags of grain from his barn each night, slipped into his brother's barn, and emptied them into his brother's granary.

About the same time, the married brother began to think, *My poor brother has no one to take care of him in his old age, while I have my wife and children to care for me. It is not right that we divide the harvest equally, for he needs more than I to save for his old age. I will give him some of my grain.* So he took three bags of grain from his barn each night and secretly slipped over to his brother's barn and emptied them into his brother's granary.

Sure enough, one night when the moon was full, the two brothers bumped into each other, carrying their bags of grain. When they realized what was happening, they fell into each other's arms with joy. And it is said that a gentle rain began to fall. The rain was God's tears of joy that two of his children should penetrate the darkness of the world around them with such great acts of mercy and kindness.

We can take a lesson from the two brothers in this Hasidic tale and become part of that great company of people who penetrate the darkness with kindness.

Thought for the Day

Be the living expression of God's kindness;
kindness in your face, kindness in your eyes, kindness in your smile.
Let no one ever come to you without feeling better and happier.

Mother Teresa of Calcutta

Be still before the Lord....
Psalm 37:7
(*New Revised Standard Version*)

Centering Ourselves in Prayer

The Society of Friends, commonly known as the Quakers, teach that there are four elements common to an effective prayer life. It is known as sitting in silence before God.

- *Sit still.* Say nothing, read nothing, do nothing.
- *Detach yourself.* Deliberately take your mind off yourself and the conditions of your experience.
- *Intentionally place your thoughts upon God.* Focus upon God's love, power, majesty, compassion, mercy, and concern. Try repeating to yourself: "God is here now, with me, within me, and all around me."
- *Be receptive to God's presence.* Allow yourself to experience the sensations of God's strength, power, love, peace, and life flowing over you and through you.

According to the Quakers and other spiritual masters, sitting in silence before God often leads to experiencing the state of mind in which one feels enlightened, purified, peaceful, directed, and filled with joy.

There is great wisdom in this technique. Behind it is the knowledge that God is worth waiting for, hearing from, and being guided by.

Thought for the Day

Forgive us when we allow our religious feelings
to become cold or lukewarm.
May they continue to glow
because our lives are deeply rooted in Thee,
the source of all light, power, and goodness.
George Fox

He is to be praised forever.
Psalm 111:10

Permanently Committed to God

Monsieur Vincent is a French film about the life of Saint Vincent de Paul. Near the end of the film, Vincent, an old man, is speaking to an equally old woman. The woman happens to be the Queen of France.

"Monsieur Vincent," she says, "when I was a greedy young princess, I wanted love and fame and riches. Now I've had all those, and I feel that I've done nothing with my life. But you, Monsieur Vincent, you've dedicated your life to God and the poor. How do you feel?"

"I, too, feel as though I've done nothing," the saint candidly replies.

"But, Monsieur Vincent," the Queen protests, "what then must one do for God?"

The saint smiles and says softly, "Always more. Always more."

It is true that we never stop serving God. In the spiritual life, there is no "retirement." Our commitment to God is permanent and lifelong. It is through our service, that God is praised forever.

Thought for the Day

Jesus did not say,
"Come to me and get it over with."
Our commitment to Christ,
however genuine and wholehearted it may be today,
must be renewed tomorrow...
and the day after that...
until the path comes at last to the river.
Louis Cassels

I will give loud thanks to the Lord.
Psalm 109:30

A Profound Lesson in Christian Love

The loudest thanks we can give to God is through acts of mercy, kindness, and compassion done in God's name. No one does this more purely than Mother Teresa of Calcutta and her Missionaries of Charity. Consider this profound example of Christian love.

Near Katmandu, Nepal, flows the Bagmati River. Hindus believe the river is connected to the Ganges River and is, therefore, holy. As a result, many poor, elderly, dying people flock to the river. They believe that unless their feet are dipped into that river at the time of death, they will not be saved. They position themselves near the river hoping that when their time comes, some kind stranger will help move them to the riverbank and dip their feet in the water.

When Mother Teresa discovered this need, she sent a number of her Sisters to the area to serve these poorest of the poor by making certain their dying wishes would be granted. The Sisters quickly found space for a simple hospice. There they placed cots, blankets, and pillows and began to care for the dying. The Sisters provide food and simple medications where necessary. And when the time comes, they carry the dying to the river for the necessary death rite.

As we move about our daily tasks, let us be alert to the needs of others. As we see these needs, let us respond appropriately. In that way, our living will give "loud thanks to the Lord."

Thought for the Day

Love pays attention.
Love notices things.
Not to notice is not to love.
John Carmody

God will put his angels in charge of you
to protect you wherever you go.
Psalm 91:11

God's Secret Agents

Several years ago, Sophy Burnham was on a skiing vacation abroad. After carefully viewing a steep slope, Burnham accepted the challenge and began to ski down. Shortly after she began her descent, however, she lost control and found herself hurtling downhill to certain injury and perhaps even death. Suddenly a mysterious black-clad figure cut in front of her, completely stopping her fall. Shaken, Burnham got to her feet and discovered to her horror that she was just inches from the edge of a cliff. A fall would have meant certain death. Without a word, her rescuer simply vanished.

"For a long time, I kept quiet about what happened," Burnham says. "I knew he was an angel, but I didn't want to even think about what seeing him implied—there was much more to this world than I was prepared to accept."

Since that event, Burnham has researched and written *A Book of Angels*. In the process, she was surprised to discover many people who had also encountered angels. In fact, nearly sixty percent of people surveyed in a recent Gallup poll believe in angels, with ten percent saying they have had a supernatural encounter.

Scripture contains many references to angels. Although they are assigned various tasks by God, their most common work is that of protection. Today's psalm provides us with the comfort of knowing that God provides a special companion to watch over us as we go about our daily routines.

Thought for the Day

An angel is a spiritual being,
created by God without a body,
for the service of Christendom and the Church.
Martin Luther

I am not afraid of the thousands of enemies
who surround me on every side.
Psalm 3:6

Maintaining Confidence in God

The Jewish activist Natan Sharansky was imprisoned by the Soviet government on false charges of spying for the United States. He was sentenced to fifteen years of hard labor. During that time, Soviet authorities tried to break his will and spirit. Yet he survived his sentence and emerged from prison stronger than when he went in.

In his book *Fear No Evil*, Sharansky explains that he was able to do this by reminding himself that the power he relied upon was greater than the power of those who kept him in prison. Although officials physically confined him to a cell, Sharansky's spirit was alive and free. Only his body was imprisoned, not his mind or soul.

Our confidence in God can bring great spiritual freedom. In today's verse, the psalmist describes an extreme situation of being surrounded by "thousands" of enemies. Yet he boldly declares, "I am not afraid." Like Sharansky, his trust is in the power of God. It is a power that sustains, stabilizes, and strengthens.

It is worth noting a similar New Testament reminder that God's power is greater than the powers that sometimes work against us. In the First Letter of John, we are assured that "the Spirit who is in you is more powerful than the spirit in those who belong to the world" (4:4). Today let us think about these verses and through them find new courage and determination to face our own particular situation.

Thought for the Day

If God maintains sun and planets
in bright and ordered beauty,
he can keep us.
Frederick B. Meyer

Sing to the L*ORD*....
Psalm 96:1

The Power of Music

A woman living in Nevada recently discovered the power of music. Her warmest childhood memory is of her grandmother singing their favorite song, *True Love*. Today the grandmother is in a nursing home, her mind lost to Alzheimer's disease.

One day when visiting, the woman knelt beside her grandmother's wheelchair and begin to sing "their" song. After a while, the granddaughter noticed a glimmer of recognition. Soon the grandmother, in spite of her impaired memory, joined in and sang the entire song in harmony. Tears flowed down the cheeks of both women as they reconnected. Now they sing the song at every visit. "It turns a sad time into a happy time again," the granddaughter says.

Scripture is filled with references to music and commands to sing. Among researchers today, there is an increasing awareness that music has a therapeutic power to lighten griefs and deepen joys.

People in biblical times understood intuitively that music nourishes the soul and brings the human spirit closer to God. Let us remember the psalmist's words "Sing to the Lord" and find new ways of using music in our spiritual growth.

Thought for the Day

Music is the medicine of a troubled mind.

Walter Haddon

Remember what the Holy One has done,
and give him thanks!
Psalm 30:4

Think, Then Thank

The deepest thanking often emerges when we do some thinking about the events of our lives. It is worth remembering that God's blessings frequently arrive incognito, disguised as misfortune, defeat, rejection, affliction, distress, and anxiety. Those who take the time to think about what has happened and what has emerged usually find reasons for gratitude and joy. This was true of Alex Haley, Pulitzer Prize winner and author of the best-selling book *Roots*.

Haley spent twenty years at sea serving in the Coast Guard. Sea duty is extremely difficult; the hours are long and the work is hard. In addition, there is great loneliness because of the separation from family and friends.

Looking back, Haley is grateful for his time at sea. When he was not working on the ship and there was nothing else to do, he used the time to write. "It started with letters to lots of people back home dramatizing my travels," he recalls. "My shipmates began to notice that I was sending a lot of mail and asked me to help them write letters to their girls. Pretty soon, I was the Cyrano of the ship, composing love letters for all these guys. That was the first notion I had that writing was something I might pursue as a career."

Thought for the Day

Receive every day as a resurrection from death,
as a new enjoyment of life...
let your joyful heart
praise and magnify
so good and glorious a Creator.
William Law

He gives sleep to his beloved.
Psalm 127:2
(New Revised Standard Version)

Gratitude for the Gift of Sleep

Physicians at a recent meeting of the American Medical Association cited the inability to get a good night's sleep as America's worst and most widespread unseen medical problem. Approximately one in three adults suffers from some type of sleep disorder. The most common problems include difficulty falling asleep, waking in the middle of the night, and excessive daytime sleepiness.

"Sleep, like nutrition and exercise, is fundamental to health," says Danyang Chen, M.D., of the National Institute of Neurological Disorders and Communicative Disorders and Stroke in Bethesda, Maryland. "Lack of it leaves us prone to accidents and stress."

In addition, a burst of new research suggests that the immune system is repaired or bolstered during sleep. Thus, prolonged or long-term poor sleep equates poor health.

In today's psalm verse, we are reminded that the ability to sleep is a gift from God. We do not achieve sleep; we receive sleep. By placing our trust in God, we reduce anxiety, worry, and fear and are able to sleep. Therefore, let us add sleep to the litany of thanks we offer to God.

Thought for the Day

Thank God for sleep!
And, when you cannot sleep,
still thank him
that you live to lie awake.
John Oxenham

You are my God; in you I trust.
Psalm 91:2

Letting God Do the Work

There is a Hassidic tale about a man walking along the road carrying a very heavy sack. Soon another man comes along driving a horse and wagon. The man in the cart, seeing the man toiling under his load, offers him a ride.

Gratefully, the man with the sack accepts the offer and climbs aboard the wagon. A few moments later, the driver turns around to see if the man is comfortable and is startled to see that the man is still standing with the sack upon his shoulder. The driver suggests to his guest, "The wagon is going to carry the sack anyway, why not put down your load and let the horse and wagon do the work?"

In light of that tale, ask yourself the following questions:

- When I turn to God in prayer, do I continue carrying my burden or do I leave it with God?
- Even though Scripture calls me to leave my cares with God because God cares for me, do I continue to be worried and anxious?
- After I pray, am I willing to trust God and let God work?

Upon completing this brief examination of conscience conclude with these affirmations:

- I am confident in God's care for me.
- I know that God is working on my behalf right now.
- I trust in God's perfect timing.

Thought for the Day

All I have seen
teaches me to trust the Creator
for all I have not seen.
Ralph Waldo Emerson

He heals the broken-hearted
and bandages their wounds.
Psalm 147:3

Cooperating With God to Heal Hurts

To be human means to experience the pain of loss. Loss and the resulting grief are intricately woven into the fabric of life. Sooner or later, we all experience the pain of a broken heart through death, divorce, disability, or the end of another important relationship. Even though such losses are a reality of being human, they can leave us deeply wounded and hurting.

Today's psalm reminds us of two important factors to consider when we are hurting. First, God is aware of our pain. Second, God is actively working to bring us healing through our wounds. Here are five ways to cooperate with God so we can be healed:

- *Accept the reality of a loss.* This does not mean liking the situation. It simply means deciding to accept the situation. Saint Paul is a good example. He had a "thorn in the flesh," yet managed to find a way to live with his thorn.
- *Remember that there is renewal beyond pain.* Even though grief produces a searing pain, there is the possibility of renewal and recovery. Recall that Christ's death was a time of confusion, anguish, betrayal, and despair for the disciples. Yet new life emerged from the grave.
- *Let family and friends help.* If we can find safe, supportive people who will let us tell our story, we can pour out our heart. Grief shared is grief diminished.
- *Express, don't repress, feelings.* Loss produces a variety of emotions. Anger, fear, anxiety, and depression are all normal. It is healthier to express these feelings than to hold them inside.
- *Be patient.* Remember God desires us to heal. Recovery usually comes gradually. It is always slower than we would like.

Thought for the Day

Earth has no sorrow
that heaven cannot heal.
Saint Thomas Moore

The L*ORD* *is my rock...*
Psalm 18:2
(New Revised Standard Version)

Trusting God's Solid Strength

One of the world's civil engineering wonders is located in the United States: Hoover Dam, built in 1935 on the Colorado River in the Black Canyon between Arizona and Nevada. The Hoover Dam is an arch-gravity dam, meaning it is an arch laid over on its side. This design makes it much stronger than a traditional dam because the more pressure that is applied against the dam, the more solidly it becomes wedged into the rock, thus becoming even stronger.

In Scripture the term *rock* is frequently connected with God. For example, today we read, "The Lord is my rock." This simple, straightforward statement tells us five things about God:

- *God is a source of strength.* We can derive staying power from God when facing difficulty. God will strengthen us so we can make wise decisions and move ahead.
- *God is a source of security.* The psalmist lived in Palestine, where huge rocks provided security from enemies. A spiritual application of this image means that God provides a secure place, inaccessible to people who would harm us.
- *God is a source of stability.* When the storms of life come our way, God becomes our anchor of hope.
- *God is a source of support.* Large skyscrapers sit on foundations of solid rock. Likewise, we are "grounded" in the reality of God, whose power is our daily support.
- *God is a source of safety.* Ultimately, God is the place of refuge during the stresses and strains of life. Those who depend upon God can find safety during times of danger.

-------- *Thought for the Day* --------

Cast yourself into the arms of God
and be very sure
that if He wants anything of you,
He will fit you for the work
and give you the strength.
Saint Philip Neri

My heart is troubled, and I groan with pain.
Psalm 38:8

The Miracle of Prayer

Perhaps the most universal prayer is one that comes from a troubled heart filled with pain. This prayer of desperation is welcomed by God.

Consider Debbie, who was told that her ten-month-old son, Eric, would probably die within forty-eight hours. Eric developed severe pneumonia after a liver transplant. His lungs were being coated with a gluelike mucous, and he was slowly smothering to death. Ninety percent of transplant patients who contract this virus do not survive.

Knowing that her son was receiving the best treatment medicine had to offer, Debbie visited the local newspaper and pleaded for the editors' assistance. They agreed, and the story in that evening's edition began, "A mother is asking for your prayers to help her baby live." It ended with a reminder that Debbie hoped readers could do what medicine apparently could not: create a healing through prayer.

The next morning, Debbie rose and prayed for strength to face whatever the day might bring. Arriving at the hospital, she was greeted with the most extraordinary news. X-rays showed that little Eric's lungs were clearing, his fever had disappeared, and his vital signs had greatly improved. By late afternoon, his physician declared, "As of now, I would say that Eric has beaten the virus."

While some might consider what happened a mere coincidence, his mother is convinced that Eric's dramatic recovery was due to his having been "bombarded with prayers" the night his story appeared in the paper.

Thought for the Day

If your knees are knocking,
kneel on them.

Graffiti in a World War II London Air-Raid Shelter

Praise the LORD, because he is good.
Psalm 135:3

God Always Gives Good Gifts

A legend from the ancient Middle East tells of a Persian king who severely injured his ankle. Although he had access to the finest physicians, none could bring him relief from pain and healing from injury.

Then one of the king's advisors told him about an imprisoned slave who reportedly had unique insights into medicine and healing powers. Because he had exhausted all traditional means of help, the king sent for the imprisoned slave. The man was brought before the king in chains and wearing prison rags.

After examining the king, the slave made a careful diagnosis and recommended a remedy that resulted in relief and healing. The king was elated and justifiably grateful for the imprisoned slave's help. In gratitude, the king sent the slave an expensive, handcrafted gift—a new set of chains made of pure gold.

Today's verse reminds us that God is not like the Persian king whose "gift" continued to imprison and oppress. The psalmist, as well as people across the ages, praises God "because he is good." His gifts are not "gold chains" that confine and limit. Rather, the gifts of God are good. They lead to freedom, liberation, and redemption. We can be certain that something is wrong with us if our faith leads us to become intolerant, insular, or narrow-minded.

Thought for the Day

The God who gave us life
gave us liberty at the same time.
Thomas Jefferson

You...understand all my thoughts.
Psalm 139:2

God Understands Us

Sandy, forty-three and the mother of two children, became a widow when Don died right before Christmas. One afternoon shortly after the holidays, a blowout on the highway forced Sandy to enter the unfamiliar world of four-ply radial tires and computerized spin balancing. Don had always taken charge of car maintenance.

Already depressed over her husband's death, Sandy felt herself slipping even lower as she dealt with the tire salesperson. With misty eyes, she softly muttered this prayer: "Lord, I hate it that Don's dead. He should be buying these tires. I really need some encouragement just now."

Sandy had left her car at the auto center and was walking to a restaurant across the street when she saw a young woman standing next to a car with its hood raised. Sandy offered help, but the young woman said that the vehicle would start when the engine had cooled. So Sandy invited the woman to join her for coffee.

Soon, Sandy was baring her soul, explaining that Don had died after sixteen-and-a-half years of marriage. The young woman asked if she and Don were truly in love. "Oh, yes, very much so," Sandy replied.

The young woman responded, "Then you've already experienced more love than most of us ever have. Think of that instead of what you've lost." Then she went on to tell about her divorce—the physical and emotional abuse, the custody battles, the continuing threats.

After the two parted, Sandy realized the truth of the young woman's observation. She did have more love than many people would ever experience. She felt her depression lift as encouragement seeped into her soul. Sandy marveled at the way God had responded to her tearful prayer. She vowed to try concentrating more on what was left instead of what was gone.

When we feel discouraged and disappointed by life, let us remember that God understands all our thoughts and feelings. And let us be prepared to experience God's encouraging intervention.

Thought for the Day

God's blessings steal into life noiselessly.
They are neither self-proclaiming
nor even self-announcing.

Henry Ward Beecher

The precepts of the L*ORD are right,*
rejoicing the heart.
Psalm 19:8
(New Revised Standard Version)

Getting Close to Scripture

Saints and mystics throughout the ages have stressed that familiarity with Scripture is essential for deepening the spiritual life. The Bible is a powerful tool that educates the mind, informs the spirit, and shapes the soul. The Scriptures provide us with guidance, inspiration, comfort, hope, help, and insight.

Every Christian should seize any and every opportunity to know the Bible better. Here are some ways to get closer to Scripture:

- Take a course on the Bible at a community college, university, or church.
- Join a Bible-study group for a specifically defined period of time: a semester, ten-week class, Lenten study group, or weekend retreat.
- Visit a religious bookstore, browse carefully, and purchase a book on the Bible that appeals to you. Then read it over the next month from cover to cover.
- Offer to lead a Bible-study group. This is not as complicated as it seems. Many excellent Bible-study books are available. Select one and organize a study group. You will benefit doubly because you will learn both through preparing for the classes and teaching the lessons.

Thought for the Day

Just as at the sea those who are carried away
from the direction of the harbor bring themselves back on course
by a clear sign on seeing a tall beacon light
or some mountain peak coming into view,
so Scripture may guide those adrift on the sea of life
back into the harbor of the divine will.

Saint Gregory of Nyssa

I pray to you, O LORD.
Psalm 5:2

The Importance of Prayer

There are many prayers in the Psalms. In fact, the Psalms consist simply of one prayer after another. The men and women of Scripture knew the importance of prayer. Here are some reasons why the Bible urges us to engage in prayer as often as possible:

- Prayer is a vital life force connecting human needs and aspirations with divine wisdom and love.
- Prayer heightens joys, deepens hopes, and lightens burdens.
- Prayer is a source of strength, stability, security, and safety.
- Prayer is an anchor in times of storm, a beacon in darkness, and a guide in the maze of life.
- Prayer makes us stronger morally and mentally, spiritually and socially.
- Prayer prepares us to receive God's guidance and to act accordingly.
- Prayer brings human will into conformity with the will of God.

In thinking about prayer, let us resolve today to incorporate more time and ways of regular prayer into our lives.

Thought for the Day

I have not the courage
to search through books
for beautiful prayers....
Unable either to say them all
or choose between them,
I do as a child would do
who cannot read—
I say just what I want to say to God,
quite simply,
and He never fails to understand.

Saint Thérèse of Lisieux

A good person…
will always be remembered.
Psalm 112:6

A Lesson in Living From Saint Valentine

Long after we are gone, it will be our small acts of kindness, courtesy, generosity, and mercy that will prompt people to remember us.

This was certainly true of Saint Valentine. Although not much is known about him, one lovely legend remains and explains why people send cards today that say, "From Your Valentine."

Valentine was a priest and physician who lived in Rome during the third century. At that time, Christianity was a minority religion and a persecuted faith. In 270, Emperor Claudius II ordered Valentine arrested and imprisoned. When he would not deny his faith, Valentine was put to death on February fourteenth.

While awaiting execution, Valentine met the blind daughter of his jailor. The priest and the little girl forged a friendship. Valentine prayed for her healing, and the girl's sight was restored. On the night of his death, he wrote his friend a farewell message signing it "from your Valentine." Thus Saint Valentine is remembered for his great act of kindness to a little girl.

We can learn a lesson in living from Saint Valentine. Like him, we must not allow personal pain and suffering to prevent us from continuing to help others. Like him, we must not become so absorbed with our hurts that we cannot see and respond to the hurts of others.

Thought for the Day

Virtue is nothing
but well-directed love.
Saint Augustine

...I walk in the presence of God.
Psalm 56:13

Creating More Time for Prayer

Today we receive a reminder that we "walk" or live in the constant presence of God. God is always around us and aware of us. Therefore, prayer should not be as complicated as it may seem. We should learn to pray at all times, maintaining a continuous attitude of prayer. Here are some gentle ways to create more time for prayer:

- *Attend church services as often as possible.* Weekly for sure, but attending additional services is a very good practice. In worship, we pray corporately and privately.
- *Use waiting time for God.* If we commute by train or subway, we can use that time for prayer. We can carry a prayer book and read the prayers.
- *Let sight and sound be reminders to pray.* Every time we hear a siren, we can pray for the officials involved and the people they are racing to assist. When we see a church, we can offer a prayer for that community's ministry. When passing a hospital, we can pray for the sick and for those who tend to them.
- *Pray while doing "mindless" tasks.* This is a wonderful lesson from Brother Lawrence, a seventeenth-century monk who was a dishwasher and prayed while doing that work. Today we engage in similar "mindless" tasks that provide opportunity for prayer. We can offer quick prayers while folding laundry, cutting the lawn, weeding, planting, washing dishes, and so forth.
- *Create a portable prayer corner.* Most of us carry purses or briefcases. We can make some space in them for a devotional book, a small Bible, or a cross. During the course of our day when there is "down time," we can seize the opportunity to read, reflect, and pray.

Thought for the Day

Prayer constantly enlarges our horizon and our person.
It draws us out of the narrow limits within which our habits,
our past and our whole personage confine us.
Paul Tournier

I will live a pure life in my house
and will never tolerate evil.
Psalm 101:3

Living Our Faith Day by Day

Today's psalm contains three resolutions that each one of us can adopt. Together, they form the path to a holy life.

First, the writer resolves to live a "pure" life. Other translations use the words "blameless life" (*New International Version*); "purity of heart" (*New English Bible*); and "integrity of heart" (*New Revised Standard Version*). No matter which phrase or word is used, the author's intent is to live a life of spiritual maturity and integrity.

Second, the writer resolves to live that life "in my house." This is an important declaration because it shows the author's intention to live the spiritual life in the home as well as the temple, in the workplace as well as the sanctuary. He will not be a "Sunday Christian" only.

Third, the writer resolves to "never tolerate evil." It is another way of stating the golden rule, to treat others as we would like to be treated. Practically, this means abstaining from gossip, judgmental attitudes, and slurs of any kind—racial, ethnic, or sexist.

Today's psalm should evoke this crisp examination of conscience:

- Do I feel a strong desire to live a life pleasing to God, or do I waver in my spiritual commitments?
- Do I live a life of spiritual and emotional integrity, or am I guilty of hypocrisy?
- Do I speak out against attitudes and actions that belittle and harm other people, or do I remain silent in their presence?

Thought for the Day

Holy has the same root as wholly,
it means complete.
A man is not complete in spiritual stature
if all his mind, heart, soul, and strength
are not given to God.
R. J. Stewart

In your goodness save me from my troubles!
Psalm 143:11

God's Faithful Help in Difficulty

In 1968, Rory Bailey was a twenty-one-year-old army private newly arrived in Vietnam. Shortly afterward, his unit was engaged in combat. Bailey remembers only searing pain and then darkness.

The battle left Bailey horribly disfigured. While in the 24th Evacuation Hospital in Long Binh, Vietnam, he was known as "the man without a face." He lost his nose and lower jaw and had only a fragment of a tongue. Initially, he could not chew and had to survive on a liquid diet. Since then, hundreds of thousands of dollars have been spent reconstructing his face.

But even after two hundred operations, Rory Bailey attracts stares. His face is dignified but masklike. The destruction of all facial muscles has left him unable to move his cheeks or eyelids. Fortunately, he can move his lower jaw and what remains of his tongue, enabling him to talk. His sight is severely impaired and he maneuvers with the help of a cane.

When asked how he managed to get through some very tough times, Bailey responds simply and sincerely, "It's because God is helping me out."

The truth is that sometimes life provides us with minimal protection. However, today's psalm reminds us that God provides us with maximum support. We will have troubles and we will also have God.

Thought for the Day

Jesus did not come
to explain away suffering
or remove it.
He came to fill it
with his presence.
Paul Claudel

How I love to do your will, my God!
Psalm 40:8

Called to Be Saints

In the early New Testament Church, the term *saint* was synonymous with *Christian*. Next it was applied to martyrs who died in defense of the faith. Later in history, the term *saint* was also used for women and men who led lives of conspicuous and heroic virtue.

Today, of course, when we think of a saint we mean a person who is clearly and completely devoted to God and who is engaged in extraordinary service to God and humanity.

Yet the reality is that each one of us is called to be a saint. As Christians, we are all called to love God and do God's will. A lofty goal and an honorable objective for each one of us is to grow into sainthood.

One way to begin this process is to read about saints, both those who are officially canonized as well as those uncanonized. By reading about godly, holy men and women, we will learn and identify elements common to saintly people. Then we can adopt their style and form into our own daily lives.

Thought for the Day

We may allow that the saints are specialists;
but they are specialists in a career
to which all Christians are called.
They are the advance guard of the army;
but we, after all, are marching in the main ranks.

Evelyn Underhill

Remove my sin, and I will be clean.
Psalm 51:7

Bringing Our Guilt to God

We must distinguish between two types of guilt. One is rational and will lead us to become better, stronger people. The other guilt is irrational and only weakens us. Consider this insight from a pastor who conducted funerals for two women in his church within a week's time. Both women had lived long, full lives.

After the funeral, the son of one of the women said to the clergyman, "I wish I had sent my mother to Florida where the sun was shining and it was warm. This cold, harsh, winter climate was the cause of her death. I feel so guilty for not sending her south."

A few days later, the son of the other woman spoke to the pastor saying, "I wish I had not sent my mother to Florida this winter. The detachment from her friends and family, the change in climate, and the long plane ride all contributed to her death. I feel very guilty over my decision."

Both sons were suffering from irrational guilt. Obviously, they wanted what was best for their mothers. In their hearts, they harbored only good thoughts and love for the women.

Rational guilt, however, emerges when we have definitely done something wrong to another or to ourselves. For those actions and attitudes, we should feel guilty. If we were unable to experience guilt, we would cease to be human and become sociopathic people.

Whenever we experience true guilt, we must quickly confess *our* transgression and ask God for forgiveness so we can be reconciled again. Such a prayer is an admission that there are some things we cannot do for ourselves. We cannot make ourselves feel good and clean. For that state of the spirit, we need God's help.

Thought for the Day

Sorrow melts away before a well-offered prayer
like snow before the sun.

Saint John Vianney

So I will not be silent;
I will sing praise to you.
Psalm 30:12

Glorifying God Through Our Actions

A woman tells about a time when she was unemployed. Although she spent a great deal of time reading the help-wanted ads, mailing résumés, and going for interviews, she still found herself unemployed after several months. In addition, she was running out of money.

When the strap on her purse broke, she decided to shop for a used purse at a nearby thrift shop. She found an acceptable replacement purse for two dollars. At home that evening, she began to transfer items from the old purse to her "new" one. When she opened the small zippered pocket inside her recent purchase, she was surprised and thrilled to find a crisp twenty-dollar bill along with this note:

> Dear Friend,
> I hope you like the purse. It's not the height of fashion, but it works just fine. The enclosed gift is just to give your spirits a boost. God bless you!

The woman reports that her spirits certainly soared, both because of the unexpected money as well as the evident goodness of the purse's previous owner.

This incident provides a strong lesson that singing praises to God can be done not only through words but actions. Whenever we do an act of kindness and mercy, we are bringing God praise. Today, let us plan to "not be silent" but "sing praise" to God through our actions.

Thought for the Day

Kind words toward those you daily meet,
Kind words and actions right,
Will make this life of ours most sweet,
Turn darkness into light.

Isaac Watts

...I will praise you
because of your goodness to me.
Psalm 142:7

Counting Pluses, Not Minuses

The people who enjoy satisfaction in life are those who know how to maximize the positive and minimize the negative. They know that negative thinking results in emotional weakness, intellectual impotence, and spiritual bareness. They are people who praise rather than curse God and life.

One woman who counted the pluses was the mother of Dr. Lee Salk, prominent child psychologist and professor of pediatrics at New York's Cornell University Medical College. Dr. Salk often recalls his mother's experiences growing up in Russia at the turn of the century.

As a girl, she was driven from her home by Cossacks in a mad frenzy of anti-Semitism. Her village, inhabited primarily by Jewish families, was burned to the ground. She fled for her life, hiding in hay wagons and huddling in ditches. Eventually, crowded in a ship's hold, she crossed the ocean to the United States. Dr. Salk writes:

> Even after my mother married and her sons were born...it was a struggle to keep food on the table....But my mother urged us to think about what we *had*, not what we didn't have. She taught us that in hardship you develop a capacity to appreciate the beauty that exists in the simplest elements of life. The attitude that she so fiercely conveyed to us was this: "When it gets dark enough, you can see the stars."

Thought for the Day

A cynic is not merely one
who reads bitter lessons from the past;
he is one who is prematurely disappointed
in the future.

Sidney J. Harris

But I am no longer a man: I am a worm.
Psalm 22:6

Growth Versus Perfection

A man filled with anxiety went to see a wise, gifted rabbi.

"Rabbi," he said wringing his hands, "I am a failure. More than half the time, I do not succeed in doing what I must do."

The rabbi listened and nodded but said nothing. So the man implored, "Please tell me something wise, Rabbi."

After a few moments of silence, the rabbi issued this command: "Go and look on page 930 of the *New York Times Almanac* for the year 1970, and you will find peace of mind, maybe."

Although it was an odd suggestion, the man located the book. This is what he found: a listing of the lifetime batting averages of all the greatest baseball players. Included was Ty Cobb, one of the best hitters in baseball history. Cobb had a lifetime average of .367.

Confused, the man returned to his rabbi and said, "I found Ty Cobb who hit .367. Is that it?"

"That's it," declared the rabbi. "Ty Cobb got a hit only once out of every three times at bat. He didn't even hit the ball half the time, so what can you expect?"

There are times when we are simply too hard on ourselves because we expect perfection. Today's psalm is a cry of anguish. Although we do not know the background of the words, the writer has probably judged himself too harshly.

Because we are human, we will experience setbacks, failures, and disappointments. We may even act inappropriately and wrongly. Rather than berate ourselves, we must learn to seek and to expect growth, not perfection. Fulfillment in life is a process of growth rather than the achievement of perfection.

Thought for the Day

Saint Seraphim of Sarov,
when asked what it was
that made some people remain sinners
and never make any progress
while others were becoming saints
and living in God,
answered:
"Only determination."

Metropolitan Anthony of Sourouzh

The Lord *rules supreme in heaven,*
greater than the roar of the ocean,
more powerful than the waves of the sea.
Psalm 93:4

Using Faith to Face Fear

Life doesn't get much tougher than it did in 1978 for Pamela Yardis. She had just returned home from the hospital after giving birth to her seventh child. Bedridden and unable to walk because nerves in her back were damaged during the Caesarean procedure, she found herself demoralized. Then her husband left for a "quick business trip" and never returned. Instead, he sent a letter declaring the marriage was over but that he'd always think of Pam as a "sister."

However, her husband's shocking letter was merely the first blow. "I soon found out that none of our bills had been paid, the cars were being repossessed, and the bank had started foreclosing on our mortgage," she remembers. With seven children under the age of eleven—the youngest two weeks old—and confined to her bed, Pamela's life was at its lowest ebb.

In spite of such desperate circumstances, Pam knew she needed to prepare herself for a career that could pay the family bills. Patching together a budget through part-time jobs, government assistance, and scholarships, Pam returned to school, eventually earning a graduate degree in computers and management. She took a job in sales and was so successful that three years later, she was offered a job for $86 thousand as vice president of a computer-programming firm.

There are times when crises come our way that are beyond our control. We can feel like a small vessel tossed about on mighty ocean waves. Yet the psalmist declares that our God is "greater than the roar of the ocean, more powerful than the waves of the sea." It is a reminder to use our faith to face fear. Faith and confidence in God's power anchor the soul in times of grave crisis. Faith frees us to weather the storm knowing that God will help us day by day.

Prayer for the Day

Loving God,
I affirm that the task ahead of me
is not as great as your Power behind me.
VMP

I am a friend of all who serve you.
Psalm 119:63

Making Friends With Saints

Children need to be surrounded by positive role models if they are to emerge as healthy adults. Likewise, the saints (canonized and uncanonized) serve as role models to help us develop our spiritual lives.

Fortunately, God provides a wealth of saintly, godly, holy people who can inspire and instruct us. We find them in the past, as well as the present.

Saintly people are a diverse group. They are young and old, male and female. Some come from great wealth, while others emerge from the poorest of families. What they have in common is an uncommon closeness to God.

Yet the saints are very much like us—fully human. Even a quick reading of the lives of saints reveals their humanity. They lost their tempers, became angry, scolded God, were impatient, made mistakes and regretted them, struggled with doubt, and experienced dark nights of the soul.

In spite of all these things, they continued moving forward spiritually. Who would not be inspired toward greater holiness of life by the words from Etty Hillesum, a young Jewish woman who died at age twenty-nine in Auschwitz. With death and destruction all around her, she wrote this prayer in a diary discovered after her death in the camp:

> The misery here is quite terrible, and yet I often walk with a spring in my step...time and again, it soars straight from my heart, this feeling that life is glorious and magnificent....You have made me so rich, O God; please let me share your beauty with open hands. My life has become an uninterrupted dialogue with you.

Like the psalmist, let us become friends with all who serve God. A good way to begin is by reading biographies of saintly, godly people.

Thought for the Day

The saints have no need of honor from us;
neither does our devotion add the slightest thing to what is theirs.
Clearly, if we venerate their memory, it serves us, not them.
But I tell you, when I think of them,
I feel myself inflamed by tremendous yearning.
Bernard of Clairvaux

Turn away from evil and do good;
strive for peace with all your heart.
Psalm 34:14

Tithing Our Talent and Time

There was a surprise in store for graduating students at the University of New York Medical Center in the spring of 1991. The commencement address, given by Dr. Frank A. Oski of Johns Hopkins University School of Medicine, was titled "Time to Tithe."

Dr. Oski reminded the young graduating doctors how fortunate they were to become part of the medical profession and how much knowledge—and therefore how much power—they had gained through schooling. He reminded them they had one of the greatest powers a human being can achieve: the power of healing.

Accordingly, he reminded them they have a serious obligation to use that power for the good of all. So Dr. Oski urged the graduates to make sharing of that power an integral part of their professional lives by being available to people who need it most: the poor, the marginalized.

Dr. Oski urged them to work in free clinics, to make that work a regular part of their weekly practice. The minimum standard he set was a tithe: one tenth of their time was to be devoted to the free care of poor people.

Although we are not all physicians, Dr. Oski's comments are appropriate to each one of us. We have all been given talents and abilities from God. Like the physicians Dr. Oski challenged, we should also consider tithing our talent and time on behalf of others.

Today, let us take an inventory of our skills and experiences. Then let us consider how they can be used to help other, less fortunate individuals.

Thought for the Day

There are scores of people
waiting for someone just like us
to come along;
people who will appreciate our compassion,
our encouragement,
who will need our unique talents.
Leo Buscaglia

"You must stop judging unjustly."
Psalm 82:2

Softening Judgment and Widening Mercy

A wise rabbi asked his pupils how they could tell when the night ended and the day began.

"Could it be," asked one of the students, "when you see an animal in the distance and can tell whether it's a sheep or a dog?"

"No," answered the rabbi.

Another responded, "Is it when you can look at a tree in the distance and tell whether it's a fig tree or a peach tree?"

"No," answered the rabbi.

"Then when is it?" the pupils demanded.

"It is when you can look on the face of any man or woman and see that it is your sister or brother. Because if you cannot see this, it is still night."

Everyone we meet is a child of God. We should remember that when we are tempted to become judgmental about another person. It is difficult to grow spiritually if we are harsh and judging in our attitudes and actions. There is an inverse relationship between judging and loving that can be stated this way: "The more one judges, the less one loves." An honorable task for every Christian is to work at softening judgment and widening mercy.

Thought for the Day

Those who judge condemn themselves.
English Proverb

The Lord is my light....
Psalm 27:1

The Power of Choice

A woman who had struggled with depression for several years attended a weekend retreat at the suggestion of her pastor. The retreat leader observed that she seemed unusually low and spoke without much energy in her voice.

Speaking privately with her, the leader learned that the woman had been treated for depression by various counselors and psychiatrists with no positive results. She continued to feel depressed and unhappy most of the time.

After reflecting upon her experience, the retreat leader responded quietly, "All of us have a choice every day—thirty choices per month, three hundred and sixty-five choices each year. Each morning we can choose whether we will be happy or unhappy, live in the light or in the darkness, be depressed or joyful." He urged the woman to consider carefully making the choice to be free of her depression each day.

For some reason, that was a new and liberating thought to her. She decided to try it. After two months she wrote to the retreat leader to say that the simple practice of choice had changed her life. Upon rising each morning, she recited a phrase from Psalm 27:1: "The Lord is my light." Then she decided to live in God's light and be happy for at least the next twelve hours.

As a result, she began truly to enjoy life again. Within sixty days, she was feeling more energetic and enthusiastic, less depressed and lethargic.

Of course, such a transformation may not come as easily to all who struggle with depression, especially when it has a physiological basis. However, it cannot hurt to try and exercise the power of choice.

Prayer for the Day

Loving and good God,
hour by hour and day by day
help me to choose good over evil,
light over darkness,
happiness over depression,
and joy over cynicism.

VMP

He will not let you fall;
your protector is always awake.
Psalm 121:3

God Watches Over Us

An eighty-five-year-old man ventured outside one snowy afternoon. Although legally blind, he could see some light and shapes. Snowflakes were especially beautiful before his eyes.

He shuffled slowly down his long driveway toward a large Douglas fir. Then he went from tree to tree shaking snow from the boughs and reveling in the sight of falling snowflakes. Suddenly, the man became aware of vague, unfamiliar shapes. He knew he had ventured too far into the woods and needed to start walking back toward his driveway.

Unfortunately, he could not remember which way he had walked and was unable to see his footprints in the snow. Everything was white and very cold! As the snow fell harder, he wiped a tear from his eye, rushed forward in panic, and shouted a desperate prayer: "Please God, help me!"

Abruptly, he stopped in his tracks and stood perfectly still as a feeling of relief broke through his fear. Then he turned around and moved in a new direction. Finally, coming to a fence he knew to be the boundary line of his property, he was able to follow it until he reached his gate and then the safety of his home.

The next morning, a young man who shovels snow for the elderly gentleman came rushing to see him. The young man was alarmed by the footsteps he had seen in the snow. The older man explained that he had gone for a walk yesterday. The young man explained that he had been alarmed because the footsteps led up to the edge of the riverbank, right where the drop-off is steepest. One more step and the older man would have fallen to a certain death.

That final step was precisely where the older man had stopped and called out to God for help. "He will not let you fall," declares the psalmist. "Your protector is always awake." The psalmist reminds us that God's power is a personal one that watches over us so that we do not stumble and fall.

Thought for the Day

What God does,
He does well.
Jean De La Fontaine

He gives me new strength.
Psalm 23:3

The Price of Freedom

A client described to his psychologist a variety of abuses that he experienced at the hands of another person. The psychologist conveyed with her eyes and body language that she truly understood each horrible offense inflicted upon the man.

When the client was finished speaking, he asked, "What should I do about all this?"

"You need to forgive the person who did these things to you," the psychologist responded candidly.

"Forgive?" shouted the client. "Didn't you hear all the terrible things I just told you that this person did to me?"

"Yes," replied the psychologist.

"Then how in the world can you possibly suggest that I forgive this person? He does not deserve to be forgiven."

"Maybe the person does not deserve to be forgiven, but you deserve to be free from the lingering pain," the psychologist said.

It was a wise and sensitive encounter. The psychologist is quite correct. All of us deserve to be free from the pains of past hurts. The price of that freedom is forgiveness.

When we find it humanly impossible to forgive, let us remember that "God gives me new strength." This means that God can empower us to do what we cannot do and what we do not want to do.

Prayer for the Day

Loving God,
give me the strength to forgive,
to let go,
to avoid resentment.
Give me the strength to be free.
VMP

Why am I so sad?
Why am I so troubled?
I will put my hope in God....
Psalm 42:5

Choosing Our Attitude

When her first child was about two years old, opera star Beverly Sills learned that her little girl was almost deaf. The little girl was cut off from the world of music that was so important to her mother. The child would never hear the sound of her mother's voice.

At almost the same time, Sills gave birth to a second child, a son who proved to be autistic. The great opera singer took a one-year leave of absence to come to terms with her dual tragedy, as well as to work with her daughter in a school for the deaf.

Asked once if she was happy, Sills said, "I'm cheerful. There's a difference. A cheerful woman has cares but has learned how to deal with them."

Beverly Sills demonstrates a rare wisdom and maturity in response to her pain and suffering. She knows that we can choose our attitudes. When we choose to be cheerful and hopeful an interesting transformation takes place: we gradually find ourselves feeling better. This is because feelings always follow actions. Today the psalmist reminds us that outward behavior influences inward feelings. The writer of the text tells us that by having a talk with ourselves, we can move from being "sad" and "troubled" to experiencing hope in God.

Thought for the Day

The longer I've counseled people,
the more I've come to believe
that a moderate amount of denial
can be salutary.
When you're discouraged,
it is remarkable
how you can change your mood
if you act enthusiastic.
Alan Loy McGinnis

How short you have made my life!
Psalm 39:5

Making the Most of Our Lives

Measured against eternity, life is very short. To make the most of living, ask yourself these profound questions:

- Have I wept over anything recently? perhaps a tear of sadness over a loss or a tear of joy over beautiful music?
- Did my heart beat faster in the presence of indescribable beauty?
- Upon seeing the spontaneous play and joy of children, did I remember to become more childlike in my living?
- Have I taken the time to reflect upon the fact I will die someday?
- Have I thought about what really is important and what is not? Have I attempted to separate the trivial from the significant?
- Am I deliberately working at cultivating new friendships while deepening old ones?
- If someone I know is suffering great pain, am I willing to pray, asking God to transfer that pain to me?

If your answer to most or all of these questions is yes, chances are you truly are living a noble, meaningful life and making the most of your years. On the other hand, if you had to honestly answer no to most of them, you may not be making the most of life. This is a good time to begin a change of direction.

Prayer for the Day

Loving God,
I thank you for the gift of life.
I ask you to guide me so that I
might live wisely,
honorably,
with love and compassion for all.
VMP

God is our shelter and strength....
Psalm 46:1

God Is With Us

A woman wrote to a newspaper advice columnist saying she and her husband had "experienced a parent's worst nightmare." They learned that one of their children has an illness for which there is no treatment. After consulting several specialists, the parents were told to anticipate their child's death.

"The pain we are feeling is indescribable," wrote the mother. "There is such a cloud hanging over our heads; it is difficult to get through the day without breaking down." She concluded with a plea for help. "How do we plan to give up a child? Although we have always been strong in faith, we are finding it particularly hard to pray."

Today's reading from Psalm 46 makes two points. First, life can be terribly unfair and disappointing. Life brings us times of trouble which can leave us feeling depleted and weakened, both physically and emotionally. Sooner or later, everyone experiences life's cruel blows: a death in the family, the end of an important relationship, a disability, a major sickness, a child who becomes terminally ill.

Second, the psalm declares that "God is our shelter and strength." When the storms of life rage and when we feel weakest, the writer reminds us that God is with us. God gives us shelter and strength.

Thought for the Day

No one ever promised us
a life free from pain and disappointment.
The most anyone promised us
was that we would not be alone in our pain,
and that we would be able
to draw upon a source outside ourselves
for the strength and courage
we would need
to survive life's tragedies and life's unfairness.

Rabbi Harold Kushner

So they are punished by their own evil
and are hurt by their own violence.
Psalm 7:16

We Reap What We Sow

There is a memorable scene in the movie *Gandhi.* It is 1947, and Mahatma Gandhi is fasting to protest the riot killings that followed the partition creating Hindu India and Moslem Pakistan. A fellow Hindu approaches to confess a great wrong.

"I killed a child," says the distraught man. "I smashed his head against a wall."

"Why?" asks the Mahatma (Sanskrit for *Great Soul*).

"They killed my boy. The Moslems killed my son."

"I know a way out of hell," says Gandhi. "Find a child, a little boy whose mother and father have been killed, and raise him as your own. Only be sure he is a Moslem—and that you raise him as one."

The grieving, guilt-racked father falls to his knees, weeping at Gandhi's feet.

We must always be careful about what we say and how we act. Evil words and actions can come back to haunt and hurt us. The writer of today's psalm reminds us of the law of life: people "are punished by their own evil and are hurt by their own violence."

Thought for the Day

From the body of one guilty deed
a thousand ghostly fears and haunting
thoughts proceed.
William Wordsworth

As for me, I do what is right.
Psalm 26:11

The Necessity of a Clear Goal

Johnny Weissmuller is best known for his portrayal of Tarzan in many Hollywood movies. Before that, however, he was a champion swimmer who set world swimming records and won several gold medals. He credits his swimming coach with teaching him an important lesson that enabled him to become successful.

The pool where Weissmuller was training was divided into lanes for competition. These lanes were defined by black tiles laid in straight lines to guide the swimmers during practice. The coach discovered that Weissmuller's time was slower whenever he swam in a pool without lines.

Rather than swimming straight to the other side of the pool, he would wobble from side to side, losing precious seconds. Without realizing it, Weissmuller had come to depend on those lane markings. To teach the young swimmer to swim straight with or without lines, the coach placed his hat at the other end of the pool. Then he instructed Weissmuller to draw a mental line to the hat and swim along that mental line just as surely as if it were a real line.

That lesson not only helped Weissmuller become a successful champion swimmer but saved his life when he was swept overboard twenty-five miles out to sea. He was able to draw a mental line to shore and swim to safety.

We, too, often find ourselves wobbling from side to side, unable to follow a straight course because we do not have a clear goal in life. By determining a worthy goal, we can then draw a mental line and follow it all the way to our objective. Although the goal may change during the course of our pilgrimage, we will discover that the true joy lies in making the journey.

Thought for the Day

To reach the port of heaven,
we must sail,
sometimes with the wind,
and sometimes against it,
but we must sail,
not drift or lie at anchor.
Oliver Wendell Holmes

Even if a whole army surrounds me,
I will not be afraid....
I will still trust God.
Psalm 27:3

How to Reduce Fear

Not enough of us share the confident view of the psalmist in today's reading. Worry and fear prevent us from taking risks, reaching out, plunging ahead. Here are several ways to reduce fear and worry in your life:

- *Write out your fears.* This simple writing exercise puts fear into a healthier perspective. Your imagination can work overtime to heighten fear. Expressing anxieties on paper deflates fear.
- *Evaluate your fear.* Take a close look at what frightens you. Ask yourself how likely it is to occur? What is the worst that could happen? Could you handle it? What can you do to minimize the risk?
- *Set a time aside just to worry.* Psychologists recommend choosing the same time each day to think about all your concerns. By scheduling your worry time you can limit it.
- *Postpone other worries for your worry period.* If you catch yourself worrying at other times during the day simply set the worries aside for your official worry time.
- *Visualize yourself as strong and successful.* An effective antidote to fear lies in creating a powerful mental image of success and strength.
- *Fight fear with faith.* An effective way to fight fear with faith is to affirm and repeat today's psalm: "Even if a whole army surrounds me, I will not be afraid.... I will still trust God."

Thought for the Day

Who lives in fear will
never be a free man.
Horace

Praise the Lord, all living creatures!
Psalm 150:6

Increasing Your Praise Quotient

The Psalms are filled with expressions of praise. There is a cause-and-effect relationship between expressing gratitude and the flow of God's blessings in our lives. People who are short on praise generally view life in negatives and do not seem to enjoy many of God's blessings.

On the other hand, those whose faith is vibrant, strong, positive, and filled with gratitude seem to receive continuous blessings from God. Why not try increasing your praise quotient by engaging in the following actions:

- If you want to know God more, give praise and thanks for God's presence in your life. Such gratitude will enable you to recognize and accept more of God's activity in your life.
- If you want more physical, emotional, or spiritual wholeness, thank God for the evidence of life and health that you already have.
- If you want more abundance, praise God for any resources and talents you can identify. Then watch and see how these multiply in new and creative ways to bring you greater abundance.
- If you are facing great trials and troubles, give God praise for the parts of your life that are not in crises, and see how your trials and troubles become more manageable and less ominous.

Find other ways to increase your praise quotient and watch how more good events, people, and experiences flow your way.

-------- Thought for the Day --------

Gratitude to God makes
even a temporal blessing
a taste of heaven.
William Romaine

You will trample down lions and snakes,
fierce lions and poisonous snakes.
Psalm 91:13

We Are Guided Through Life's Many Perils

Sixteen-year-old Chris was riding her bike to the YMCA when she felt something hit the back of her head. In an instant, she realized a copperhead snake was wrapped twice around her neck. Somehow the snake had gotten caught in the back wheel of her bike, which had no fender, and was flipped onto the back of her neck.

She could see the snake's head just inches from her face, poised to strike. The teenager knew she had to get the snake away from her face. A snakebite that close to the heart could be fatal. So she grabbed the snake hoping to seize it just behind its head but in her haste wrapped her hand around the snake's head. The creature sank its fangs deeply into the first finger of her right hand.

Chris was able to fling the snake hard to the ground. However, she knew the snake had to be trapped so physicians could determine what kind of medicine to give her. She pinned the snake under the back tire of her bike. Although she felt dizzy and disoriented, Chris managed to run home. By the time her parents got her to the hospital, Chris' arm was two and one-half times its normal size. She received treatment and recovered.

Physicians say the young woman's quick, skillful thinking spared her from numerous surgeries to remove dead tissues and may even have saved her life, since the snake was a poisonous copperhead.

Today's reading may sound odd: "You will trample down lions and snakes, fierce lions and poisonous snakes." Yet it is simply the ancient writer's way of saying that, although life is filled with many perils, as we learn to trust and depend on God, we can grow to feel secure. When we are faced with great danger, our God is present to guide our thinking and our acting.

Thought for the Day

To those who dwell in God
evil forces become harmless;
they wear a charmed life
and defy the deadliest ills.

Charles H. Spurgeon

The LORD *is...*
blessing us with kindness and honor.
Psalm 84:11

Ten Self-Affirming Beliefs

Even though today's reading, as well as various other passages in the Bible, states clearly that God values, loves, honors, and respects us, many women and men continue to suffer from a low self-image. Here are affirmations that can help bolster self-esteem:

- I am a good, valuable, worthy individual.
- God has made me fully capable of achieving all goals that I set for myself.
- I am a responsible, trustworthy person.
- Happiness is a choice, so regardless of what may happen I have decided to be a joyful person.
- My spirit, mind, and body form a powerful team enabling me to set and accomplish high goals.
- I trust my judgment and am willing to take risks.
- I view problems and setbacks as opportunities for learning and growth.
- Every day in every way, my emotional, spiritual, and intellectual life deepens.
- Day by day I acknowledge and respond to God's goodness, kindness, and love for me.
- God loves me, so I love and accept myself.

Thought for the Day

Consider then thyself,
O noble soul,
and the nobility within thee,
for thou art honored above all creatures
in that thou art an image of God...
thou art destined to greatness.
Meister Eckhart

He is the God who makes me strong.
Psalm 18:32

Turning Weakness Into Strength

If you have ever been stung by critical comments that point out a weakness or flaw in you, think of this story about football coach Vince Lombardi. When he took over as coach of the Green Bay Packers, Lombardi chose a young man named Bart Starr to be his quarterback.

Lombardi made that decision in spite of Starr's noticeable weakness in throwing long passes. Wisely, Lombardi believed that once a weakness was identified, practice and hard work can turn it into a strength.

Consequently, he and Starr concentrated all their practice time on long passes. Eventually, the quarterback greatly improved both his confidence and his physical ability. Bart Starr, of course, became one of the best all-around quarterbacks in the history of football.

Rather than be hurt by criticism, try evaluating the comment. Is it valid? If not, then dismiss it from your mind. However, if there is truth to it, remind yourself that any weakness can be converted into a strength. Like Vince Lombardi and Bart Starr, do whatever it takes to make that transition.

-------- *Prayer for the Day* --------

Loving God,
I affirm you are for me and with me.
I affirm you seek the best for me.
Guide me as I ever work to transform
weakness into strength,
pain into power,
despair into hope, and
indifference into love.
VMP

They do not speak in a friendly way.
Psalm 35:20

Heart Service Instead of Lip Service

In the New Testament, it is clear that Jesus was a true friend to outcasts, those on the fringe of society. He genuinely valued and accepted them. Today's psalm refers to people who choose not to befriend others. This contrast between Jesus' attitude and those cited in the psalm provides an opportunity for an examination of conscience. Let us sincerely ask ourselves:

- Do I give true heart service or mere lip service?
- Are my actions consistent with my statements?
- Do I seek to cultivate boundless love and unconditional acceptance of others?
- Do I view the harassed and helpless with deep compassion and mercy?
- Do I try to see others with the spiritual vision of wholeness, with the eyes of Christ?
- Do I actively work at softening my judgmental attitudes while broadening attitudes of love and kindness?
- Do I try to express God's compassion for all, especially for those who experience soul-deep feelings of inadequacy, low self-esteem, and unworthiness?

Prayer for the Day

Loving God,
In all things,
let my creeds match my deeds,
my words match my works,
my belief match my behavior.
VMP

Rescue me from their attacks.
Psalm 35:17

The Healing Power of Acceptance

A blood transfusion during childbirth infected Elizabeth Glasser with the AIDS virus, which was then passed on to two of her children. Ariel, her oldest daughter, died from AIDS shortly after her seventh birthday; Elizabeth died in the fall of 1994. Elizabeth, her husband, Paul, and their children experienced the cruelty of rejection by others because they are an AIDS family.

However, Elizabeth spoke out on behalf of people who suffer from AIDS, urging society to adopt compassionate attitudes. She shared a powerful incident of unusual acceptance when she and her husband met with two hundred parents from their son's school. When they told the parents about their little boy's diagnosis, the Glassers had no idea how the adults would react. In the past, they had been deeply hurt by the fear and rejection they experienced.

Upon completing their talk, Elizabeth asked whether anyone had any questions. An uneasy hush fell over the room. Finally, a man raised his hand and said, "Yes, I have a question." Elizabeth's chest tightened, but the man continued, "When can your son come to our house to play?"

When Elizabeth would retell that story, tears would form in her eyes. It was a powerful moment of acceptance that restored her spirit.

Let us remember the man who responded positively and compassionately to the Glassers' pain. May we view with the loving eyes of Christ those whose lives are a desperate struggle. Keeping in mind today's psalm, "Rescue me from their attacks," let us be people of compassion who rescue women and men from the "attacks" of others.

Thought for the Day

Your voice falls on me as they say love should,
like an enormous yes.

Philip Levine

Wait for the LORD.
Psalm 27:14
(*New Revised Standard Version*)

The Virtue and Value of Patience

The ability to be patient is a vital life-skill through which dreams can be transformed into reality. The exercise of patience is a powerful defense against easy defeat. Consider the example of country music star Randy Travis. His wife and manager, Lib Hatcher, remembers long lean days waiting for Randy to be "discovered."

During that decade—3,650 days—Lib sold her jewelry and pooled all her cash to keep her nightclub open long enough for someone to discover what she had discovered: the voice of Randy Travis.

For ten lonely years, she promoted Travis while he fried catfish, washed dishes, and sang in their nightclub. Then it finally clicked. He had a hit called "On the Other Hand," followed by an album contract, an offer for a tour, and even a movie deal. Detached observers called Randy an overnight success, never realizing that he worked toward stardom for ten years.

Thought for the Day

There are some favors
that the Almighty does not grant
either the first or the second or the third time
you ask Him,
because he wishes you to pray
for a long time
and often He wills this delay
to keep you in a state of humility...
and to make you realize
the value of his graces.
Jean Eudes

Why am I so sad?
Why am I so troubled?
I will put my hope in God.
Psalm 42:11

Managing the Blues

Depression, commonly referred to as "the blues," is experienced by most people. However, for some, depression is debilitating because it obstructs hope and impairs daily life. One man describes his depression this way: "I feel I am the saddest, loneliest person on the planet. There are days when it's difficult to get out of bed. I don't feel enthusiastic or hopeful about anything. I can't even stop to smell the flowers because I don't have any."

Although feelings of depression afflict most people, the good news is that those feelings can be managed and even transformed. In today's psalm, the writer is feeling depressed but takes charge of his feelings by talking back to them. The next time you are feeling depressed, take charge of your emotions by using some of these techniques:

- Remind yourself that you are not alone, that many people live with and manage depression.
- Focus on something besides your feelings, your pain, your experience.
- Write an uplifting letter of praise and compliment to someone.
- Take an inventory of your blessings and recite reasons to live a life of gratitude.
- Read some inspirational books and magazine articles.
- Tell yourself, *It's only depression*, and then get on with your day.

Thought for the Day

Anyone can carry a burden, however hard,
until nightfall.
Anyone can do work, however hard,
for one day.
Anyone can live sweetly, patiently, purely,
till the sun goes down.
Robert Louis Stevenson

Give me understanding. . . .
Psalm 119:169

Maintaining Good Relationships

June, a woman in her thirties, learned she was HIV-positive. Her life has been a roller coaster of emotions ever since, but she is slowly coming to terms with the realities of AIDS. She is currently in good health, and feels that with proper diet, exercise, medication, and a positive attitude, she will remain that way for a long time.

However, over the last few years she has become estranged from several friends who had meant a great deal to her. "Most of the trouble I've had with these friends could be blamed on me," she confesses.

Facing the possibility of death from AIDS, June wants to reconcile with the people "I treated shabbily," she says. "It is important to me that I leave this world with all my fences mended."

Consequently, she is courageously contacting each person she has offended. June expresses regret for her actions, for the estrangement, and expresses her desire to reconnect.

June's attitudes and actions are commendable. We can all learn from her example. However, we do not need to have an incurable condition to make us think more deeply about the importance of maintaining good relationships. That is something we should be working for at all times. Like the psalmist, we should pray often "Give me understanding," and God will give us the wisdom we need to manage and maintain our relationships so that when we are wrong, we will make amends. Likewise, when we are wronged, we will have the courage to confront in order to redeem the relationship.

Thought for the Day

I have learned...
that the head does not hear anything
until the heart has listened,
and what the heart knows today
the head will understand tomorrow.
James Stephens

Do not let proud men attack me....
Psalm 36:11

God Disarms Our Adversaries

During the early 1960s, educator Robert Coles interviewed black children when their southern schools were being forcefully integrated. Dr. Coles was astonished by their courage in the face of daily threats from angry mobs of white adults.

One eight-year-old girl from North Carolina told of a time when she was "all alone, and those [segregationists] people were screaming, and suddenly I saw God smiling, and I smiled." The little girl went on to say that a woman in the crowd shouted at her, "Hey, you little nigger, what you smiling at?" The eight-year-old responded simply and sincerely, "At God." The white woman looked up into the sky, then looked at the little girl and stopped shouting and threatening her.

Those who wrote the Psalms often asked God to disarm and neutralize their enemies. We may not be facing a life-or-death situation or something of the magnitude of the struggle for integration. However, there are times when we face our own perils and dilemmas.

There are times when we find ourselves in the presence of an "enemy"—a threatening stranger who could hurt us physically, an employer who abuses us emotionally, or even a family member or friend who takes advantage of us in other ways. In those moments, we must remember to call on God for strength, protection, wisdom, safety, and security.

Thought for the Day

You need not cry very loud;
he is nearer to us than we think.
Brother Lawrence

Teach me, Lord....
Psalm 27:11

Controlling the Critic Within

A woman, now in her forties and at the height of her career as an astronautical engineer, laments that she does not have a good relationship with her mother. "When I was growing up, all she did was criticize me for everything I did and didn't do. She created an oppressive atmosphere in the house. I hated to come home after school and face her."

Most of us have a tendency to be overly critical. We especially tend to overcorrect the people we love. While we do that to help them become the best people possible, too much criticism can stifle the personality and strangle the spirit.

The problem is that what we perceive as a constructive criticism can be experienced by another as an attack. Consequently, our relationship with others will suffer under the burden of negativity.

An effective way to soften and sweeten our relationships is to reduce the volume of criticism, judgment, fault-finding, and castigation. Before speaking out, try to assess if the issue is important or trivial, large or small. If it is trivial or small, remain silent. Like the psalmist, we should pray, "Teach me, Lord."

If your daughter's hair is dreadful, if you son's clothing does not match, if your husband has bored everyone at the table with his jokes, don't be the one to tell them. When we control the critic within us, life becomes lighter and more joyful.

Thought for the Day

See everything, overlook a lot, correct a little.
Pope John XXIII

I will sing with joy because of you.
Psalm 9:2

Cultivating Happiness

Recent research indicates that factors usually associated with a sense of well-being, such as age, race, sex, and income, have much less effect than previously thought. According to research published in *Psychology Today*, the following are recommended as important contributing factors to overall happiness and satisfaction in life:

- *Enjoy the present.* Take time to enjoy everyday small pleasures rather than delaying joy for some future time.
- *Control your time.* Research reveals that unhappy people tend to be unfocused in their thinking and planning. Those who are happy generally have plans, large and small, and work toward achieving those goals.
- *Exhibit happy behavior.* Thinking and acting in positive, optimistic ways leads to greater happiness.
- *Get physical.* Physically fit people cope with stress better and are more self-confident than the physically unfit.
- *Get enough rest.* People who give themselves enough time for restorative rest and solitude are happier.
- *Cultivate close relationships.* Friendships are extremely therapeutic. Happy people have good friends they can turn to and confide in.
- *Exercise your faith.* There is a powerful link between faith and happiness. While faith does not prevent suffering, it can evoke meaning and purpose in life. Faith also provides a focus beyond oneself.

Prayer for the Day

Loving and eternal God,
Help me to know life's simple joys.
Open my eyes to see the beauty of the sun,
the innocence of children,
the delight of friendship,
the opportunity of service,
the gift of life.
VMP

Give us success in all we do!
Psalm 90:17

See a Need and Respond

Several years ago Steve Wallenda, of the famous flying Wallendas high-wire circus act, learned that a good friend needed a heart transplant. This friend had neither money nor insurance coverage to pay for the expensive procedure.

Immediately, Steve Wallenda came up with a fund-raising plan of action. He arranged to have a forty-foot high wire set up in the parking lot at the Rawhide Amusement Park in Scottsdale, Arizona. Wallenda told his friend as well as the press that he would mount the high wire and stay up there for four days in a fund-raising effort to help pay for his friend's surgery.

Wallenda did not wait for anyone to tell him how he could help. He saw a need and responded.

Let us be guided by that inspiring action. Whenever we come across someone who needs assistance, let us respond spontaneously, boldly, and courageously. Let us remember also to do acts of kindness and compassion with a prayerful, humble spirit. We must ask God to guide us, bless our effort, and "grant us success" as we seek ways to help a needy individual or family.

Thought for the Day

If you truly want to help the soul of your neighbor,
you should approach God first
with all your heart.
Ask him simply to fill you with charity,
the greatest of all virtues;
with it you can accomplish
what you desire.
Saint Vincent Ferrer

They are like trees that grow beside a stream,
that bear fruit at the right time....
Psalm 1:3

Expanding Your Horizons

Our relationships improve and take on deeper dimensions as we expand our horizons and have more to bring to them. Because life is always a constricting, conservative force, we need to force ourselves out of comfortable ruts and routines of family, home, friends, job, and so forth.

Here are some ideas for expanding your horizon:

- Spend a few minutes each day with a book that challenges, expands, and nourishes the mind and the soul.
- Take a class in a serious subject that interests you—something you've never studied before.
- If you live in a community that has a museum or art gallery, become a member. Visit frequently, taking advantage of special exhibits and lectures.
- Express yourself through art or music. Learn to paint. Take up a musical instrument. Study pottery making.

When you choose to expand yourself you enrich your relationships. Remember that relationships are not just about shared bodies, shared bank accounts, shared dinner tables. They are richest when they are about shared experiences and shared ideas. In this way you will be "like trees that grow beside a stream, that bear fruit."

Thought for the Day

To learn is a natural pleasure,
not confined to philosophers,
but common to all.
Aristotle

A good person…
will always be remembered.
Psalm 112:6

Using Our Power to Help Others

Too often power is used to hurt or hinder others. Yet we all have personal power and should remember to use it on behalf of others. Normally, roles are quite limited for older women in television and Hollywood. Yet Angela Lansbury has experienced unusual success, enjoying ten smash seasons on CBS's "Murder, She Wrote."

Lansbury has used her influence to establish a more humane work schedule. Her own limit is twelve hours a day, down from seventeen. She has ensured guest shots for friends from her film days, many of whom are unable to find film roles.

Recently, she learned that actress Madlyn Rhue was suffering from multiple sclerosis and needed a part in order to keep up her Screen Actors Guild health benefits. Lansbury quickly signed Rhue to play a librarian in an episode of her series.

Personal power is a privilege. We must learn to use it on behalf of others. Creating acts of kindness and mercy is always a proper use of power.

Thought for the Day

O! it is excellent
To have a giant's strength;
But it is tyrannous
To use it like a giant.
William Shakespeare

I had hoped for sympathy, but there was none.
Psalm 69:20

Being More of a Giver, Less of a Martyr

Have you ever heard yourself using sentences such as the following: "I am tired of being taken advantage of"; "I'm always the one who is asked to help"; "I'm the one that always goes the second mile"; "If I don't do it, no one will?"

Those sentences reveal a person who is a martyr rather than a true giver. Of course, if they contain truth, then it is appropriate to become more assertive of one's personal rights.

Often, however, such statements simply indicate that we expect too much from others and do not demand enough from ourselves. We are martyrs when we expect praise and recognition for what we give. "I had hoped for sympathy, but there was none," is the psalmist's lament. One critical aspect of a meaningful life is to be more of a giver and less of a martyr.

We become martyrs when we give in order to win love or merely to meet some social expectation. We sacrifice ourselves when we act because of our need for approval from others.

However, true giving is a joy and leads to a life filled with meaning. When we honestly act to help others, we are actually offering our lives as a gift to be shared. One effective way to become less of a martyr and more of a giver is to have a daily goal to give in small ways. Here are some examples:

- Send a note of encouragement to someone who is down.
- Write a letter of congratulations to acknowledge a friend's victory.
- When making your lunch for work make an additional one to give away to a homeless person.
- Make a grand gesture by offering to look after other people's children so they can go on a retreat or have a quiet weekend.

Thought for the Day

To give and then not feel that one has given
is the very best of all ways of giving.
Sir Max Beerbohm

I had nearly lost confidence;
my faith was almost gone....
Psalm 73:2

Living by Faith, Not by Sight

What we see around us can cause us to lose confidence in ourselves and diminish our ability to trust in God. For that reason, it is vital that we learn to live by faith and not by sight.

Bobbie Green Kilberg, who was a deputy assistant to former President George Bush, was asked to share her thoughts about the glamour and excitement of working daily in the White House.

Interestingly, the event which Kilberg says she will always remember was a visit to the White House from Polish leader Lech Walesa. He was in the country to receive the Medal of Freedom.

"He told us about the time police were waiting downstairs to take him to prison," recalls Kilberg, "and he went upstairs and made the sign of the cross on each of his children. The emotion in that room was extraordinary; we all felt it."

Walesa's action is a good example of living by faith and not merely by sight. At that time, all he could see was that the power of a hostile state was set in motion against him, his family, and his movement. Yet in rushing upstairs to pray quickly for his children, Walesa demonstrated his faith in God. Even though great powers were aligned against him, he knew that a Higher Power would guide and provide for him and his family.

Let us remember to walk and live by faith, not only by sight. Let us remember that God's love and power will manifest themselves no matter what our circumstances might look like.

Prayer for the Day

Loving and eternal God,
I affirm you are with me.
I affirm you are holding me.
I affirm you are guiding me.
Therefore, I will live by faith
and not by sight.
VMP

He gives generously to the needy,
and his kindness never fails.
Psalm 112:9

What Does Love Look Like?

Today's psalm reading is a picture of love:

- Love has hands that reach out promptly to those who hurt and suffer.
- Love has feet that move rapidly toward those in need of help and assistance.
- Love has eyes that see the poorest of the poor among us and respond with compassion.
- Love has a heart that beats in tune with the very heart of God. It is filled with kindness, mercy, and tenderness.
- Love has ears that hear the groaning and sighing of hurting women, men, and children.
- Love has a mouth and a voice that offer cheer, praise, encouragement, and support to those who feel defeated.
- Love has arms wide enough to include and embrace those on the fringes of society.

What does love look like? Love looks like you!

Thought for the Day

Our business is to be
the hands and feet and mouth
of One who has no other hands or feet or mouth
except our own.
Frederick Buechner

Be patient...
don't be worried about those
who prosper.
Psalm 37:7

The Power of the Three *P*'s

Today's psalm offers good advice for any of us who are tempted to compare ourselves with others. Too often, doing that leaves us feeling as though we are not as successful or have not advanced as quickly.

The psalm reminds us about the power of the three *P*'s: patience, perseverance, and persistence. Dreams come true only for those who are able to work faithfully and then wait for the fruit of their labors to blossom. Consider the example of Nathan Birnbaum.

Nathan Birnbaum was regarded as a poor vaudeville comic who was thrown out of one theater after another. Theater owners and managers wouldn't hire Nathan after they saw his routine. He had to keep changing his name to get jobs.

Yet he refused to give up. Nathan continued to polish his act, teamed up with a woman named Gracie Allen, and then changed his name to George Burns. Now, of course, he is extremely successful. But it took patience, perseverance, and persistence on his part.

When we see others whose success is impressive, let us take them as inspiring examples of what we, too, can become. Let us remind ourselves that everything worthwhile has its price. And the price for seeing dreams become realities is working and waiting.

Prayer for the Day

Loving and glorious God,
Day by day remind me
that the prospering presence of God
is always with me.
Because of you,
I am already wealthy in body,
in mind, and in spirit.
Today, bless my labor
and let all that I do bring you
glory and honor.
VMP

Strive for peace with all your heart.
Psalm 34:14

Practicing the Art of Forgiveness

One man decided it was time to unclutter his spiritual life so he decided to let go of past difficulties by forgiving people. He compiled the following list of forgiveness statements:

I forgive a doctor for doing a sloppy operation.
I forgive an old girlfriend for marrying someone else.
I forgive a family member for treating me badly.
I forgive myself for being unkind to my dad.
I forgive someone who sued me in a frivolous lawsuit.
I forgive myself for punishing and abusing myself.

A sure and definite sign of spiritual and emotional maturity is our ability to forgive wrongs, large and small. Daily forgiveness is an honorable goal for all of us. It is the path to inner peace. Begin today by

Forgiving a family member who hurt you
Forgiving a colleague who betrayed you
Forgiving a friend who divulged a confidence
Forgiving a parent who was unkind, even cruel
Forgiving a relative who gossiped about you
Forgiving an employer who terminated your job
Forgiving a stranger who was unkind and uncaring
Forgiving whomever for whatever

Thought for the Day

Forgiveness is not something
you work toward
to let someone else off the hook.
Forgiveness lets you off the hook,
the hook of your own rage.
Judith Sills

I have done what is right and good.
Psalm 119:121

Small Deeds Have a Large Impact

Very few of us will be called upon to act in heroic, courageous ways.

Very few of us will ever receive a ticker-tape parade honoring us for some great achievement.

Very few of us will have the opportunity to perform a great sacrifice.

Very few of us will find our names engraved in bronze or granite or placed in a hall of fame.

Yet all of us will have ample opportunities to do good.

All of us will have opportunities to exercise gentleness, kindness, and compassion.

All of us will have opportunities to offer words of praise, encouragement, and hope.

All of us will have opportunities to soften the blows of life by providing friendship and support.

All of us will have opportunities to help others fight off discouragement, disappointment, and despair.

Daily life is filled with opportunities to do what is "right and good." They may be small deeds, but every small deed has a large impact.

-------- *Thought for the Day* --------

In fact, to this very day,
common sense in religion is rare,
and we are too often trying to be heroic
instead of being just ordinarily good and kind.

Dorothy Day

. . .you defend the cause of the poor
and the rights of the needy.
Psalm 140:12

Small Starts Can Lead to Large Results

Yesterday we considered how small deeds can have large impacts. Today let us consider how small starts can lead to large results. In the last century, a physician donated his time at a mission in London's east end, the poorest section of the city.

One night as he turned off the lights in the mission, the doctor saw a little boy huddled inside the door. The youth, a homeless orphan, begged the doctor to let him sleep inside because he had nowhere else to go. The boy told the physician that he had been living in a coal bin with several other youths.

As he won the confidence of the child, the doctor persuaded the boy to take him to the coal bin where other boys had been living. After going through several darkened alleys, they came to a hole in the wall of a factory. Crawling inside, the doctor found thirteen boys huddled under rags to keep warm. All were asleep.

Because of that experience, the doctor's heart was burdened to begin a home in London for abandoned, orphaned, and homeless children. By the time he died, Dr. Thomas Barnardo had founded homes for over eighty thousand homeless boys and girls.

That great work began with his compassion for one frightened, cold child. He was led by God to "defend the cause of the poor and the rights of the needy." Soon his compassion extended to thirteen more boys and grew to a crowd of over eighty thousand. In the hands of God, our small starts can sometimes lead to large results.

Thought for the Day

Holiness consists
of doing the will of God
with a smile.

Mother Teresa of Calcutta

I put my hope in you.
Psalm 39:7

Crusaders for Hope

Sooner or later, sadness, sorrow, and suffering enter every life. Ultimately, no one can escape some trial, trouble, or trauma. When others experience such difficulty, we should act to become crusaders for hope.

Let us give strength to those who are weakened by life.

Let us speak with love to the frightened, for love conquers fear.

Let us act with sensitivity to those who are grieving.

Let us offer words of wisdom to those who are confused and uncertain.

Let us keep the faith for those whose faith is diminishing and faltering because of some life event.

Let us live with God's joy in our hearts, giving others a reason to smile and laugh once again.

Let us pray deeply and fervently for those whose pain is great.

When we respond with compassion to the suffering of others we not only help strengthen and stabilize them, we empower them to place their hope in God.

Thought for the Day

The love of our neighbor
in all its fullness
simply means
being able to say to him or her:
"What are you going through?"
Simone Weil

...he will give you your heart's desire.
Psalm 37:4

Dreaming Great Dreams for God

Many people today experience life as empty and shallow. Many feel their existence is devoid of meaning. Consequently, they simply drift along without plan or purpose. Yet God calls all of us to achieve our potential and contribute to the common good. God's intent is to "give you your heart's desire."

If you are having difficulty finding a focus for your life, here are some questions that can open up new directions. Ask yourself each question and pause to think before moving on to the next question.

- What do I care about deeply?
- What brings a tear to my eye?
- What quickens my pulse?
- What brings me joy and pleasure?
- What did I want to be when I was a child?
- What makes me feel good about myself?
- What injustice makes me want to help others?
- As a child, what did I love to do?
- If I had only a few months to live, what would I do?

After asking yourself these questions, listen carefully to your inner spirit. It has a wisdom all its own about what is and is not right for you. Your inner spirit will share its insights with you through signals of comfort and discomfort. The discomfort could be physical pain, emotional distress, or general malaise. The negative signals can be corrected by making a life adjustment. The positive signals should be followed and obeyed. They will lead to life in all of its fullness.

Prayer for the Day

Eternal and glorious God,
I affirm that your divine love
inspires me to make wise choices,
guides me to live wisely,
energizes my daily life,
sustains and upholds me.
VMP

I delight in following your commands
more than in having great wealth.
Psalm 119:14

Establishing Healthy Priorities

After Derek Bok retired as president of Harvard University in 1991, he spent a year at Stanford University researching and writing a book, *The Cost of Talent*. Focusing on the career choices of society's most talented college students, Bok concluded that they appear to be motivated and lured by careers that offer the most money.

During the past twenty-five years, the "best and brightest" young people have turned to careers in law, medicine, and business rather than to teaching, government, ministry, and other public service occupations.

Dr. Bok notes that in 1970 approximately forty percent of incoming college students listed "being very well off financially" as a "very important" goal. By 1990 that figure rose to seventy-five percent of first-year college students. The former Harvard president is dismayed and concerned because of the diversion of society's best minds from the needs and opportunities of public service.

People who are spiritually wise and mature know the importance of establishing healthy priorities. Of course, there is nothing wrong with a career in law, medicine, or the corporate world. However, the decision to enter those fields should be based upon an inner calling rather than upon the craving for material wealth.

Today let us review our career choices in light of Psalm 119:14. Can we say, like the psalmist, "I delight in following your commands more than in having great wealth"?

Prayer for the Day

Holy God,
Rather than simply building a career,
help me build a life.
Rather than merely seeking financial
security for myself and my family,
help me remember
the needs of others as well.

VMP

My cup overflows.
Psalm 23:5
(New Revised Standard Version)

Emptying and Filling the Mind

There are times when we must consciously empty the mind of all negative emotions in order to fill it with God's peace and joy. One by one, we must remove all that holds us back from God's abundant life. Try practicing the following method of emptying and filling.

Today I empty myself of all
anger, fear, self-pity,
doubt, jealousy, worry,
discouragement, disappointment,
sadness, unhappiness, selfishness,
insecurity, anxiety, disappointment,
coldness, callousness, insensitivity.
Today I empty myself of all tears.

Having emptied myself, I now refill myself with
peace, power, prosperity,
wisdom, insight, knowledge,
love, warmth, friendship,
living, learning, laughing,
caring, sharing, helping,
forgiving, accepting, affirming.
Today I fill myself with God's abundance.

Prayer for the Day

Holy and loving God,
You are filling my mind with
peace, courage, assurance.
You are with me now and always.
You are my constant companion.
You fill the cup of my life
to overflowing.
VMP

Praise him for the mighty things he has done.
Psalm 150:2

Spreading Sunshine

Shortly after a man and his wife moved into a one-hundred-eighty-two-family condominium development in San Diego, California, he had to have surgery. A week later, he received a cheerful get-well card signed simply "The Sunshine Lady." He had no idea who the sender was. A few months later, his wife was ill with the flu. Soon another bright greeting card was delivered. Again it was signed "The Sunshine Lady."

When he asked a neighbor about the mystery card sender, he was told "That's Bianka Rothschild. Ever since she moved into this condo in 1980, she's been sending cards to everyone who is confined to a bed." The man visited Mrs. Rothschild to thank her for such unexpected thoughtfulness and asked why she had taken on the monumental task of tracking the sick and then sending them cards. The woman surprised him with her explanation.

Mrs. Rothschild was born to a Jewish family in Poland. While growing up, she experienced the love of her parents and a large extended family. Of all that family, she alone survived the Holocaust. While in a concentration camp awaiting death, she read from a tiny Jewish prayer book that she kept hidden. This passage spoke to her heart: "We have a right to the joy of giving so others may receive. We can give material things, we can give moral support, we can give a friendly ear, and best of all, we can give love."

She bargained with God to give of herself in a true and loving spirit if God helped her through the terrible ordeal of surviving in a concentration camp. When she moved into the condominium complex, she made a personal commitment to carry out her promise. "In a complex with one hundred eighty-two families, you have lots of nice people who sometimes need a ray of sunshine," she said.

Like Mrs. Rothschild, God has blessed us abundantly. Like Mrs. Rothschild, why not be the first to spread sunshine into the lives of people who experience times of discouragement and darkness?

Prayer for the Day

Holy God and loving Creator,
Today I let your hope flow through me to one other person.
Today I let your love flow through me to one other person.
Today I will be the ray of sunshine to one other person.
VMP

I am...despised and scorned by everyone!
Psalm 22:6

The Power of a Note

A spoken compliment always brightens one's day and mood. However, a compliment written in a note has a longer, lingering impact because it can be read over and over and over again.

One busy person who makes time to write notes of praise and compliments is Donald Peterson, the former CEO of the Ford Motor Company. Peterson, who is largely credited for turning the company around in the 1980s, made it a practice to jot positive messages to associates each day.

"I'd just scribble them on a memo pad or the corner of a letter and pass them along," he says. "The most important ten minutes of your day are those you spend doing something to boost the people who work for you."

The truth is that people thrive on a compliment. One sure way to strengthen all our relationships is to express appreciation and praise toward members of our family and circle of friends.

So today why not consider sending off a short inspirational note to someone who needs a word of cheer? Keep in mind that too many people receive plenty of criticism and judgment but far too little praise and encouragement. Often people feel like the psalmist, "despised and scorned by everyone." A note of praise can soften such negative feelings.

Thought for the Day

The drawback with phone calls, of course,
is that they don't last.
A note attaches more importance
to our well-wishing.
It is a matter of record,
and our words can be read more than once,
savored, and treasured.

Fred Bauer

If I lay down in the world of the dead,
you would be there.
Psalm 139:8

The Five W's of Our Spiritual Life

In the world of journalism, a good news story responds to five W's: who, what, when, where, and why. The spiritual life can also be deepened by considering the same five W's.

Who. Who am I? Am I merely the product of parental upbringing? While parents have a great influence over us, that is only a partial answer. The greater reality is that we are the children of God. As such, we are profoundly loved, valued, and respected. This reality should animate our living.

What. What am I? I am first and foremost a spiritual being. Therefore, with God's help, we can manage my life. We can cope with change, overcome negative forces, heal from pain, change our minds, and even change our lives.

When. The answer is "now." As faith-filled people, we can let go of the past and experience God's abundant life right now. We plan for the future while letting go of our own rigid plans.

Where. Where do I go for spiritual nourishment and insight? Obviously, we can grow spiritually by attending church, participating in prayer or Bible-study groups, doing spiritual reading, making retreats. We can also be aware that God is everywhere. There is no place we cannot experience God's comforting presence. "If I lay down in the world of the dead, you would be there," reminds the psalmist.

Why. Why am I here? The answer is simple: It is our lifelong mission to make Christ real in this world.

Thought for the Day

Put yourself completely
under the influence of Jesus,
so that he may think his thoughts
in your mind,
do his work through your hands,
for you will be all-powerful
with him to strengthen you.

Mother Teresa of Calcutta

. . . I am ready to give up.
Psalm 143:4

Exercising and Expressing Our Gifts

In spite of a thirty-year age difference, artists Henri Matisse and Pierre Auguste Renoir were good friends. When the elder Renoir was confined to his home during the last decade of his life, Matisse visited him almost daily.

At that time, Renoir was paralyzed by arthritis but continued to paint in spite of his infirmities. One day as Matisse watched the elder painter working in his studio, fighting tortuous pain with each brush stroke, Matisse blurted out: "Auguste, why do you continue to paint when you are in such agony?"

Renoir answered simply and eloquently: "The beauty remains: the pain passes." And so, almost to his dying day, Renoir painted. One of his most famous paintings *The Bathers* was completed just two years before his death and fourteen years after he was stricken by arthritis.

We do not need to allow physical or emotional issues prevent us from expressing and exercising our God-given talents, whatever they may be. Like Renoir, let us continue to use the gifts God has given us.

Prayer for the Day

Eternal and gracious God,
I choose not to be quickly deterred
or defeated;
I choose not to give up easily
or prematurely;
I choose to use the gifts
you have graciously given me.
VMP

Let us sing for joy to God!
Psalm 95:1

The Ingredients of Happiness

True happiness never comes from without but always from within. We are happy as a result of our own efforts. Here are some ingredients of happiness:

a simple lifestyle and tastes
courage in the face of fear
the desire to love and be loved
an ability to delay gratification
some self-denial
accepting a challenge
overcoming a major problem
the gift of laughter, especially at yourself
engaging in meaningful work
cultivating and maintaining friendships
accepting what cannot be changed
faith in God
a clear conscience

-------- Thought for the Day --------

When one door of happiness closes,
another opens;
but often we look so long at the closed door
that we do not see the one
which has been opened for us.
Helen Keller

Praise the LORD's glorious name;
bring an offering....
Psalm 96:8

Offering God a Life of Service

In 1798 British comedian John Bernard was touring the United States when he came across an overturned carriage on a Virginia road. An unconscious woman was lying beside it. Bernard reported seeing an elderly man straining to help the woman and free the carriage from the half-ton of luggage burying it. The comedian quickly assisted.

After they had completed their mission of mercy, the elderly man invited Bernard to rest at Mount Vernon. Only then did Bernard realize that the elderly man was George Washington, the most famous living American.

Bernard was impressed by Washington's thoughtful remarks and even more by his behavior, which was so different from that of most country gentlemen who would have sent their servants to help. The former president saw a need and met it.

Let us know that in the eyes of God, greatness is measured by loving action, not by reputation. The greatest offering we can bring to God is a life of service to others.

Prayer for the Day

Continuously teach me, good Lord,
to see a need and meet it,
to see a pain and heal it,
to see a wound and bandage it,
to see a hurt and treat it.
VMP

You have sent troubles and suffering on me,
but you will restore my strength.
Psalm 71:20

God Uses Life's Bruises

At the turn of the century, British naturalist Alfred Russel Wallace wrote about a lesson he learned by observing cocoons in which moths were developing. He noted that one of the larger moths was beating desperately with its undeveloped wings, trying to break out of the cocoon.

After several hours, Wallace could not bear to watch the struggle any longer. Using a sharp knife, he gently split the cocoon, freeing the moth from its desperate struggle.

However, in the ensuing days, Wallace discovered the moth was not developing naturally. Missing were the beautiful tints and shades of color that should have come into the wings. Also, the wings' growth was severely stunted, and they remained underdeveloped. After a few days, the moth died long before its time.

Wallace learned that the struggle against the cocoon, which he had interrupted, was nature's way of strengthening and developing the moth's wings.

The same is true for us when we struggle because of some life crisis. The struggle itself makes us stronger, wiser, more resilient, and less weakened. So we should try not to feel frustrated and angry when trouble comes our way, but rather try to view it as a strengthening opportunity.

Thought for the Day

The harder the conflict,
the more glorious the triumph.
What we obtain too cheaply,
we esteem too lightly.
I love the man that can smile in trouble,
that can gather strength from distress
and grow brave by reflection.
Thomas Paine

Light shines on the righteous....
Psalm 97:11

Are You Putting Out Your Light?

Here is a sobering thought: if we know what to do in a given situation and choose not to do it, the light that is within us is diminished. Furthermore, if we consistently fail to act and respond as we should, the light that is within us will become completely darkened.

Today examine your conscience by asking,

- By my thoughts and actions am I putting out the light?
- When I see a need, do I seriously attempt to meet it?
- When I witness an injustice, do I seek to create understanding, goodwill, and justice?
- When I know someone is hurting, do I try to become a source of hope and healing?
- When my heart is moved to compassion, do I act?
- When there is an opportunity to be a peacemaker, do I step forward?

-------- *Prayer for the Day* --------

Glorious and loving God,
Let your light continuously glow in my life.
Let me be the one who brings your gifts of
love and joy,
peace and power,
hope and faith
into our needy world.
VMP

As for me, I do what is right.
Psalm 26:11

Doing the Right Thing

While window-shopping at a southern California mall with her husband, Tom, and their eleven-year-old son, Jason, Pauline Nichter found a wallet containing two hundred dollars. After discussing options, the Nichters took the wallet to the police station.

There they discovered that a secret compartment in the wallet held an additional two thousand dollars. When the owner came to the police station to claim the wallet, he thanked the Nichters and went home.

Although it is a noble story in itself, what made it newsworthy was the Nichters' desperate financial circumstances. They were window-shopping because that was all they could afford to do. Tom, a printer, had not been steadily employed for five years. Pauline had been laid off from her warehouse job the previous year. Homeless, they had moved in with Pauline's parents.

Pauline admits that on the way to the police station they discussed simply keeping the money. Of their decision not to, she says, "We just did what you're supposed to do, what was right!"

The world needs more people like the Nichters and like the psalmist, who declares, "As for me, I do what is right."

Thought for the Day

A commentary on the times
is that the word honesty
is now preceded by old-fashioned.

Larry Wolters

Relieve the distress of my heart.
Psalm 25:17
(*Jerusalem Bible*)

Making and Keeping Friends

Friendship relieves the distress of our hearts. A friend can help you make wiser decisions, soften life's blows, and ease anxiety. Here are ten guidelines for making and keeping friends:

- *Extend yourself.* Making new friends means extending ourselves beyond normal comfort levels. Be willing to attend a neighborhood party where you don't know anyone.
- *Connect to someone with common interests.* The strongest friendships are based on common interests. Look for people who enjoy your hobbies, social activities, work.
- *Show interest in the other person.* Many people are shy and timid. If you identify someone with whom you would like to have a friendship, let her or him know through a smile or a shared comment. Take the first step.
- *Make the other person feel important.* Point out another person's talent and express your appreciation and admiration.
- *Minimize your insecurities.* Don't worry about whether the other person likes you or not. Just reach out and be natural.
- *Be a good listener.* Listening helps another person and bonds two people tightly.
- *Don't keep score.* When you do something for a friend, never expect something in return. Good friendships have a way of balancing themselves.
- *Value differences.* Don't try to change your friend. Enjoy the diversity.
- *Apologize and forgive.* Two people can hurt each other through words and actions. Learn to apologize. Be quick to forgive.
- *Work at the friendship.* Developing a friendship is like growing a plant. Both need attention and nurturing.

Thought for the Day

Friendship is a thing most necessary to life since without friends no one would choose to live, though possessed of other advantages.
Aristotle

...keep me from falling.
Psalm 119:133

Avoiding Bad Habits

The story is told of a proud eagle perched high on the tip of an iceberg floating swiftly down the river. The big bird seemed oblivious to the tremendous waterfall that lay ahead. At the same time, an Indian hunter was walking along a path at the river's edge. Seeing the large bird perched on the iceberg, the Indian clapped his hands and cried out, "Fly away, eagle! There is danger ahead."

The eagle merely shrugged his great wings as if to say, "Don't bother me. I know what I'm doing." As the iceberg moved closer to the waterfall, the Indian cried out again, "Fly away, eagle! There is a waterfall ahead."

Once again, the eagle merely shrugged his wings.

At that moment, the eagle looked down just in time to see that the iceberg had reached the brink of the waterfall and was about to go over the edge. The big bird spread his wings and prepared for immediate takeoff. However, he was unable to rise. His claws were frozen to the ice, and he went down with the iceberg to a certain death. Clearly, the eagle should never have perched on a floating iceberg. Then, when warned, the bird should have responded. His death was due entirely to his own negligence.

This story is a parable about bad habits. We can start them innocently and naively. Yet when we allow them to continue, they can, like the bird on the ice, trap us and even destroy us.

The most effective solution is to avoid engaging in any questionable behavior in the first place. Further, we should listen to the advice and warnings of others who may be able to see our predicament more clearly than we do. They may be sent our way to "keep us from falling."

Thought for the Day

Sin is not a distance,
it is a turning of our gaze
in the wrong direction.
Simone Weil

Teach me, LORD....
Psalm 27:11

Nurturing a Sensitivity to the Spiritual World

Spiritual growth is like an indoor houseplant. Both need a healthy environment, proper nourishment, and exposure to light to grow, develop, and bloom. Here are some simple suggestions for intentionally nurturing a sensitivity to the spiritual world:

- *Clear your life of clutter.* Take a look at your lifestyle and see where you can simplify. Being preoccupied with too many things and too many activities can squeeze out opportunities for spiritual growth.
- *Act on the truth you already understand.* Listening and obeying are inexplicably linked to each other. Deeper truths are unlikely to be recognized until you respond to the truths you already understand.
- *Beware of self-rejection.* Do not be too harsh and critical of yourself. Spiritual growth is greatly reduced if you view yourself too negatively.
- *Learn from a spiritual mentor.* This can be as informal as associating with people who hear and see the spiritual world more clearly than you do. Or it can mean placing yourself under the guidance of a spiritual director.
- *Have a soft heart.* Guard against becoming calloused or immune to the sufferings of others. Let your heart remain soft, tender, and receptive.

Thought for the Day

Faith may be developed in action,
endurance in the midst of storms and turmoil.
Courage may come in the front lines of battle.
But wisdom and understanding and revelation
unfold as dew forms on the petals of a rose—in quietness.
Peter Lord

If you kept a record of our sins,
who could escape being condemned?
But you forgive us....
Psalm 130:3-4

Peace and Healing Through Forgiveness

A parish gave its pastor a sabbatical leave, which he used to study in Israel. While sitting on a hillside overlooking the Sea of Galilee, the pastor became aware of a woman nearby. She looked distressed, tired, and emotionally worn out. They engaged in a conversation.

The pastor learned that the woman was a nurse from Belfast, Northern Ireland. She worked in a children's ward where she frequently cared for the small victims of terrorist bombings and sniper fire. The woman hated the IRA.

One day she was called to an adult male ward and asked to help turn a seriously wounded patient in bed. As others turned his legs and body, she was to turn his head. The physician warned that the maneuver had to be done in concert, or the patient could be paralyzed or even die. Suddenly, the nurse recognized the man as a leader of the IRA. He was responsible for the suffering of the children she nursed.

The woman felt deep hatred well up within her. She wanted to kill the IRA leader. This was her opportunity, because it would appear as an accident. She did not harm the patient, but afterward had to get away. "The cancer of hatred is eating me alive," she told the pastor.

As the woman and the pastor spoke, they became more comfortable with each other. So the pastor led the woman to repeat four three-word prayers: *Lord, forgive me. I forgive myself. I forgive them. Lord, forgive us.*

It was not easy for the woman to offer those prayers, yet after doing so, she was able to smile again. As the two continued to speak, the woman laughed for the first time in many months. Peace and healing had come to her soul.

Thought for the Day

Forgiving is love's revolution
against life's unfairness.
When we forgive,
we ignore the normal laws
that strap us to the natural law
of getting even
and we release ourselves
from our own painful pasts.
Lewis Smedes

You see me, whether I am working or resting.
Psalm 139:3

God Is Present at All Times

Too often we forget that God is present in all places and at all times. Too often, we feel that we have to go somewhere or do something to reach God. Scripture clearly states that God's presence is pervasive. The psalmist declares, "You see me, whether I am working or resting.

Let us be mindful of the truth that God is present

in the car
in the city
in the hospital
at the stoplight
on the crowded bus
at the dinner table
in moments of joy and peace
in the doctor's waiting room
in the hospital's operating room
during the night when we sleep
in times of distress and despair
at the factory and in the office

As we go about our daily lives, let us be comforted and guided by the reality that God is with us. God sees us whether we are resting or working; whether we are aware of him or not.

Affirmations for the Day

Divine love is present everywhere.
Divine love fills me with peace.
Divine love provides me with order and harmony.
Divine love instills me with wisdom.

VMP

Trust in the Lord.
Have faith, do not despair.
Psalm 27:14

Living by the Persistence Principle

A quick dictionary check of the words *persist* and *persistence* reveals these definitions: "To refuse to give up"; "Stubborn continuance; tenacity." People whose dreams come true have an amazing ability to persist.

Benjamin Bloom and a team of researchers at the University of Chicago analyzed the careers of concert pianists, sculptors, research mathematicians, neurologists, Olympic swimmers, and tennis champions to determine what processes led to high levels of achievement.

The research team discovered that successful professional musicians worked an average of 17.1 years from the day they began taking piano lessons to the day they won a major competition.

Their example reveals that talent alone doesn't guarantee success. In addition to skill, the ability to persevere leads to success. In today's psalm we are reminded to "trust in the Lord," to "have faith," and "not to despair." Let us persevere, trusting in God's perfect timing.

Thought for the Day

Genius, that power that dazzles mortal eyes,
is oft but perseverance in disguise.
Henry Austin

You will reveal the path of life to me,
give me unbounded joy in your presence....
Psalm 16:11
(*Jerusalem Bible*)

Using the Therapy of Laughter

People who truly enjoy living know how to have a good laugh. The spiritually and emotionally healthy laugh comes easily and naturally. There is something therapeutic about laughter. That may be why Saint Ignatius of Loyola, founder of the Society of Jesus, advised, "Laugh and grow strong."

Most of us need to take ourselves less seriously. A good model is former boxing heavyweight champion Muhammad Ali. Although he suffers from neurological problems related to years in the ring, Ali has not lost his sense of humor.

Actor Michael Caine tells of meeting Muhammad Ali at a dinner party. "He was a great joker and at one point said to me, 'Do you want to see my right hook?' " Caine recalls.

"A bit apprehensive, I said yes, hoping that he would miss my chin in the demonstration. He stood absolutely still for a second or two and then said, 'Do you want to see it again?' "

The next time you are feeling gloomy and sad, find something that will make you smile and laugh. When events prompt you to feel disturbed and depressed, remember that the life of faith is first and foremost a life of joy. The closer you are to God, the more reasons you have to sing, rejoice, and laugh. After all, God has revealed to you the "path of life" and given you "unbounded joy."

Thought for the Day

To be a saint, one must be beside oneself.
One must lose one's head.
Saint John Vianney

How much longer, Lord, will you just look on?
Rescue me....
Psalm 35:17

Thanking God for the Darkness

No one welcomes a life crisis. When one comes, we share in the prayer of the psalmist: "How much longer, Lord, will you just look on? Rescue me...." However, our greatest growth usually takes place during life's difficult times. Too often we forget that when Paul advises us to "be thankful in all circumstances" (1 Thessalonians 5:18), he is including times of struggle through darkness. Here are some important reasons to thank God for the dark times:

- It is in the darkness that we let go and turn to God. Our society places a high value on independence, self-sufficiency, and achievement. While those qualities may be positive, they can also prevent us from truly relying upon God.
- It is in the darkness that we become less judgmental and more accepting of others.
- It is in the darkness that many of the deepest insights are learned and where our most significant growth takes place.
- It is in the darkness that we shed our arrogance and learn true humility.
- It is in the darkness that we experience the fullness of God's grace and guidance.
- It is in the darkness that we learn how to love as God loves. When we emerge from the darkness, we often have a deeper desire to help others who are suffering.
- It is in the darkness that spiritual discernment emerges and where we experience blessings absent in the "sunshine."

Thought for the Day

I pray that God may open your eyes
and let you see what hidden treasures he bestows on us
in the trials from which the world thinks only to flee.

Blessed John of Avila

We put our hope in the LORD.
Psalm 33:20

The Power of Hope

Popular Country-Western singer Naomi Judd had to give up her musical career because of chronic active hepatitis. Although she and her daughter, Wynonna, were at the top of their careers with five platinum albums and more than a dozen hit singles, physicians advised Naomi to call it quits.

Along with the best care that medicine had to offer, Naomi prayed for healing and recovery. Now her hepatitis appears to be dormant, and she is gradually returning on the stage. Both before her bout with hepatitis and afterward, Naomi had experienced the power of hope. She describes it this way:

> Hope has been my constant companion. Hope is what's gotten me through all the struggles. It's what allowed Wynonna and me to fulfill this implausible dream of becoming country stars. It's what got me off welfare. It's what got me out of hideous relationships.

Christian hope is optimism fueled by faith. Hope is grounded in the reality that God is working in all of life's tragedies and troubles seeking to evoke good from them. It is because of God that we can rightly expect something better to emerge from pain and suffering.

Like Naomi Judd and the psalm writer thousands of years earlier, let us hope by trusting God to guide us and lead us through every dark time.

Prayer for the Day

I praise God
for the love that sustains me.
I praise God
for the light that illuminates me.
I praise God
for the life which fills me
with unlimited hope and faith.
VMP

Find out for yourself how good the LORD is.
Psalm 34:8

Awareness of God's Presence

God is forever present in our lives no matter what "evidence" there may be to the contrary. And God is present in our lives even if we consciously or unconsciously choose to drift away.

God is forever seeking to establish and maintain communication with us. God is aware, sometimes sadly and painfully, when we pull away or move in the wrong direction.

God is forever seeking us, as we divert from, and redirect our paths. Like a very good friend, God remains loyal to us.

God is forever present, as we search for solutions to problems that confuse us.

God is forever available when we feel lonely, alienated, and lost. God is present to provide companionship and guidance through life's many dilemmas.

God is forever standing by the door of our lives seeking an entry point to support, sustain, and strengthen us.

God is forever present even when we are indifferent toward him and feeling great independence and self-sufficiency.

God is more anxious to confer his blessings than we are to receive them.

As we go about our daily living, let us know and be aware of God's real presence. "Find out for yourself how good the Lord is."

******** *Thought for the Day* ********

We do not seek God–
God seeks us.
Frederick William Robertson

I come to you, LORD, for protection.
Psalm 31:1

Looking in the Right Direction

After the bombing of Pearl Harbor, British intelligence learned that Japan would attack Singapore, which was under British protection. Although the British knew that an attack was planned, they were unconcerned. Authorities believed that Singapore was safe because it was built at the end of the Malay Peninsula. The jungle protected it from behind, and massive British guns aimed toward the sea protected it from a naval invasion.

Yet on February 24, 1942, Singapore was attacked not from the ocean where the large guns provided protection, but from the jungle. Japanese soldiers made their way through the woods. In ten days, Singapore fell to the Japanese because the British guns were pointed in the wrong direction.

This story can be a parable for our living. As long as we are looking in the right direction, we will enjoy the abundant life Christ spoke about. However, it is when we shift our gaze and look elsewhere that our problems feel insurmountable and overwhelming. At all times and under all circumstances, let us look to God who is our defender and protector.

Affirmations for the Day

I look to God for peace in my life.
I look to God for joy in my life.
I look to God for love in my life.
I affirm and give thanks
for God's gracious presence in my life.
VMP

You are a righteous God;
save me, I pray!
Psalm 31:1

The Importance of Expressing Our Needs

Three different people facing diverse situations asked others to pray. Here are the results.

The first person, a woman worried about her son-in-law, asked for prayers to help him find employment. Jobs were scarce, and he had been unemployed several months. The man and his family were deeply in debt and had received a notice of eviction. To make matters worse, the wife developed an ulcer because of the stress. Shortly after asking a group to pray, the son-in-law found employment in another part of the country. The family was relocated with all expenses paid.

The second individual was a man who had lost an important book containing financial reports. They could never be replaced and were vital to his organization. He asked for prayer. After ten minutes, he says, "It seemed as though a veil was lifted and my mind cleared." Immediately he recalled where he had placed the book.

The third person was a woman whose daughter was to have surgery. Physicians believed the younger woman had ovarian cancer, so they were going to remove her ovaries. Friends prayed while doctors performed surgery. To the physicians' surprise, the growths on the ovaries had shriveled up and were later found to be benign.

God invites us to make all our needs known. We must not be too proud or too stubborn to ask for help. Like the three persons cited, we must express our needs and ask God to help.

Thought for the Day

Prayer, rightly understood,
prepares the soul for action,
sustains her on life's road
when weary and worn,
and arms her for the fight
when the foe assails her.

Joseph Mercier

See what happens to those who trust in themselves....
Psalm 49:13

Guidelines for Self-Discovery

After vigorously pursuing a career for nearly two decades, a frustrated corporate attorney lamented, "Now that I have firmly established myself, I'm still unhappy and don't know what I want out of life."

Many people share his dilemma. Listed below are some guidelines for self-discovery. Using paper and pencil write your responses to the following questions:

- What do I want the most?
- What do I think about a great deal?
- How do I use my money?
- How do I spend my leisure time?
- Whose company do I enjoy and why?
- Whom do I admire and why?
- What issues stir me and how would I like to respond to those issues?

After writing your answers, look over them carefully. Pray about them, using the information as the basis of a consultation with a trusted spiritual guide. Together you can discern what God may be calling you to do with your time, talents, and life.

Affirmations for the Day

The spirit of God calms my mind
and helps me think clearly.
The spirit of God illumines me
so that I think and act with wisdom.
The spirit of God lifts me
to greater understanding.

VMP

Whenever I am anxious and worried,
you comfort me and make me glad.
Psalm 94:19

Angels in Green Scrub Suits

The doctor announced to a mother that the pain in her little son's ear was caused by a button he had somehow shoved deep inside. Surgery would be required to remove the button.

Although the worried mother wanted her son's problem corrected, she hesitated. She is a single parent and has cerebral palsy. Since she had no medical insurance, she knew that the hospital and physicians would ask for the money up-front. Because she had two part-time jobs, she was able to arrange for a loan to cover the medical expenses.

The additional expenses created a great deal of stress for her. The new bills would mean no extras of any kind for her son or herself: no birthday presents, no Christmas gifts, no eating out. Life felt very oppressive to the young mother.

As she was sitting in the hospital lounge waiting for her son to recover from the surgery, the anesthetist came out, handed her an envelope, a prescription, and instructions on how to care for the injured ear.

When she returned home, the mother put her son to bed and opened the anesthetist's envelope. Inside was the check she had made out to the doctor along with a note saying he would not accept payment for his services.

"God's goodness as expressed in that physician's compassion came through loudly and clearly," she said. "I realized that some of God's angels wear green scrub suits!"

Let us remember that when we become anxious, worried, and fearful about our needs and how to meet them, God takes note of our anxiety—and God works in unique and mysterious ways.

Affirmations for the Day

The light of God glows within me
and creates miracles in my life.
The love of God goes before me
and prepares the way.
I thank you, God,
for your light and your love,
which bless me daily.

VMP

Happy is the man who...
depends on the LORD his God.
Psalm 146:5

Staying in Touch With Hope

The daily newspaper, television news, and even the events of our own lives can conspire to reduce and eliminate hope. We need to work consistently at staying in touch with hope.

Hope is the answer when problems and difficulties emerge in our lives and in our world.

To have hope is to move from "Why did this happen?" to "What can I do now?"

To have hope is to move forward in faith and not remain stuck in despair.

To have hope is to find strength in God and in ourselves.

To have hope is to take the focus off present hardships and turn them over to God's love and guidance.

To have hope is to look farther down the road and know that God is working for a greater good.

To have hope is to experience a place of peace, a reservoir of power, a source of strength, additional courage, and spiritual wisdom.

Staying in touch with hope is staying in touch with the God who is always present in the darkness and who is present as we move toward brighter future. That is why the psalmist writes, "Happy is the man who...depends on the Lord his God."

Thought for the Day

Hope means expectancy
when things are otherwise hopeless.
G. K. Chesterton

Teach me, Lord....
Psalm 86:11

Thanking God for Our Teachers

A legend tells of a compassionate king who decided to set aside one day each year to honor the greatest of his subjects. Groups of citizens were asked to present people who, in their opinion, were worthy of the honor.

When the special day arrived, a large crowd of people from all walks of life gathered in the palace courtyard. As his subjects cheered, the king sat down on the royal throne and asked the various citizen groups to present their candidates.

The first person presented was a man of immense wealth who had given much money to the poor. The second person presented was a celebrated physician who faithfully tended the sick and never turned anyone away. The third person presented was a judge whose sense of fairness and wise decisions were renowned.

Finally, an older woman was presented. Although she was poorly dressed, she carried herself with dignity. The king asked, "Who is this candidate?" The civic group who presented the woman answered simply, "She was the teacher of the wealthy man, the physician, and the judge."

Today let us reflect on the various teachers God has sent into our lives, people whose instruction and example have inspired us and contributed to our growth. It may be a schoolteacher, a pastor, a friend, a work colleague, a counselor, even a child. Then let us thank God for sending teachers our way.

Thought for the Day

A teacher affects eternity;
he can never tell
where his influence stops.

Henry Gardiner Adams

Come and see what God has done,
his wonderful acts among men.
Psalm 66:5

Compassion That Transcends Personal Need

Out of the Los Angeles earthquake of 1994 comes this remarkable, inspiring, and wonderful act of compassion.

When sixteen people were killed in an apartment building, a group of people in Michigan decided to help financially. Quickly, they raised money and sent two representatives to Los Angeles. They presented six checks for eight-hundred-fifty dollars each to those who had lost loved ones and three checks for one-hundred-fifty dollars each to other hard-hit residents.

Jim Enos was given an eight-hundred-fifty-dollar check. His wife, Darla, was killed in the quake. However, Enos quietly slipped his check into the hands of Hyun Sook Lee, another resident, whose husband and fourteen-year-old son were killed and whose twelve-year-old son was seriously injured. When asked about his outpouring of generosity, Enos replied simply, "She lost her entire family. I lost my wife, but she lost more."

We can take a lesson from Enos' remarkable act: we can be compassionate in spite of our own needs and hurts. We must not allow anything to dim our sense of compassion for others. As Christians, we must never take what Saint Ignatius of Antioch calls "a merely natural attitude" toward our neighbor.

Thought for the Day

Let none of you
take a merely natural attitude
toward his neighbor,
but love one another continually in Christ.
Saint Ignatius of Antioch

My prayers go up to you;
show me the way I should go.
Psalm 143:8

Prayer Plus Perseverance Produces Results

In January 1921 the eminent African-American agricultural chemist George Washington Carver was invited to Washington, D.C., to speak before a congressional committee about the possibilities of the peanut as a commercial product.

Sadly, he was greeted with hostility by some white southerners who sat on the committee. One shouted, "I suppose if you have plenty of peanuts and watermelons, you're perfectly happy!"

Amid the laughter of the committee members, Carver spoke a silent prayer asking for God's guidance and support. Told he had only ten minutes in which to make his case, Carver quickly opened his display case and began his presentation while observers continued to speak in a condescending manner.

However, as Carver continued, the atmosphere began to change. Because he spoke with authority and was so convinced about the experiments he had conducted, his ten minutes were extended, and his presentation lasted nearly two hours. During that time, he gained the respect of the entire committee.

As a result of George Washington Carver's devotion to his work, peanuts came to be grown commercially here in the United States, becoming an important financial resource to several states.

It was Carver's faith in himself, in his product, and most importantly in his God that enabled him to persevere through opposition and win over skeptics. Prayer coupled with perseverance makes a world of difference.

Thought for the Day

Success is to be measured
not so much
by the position that one has reached in life
as by the obstacles
which he has overcome
while trying to succeed.
Booker T. Washington

When I lie down,
I go to sleep in peace.
Psalm 4:8

Givers Sleep Well

"If you don't share, you may have material success, but you'll be very poor in spirit," observes professional golfer Chi Chi Rodriguez. He recalls learning this lesson as a young boy growing up in a tiny, tin-roofed shack in rural Puerto Rico.

The lesson took place when his father awakened him at two o'clock one morning. He heard someone out back. The two crept outside and found a machete-wielding neighbor standing beside the small banana grove that fed their family.

Despite the fact that the intruder could have killed him, the elder Rodriguez commanded, "Give me the machete." Then Chi Chi's father cut a bunch of bananas and handed half of them to his neighbor. "From now on," he said, "anything you want back here, you come to my door and ask for it. And make sure you leave some for my kids too."

Chi Chi Rodriguez says that the compassionate way his father handled that incident permanently influenced his life. "That night, he taught me that takers eat well, but givers sleep well."

Thought for the Day

A generous action is its own reward.
William Walsh

So I will not be silent;
I will sing praise to you.
Psalm 30:12

Returning God's Gifts

Every Sunday afternoon for several years, the Reverend William Waffles, a Methodist pastor in Ohio, would conduct services at a nearby prison. Then he would visit with the incarcerated men, developing friendships with many of them.

For some time, he and his wife had been saving for a trip to the Holy Land. On the Sunday afternoon before they were to leave, he told the prisoners of their trip, explaining that he and his wife had worked hard to save the money. Although he would not be at the prison for several weeks, he assured them of his prayers while away.

The prisoners were delighted for him and immediately gathered around Reverend Waffles. They hugged him, patted him on the back, shook his hand, and jostled him lovingly with affection and camaraderie. As he was getting ready to leave, a prisoner came forward with a package that had been hastily wrapped. The man explained, "We didn't have time or money to get you a gift, but this is the best we can do. Please don't open it until you get home."

Reverend Waffles thanked them and took the package home, where he opened it with his wife. Inside he found his wallet, his pen, his watch, his eyeglass case, and his pocket knife. When the prisoners had gathered to congratulate the minister, they picked all his pockets. Then they gift-wrapped the items they had taken and gave them back as a sign of their love, as if to say, "It's all we have to give."

All of us have picked the pockets of God. Like those prisoners, we should remember to "wrap up" the things we have received and give them back to God through our love, service, time, and tithes. That way, we do not remain silent, taking God's gifts for granted.

Thought for the Day

God's blessings steal into life noiselessly.
They are neither self-proclaiming
nor even self-announcing.
Henry Ward Beecher

Praise God with shouts of joy, all people!
Psalm 66:1

Ways to Face and Erase Worry

Everyone has plenty of reasons to worry about something or someone. Yet some individuals seem to flow with life more easily than others. Here are some ways to face and erase worry.

- Remind yourself that worry is a bad habit, and—like any habit—it can be broken.
- Before rising from bed each morning, repeat five times the psalmist's affirmation, "Praise God with shouts of joy, all people!"
- Pray and place into God's hands the new day, your life, the lives of your loved ones, your work.
- Tell yourself that you are in God's hands and that God will help you deal with whatever comes along.
- Think and speak positively about yourself. Do not allow yourself to say, "I'll never be able to…"
- Go through your Bible, highlighting passages that speak to you about faith, hope, joy, and peace.
- Cultivate friendships with people who are optimistic and who radiate serenity.
- Help another person become free from a worry. This will give you more power over your concerns.
- Each day visualize yourself as living in partnership with God. Keep foremost in your mind the reality that God is with you in all circumstances.

Thought for the Day

There are Christians
who have hysterical reactions,
as if the world
would have slipped out of God's hands.
But we believe in history;
the world is not a roll of the dice
going toward chaos.
A new world has begun to happen
since Christ has risen.

Luis Espinal

Whenever I am anxious and worried,
you comfort me....
Psalm 94:19

Living One Day at a Time

Yesterday we considered ways to deal with worry. So many worries result from anxiety about the future—what it may or may not bring. Another effective way to eliminate those worries is to consciously live one day at a time. No one ever sinks from carrying daily responsibilities; it's only when tomorrow's responsibilities are added to today's that the weight becomes unbearable.

A master of living one day at a time is comedian Jay Leno. As successor to Johnny Carson on NBC's "Tonight Show," Leno is aware that the slightest dip in ratings could mean his job. In spite of that pressure, however, he works with confidence and tranquillity saying,

> To me every show is still a one-nighter. I come in, I do my work, and I go home. My attitude is always, "If they ask you to leave, fine." There's nothing of mine, no personal effects, in my office at NBC. My dressing room is not even locked because there's nothing in there. I carry all my stuff in each day, and I carry it out each night. I don't leave anything behind.

Leno shows great wisdom in that approach. Worry is a completely negative emotion. It drains energy, reduces confidence, heightens fear, and makes problems larger than they really are. Today make the commitment to live just one day at a time, trusting God completely.

Thought for the Day

Anxiety does not empty tomorrow of its sorrows
but only empties today of its strength.
Charles Haddon Spurgeon

Your presence fills me with joy
and brings me pleasure forever.
Psalm 16:11

Adding Humor to Life

The sting of many of life's hurts and irritations can be reduced and eliminated by viewing events with a touch of humor. Opera star Beverly Sills was able to do this effectively when someone critically observed that Sills' elder brother, a well-known obstetrician, did not attend many of her performances. The soprano responded, "Why should he? I don't attend his deliveries!"

Not only does laughter soften life's blows, scientists believe that laughter contributes toward good physical health. "Laughter makes the unbearable bearable and a patient with a well-developed sense of humor has a better chance of recovery than a stolid individual who seldom laughs," notes physician Bernie Siegel in his book, *Love, Medicine, and Miracles*.

Although Scripture does not specifically cite laughter as one of life's important ingredients, there are many references and commands about praise, joy, and happiness, all of which are connected to humor. Today's psalm is an important reminder that people who remain close to God are filled with joy and experience pleasure. So let us deliberately lighten up and see the humor in events that come our way.

Thought for the Day

Mirth is God's medicine.
Everybody ought to bathe in it.
Grim care, moroseness, anxiety—
all this rust of life—ought to be scoured off
by the oil of mirth.

Henry Ward Beecher

But I am in pain and despair;
lift me up, O God. . . !
Psalm 69:29

Transforming Pain Into Power

Life can be brutally unfair and unkind. Some problems lie beyond our power of control. Although it is true that we cannot control what life sends our way, we do have a choice over how we respond to life's injustice and cruelty.

We can become worried, anxious, and fearful. Or we can choose to transform pain into power and a negative into a positive.

Consider Dr. Elisabeth Kübler-Ross, well known for her compassionate work with people close to death. What is not so well known is that Dr. Kübler-Ross came to be interested in death and dying when her beloved brother-in-law, Seppli, died of cancer.

"Seppli was one of the highest motivating forces that led me to become a compassionate, listening physician which enabled me to work with dying patients and their families," she says. "Looking back at this painful experience, I can say that the thing that carried me through was the ability to turn a painful and negative experience into something positive and creative."

Nothing is ever wasted when we turn it over to God. God can help us take the painful experiences of life and transform them into power. What has caused us great hurt can be transformed into a tool to bring great healing for others.

Affirmations for the Day

God is working through me right now.
God is transforming my pain into power.
God is moving me from hurting to healing.
Therefore, all darkness and despair in my life
gives way to God's love and light.

VMP

Don't stay so far away, O God.
Psalm 71:12

Living "As If"

John Wesley, the Anglican priest who became the founder of Methodism, came to a place in his life where he was spiritually empty. His faith had shriveled up, his spirit sagged, and he felt he could no longer preach.

Rather than abandon his faith and his calling, he met with his spiritual director, Peter Bohler, who gave him this advice: "Preach faith until you have it, and then because you have it, you will preach faith."

Bohler meant that Wesley should act "as if" he had great faith and hope. Then, Bohler believed, Wesley would grow into the role he adopted.

That is, in fact, precisely what happened. In the midst of low-level faith and spirit, Wesley continued to preach, teach, write, and minister. He lived an "as-if" faith, acting as if he felt God's love even when he didn't.

Gradually, he discovered that God's love was indeed there all along. Slowly but surely, his faith increased, his hope deepened, and his spirit began to soar.

There are two important lessons for us to consider from Wesley's example. One is that all people, including those with deep piety, experience times of dryness when God feels remote or absent from our lives. "Don't stay so far away, O God," cried the psalmist in his darkness of the soul.

The other is that we must struggle to be faithful to God and our calling regardless of how we may feel. There are simply times when we have to go on "automatic pilot" when it comes to our faith. Then, like Wesley, we will discover anew God's love and care for us.

Thought for the Day

In time of desolation
one should never make a change,
but stand firm and consistent
in the resolutions and decisions
that guided him
the day before the desolation.
Saint Ignatius of Loyola

We have escaped like a bird from a hunter's trap.
Psalm 124:7

God's Protective Nature

All good parents have strong and natural impulses to protect their children from all danger, disease, and trauma. Likewise, as our loving parent, God has a strong and natural protective nature toward us.

Consider the experience of a Florida woman. She and her husband were driving across the country, from Florida to California. After lunch each day, the couple usually switched driving responsibilities. However, one particular day the husband said he was not tired and insisted on driving.

The woman then reclined in her seat, relaxed, and went to sleep. Shortly, she opened her eyes and saw the image of her niece's face on a mountain ahead. Her niece had died thirty-five years earlier! The image startled the woman, and she looked toward her husband who had just fallen asleep.

When she called out his name loudly, he awakened suddenly but lost control of the car. "We spun around into oncoming traffic, but we escaped death," she says. "Had the image of my deceased niece not appeared to me I would never have awakened my husband, and we would probably have been killed or seriously hurt in an accident."

Today's psalm is a reminder that life holds many dangers for us. Like a small bird, we may not even be aware of the "hunter's trap." Yet our God is aware. Our God watches over us day and night.

Thought for the Day

Through many dangers, toils, and snares,
I have already come;
'Tis grace has brought me safe thus far,
and grace will lead me home.
John Newton

"Praise him, you servants of the LORD!
Honor him. . . !"
Psalm 22:23

Committing Random Acts of Kindness

A current popular movement invites people to "commit random acts of kindness and senseless beauty." One woman who was the recipient of such an act shares her story.

While on her way to work during rush hour, she noticed two pickup trucks—one behind her, the other ahead. Both were signaling her to pull over. Thinking at first that the two drivers were communicating with each other, she ignored their signals.

Then one of the trucks started to follow her and motioned for her to pull to the curb. Since it was daylight and rush hour with many other drivers around, the woman pulled over and stopped.

When she emerged from her car, one of the drivers said that he had noticed a purse on top of her car. When it fell off, the other trucker had stopped to retrieve it, while the first one followed her to let her know.

"How wonderful that these two men took the time to do the right thing," the woman says.

Today is a good day to make ourselves available to God to commit a random act of kindness. In this way, our lives bring God praise and honor.

Thought for the Day

Do not wait for extraordinary circumstances
to do good. Try to use ordinary situations.
Johann Paul Friedrich Richter

All you that are righteous,
shout for joy for what the LORD has done.
Psalm 33:1

Bearing Witness to Our Faith

The world will be a better place only when we live our faith and bear witness to it. Here are five ways to touch others with your faith.

- *Be a positive role model.* Set the example for what it means to be a person of honesty, integrity, compassion, and kindness.
- *Be a generous forgiver.* Although forgiving others for hurts inflicted can be difficult, it is a requirement of faith to be a generous forgiver. Ask God to help you do this.
- *Be loving and caring.* In the home and in the workplace, sincerely love and care for others. A loving spirit is a powerful witness to God's greater love.
- *Be a person of prayer.* Maintain a regular prayer life. Include in your prayers those who are ill, troubled, and without faith.
- *Share your faith verbally.* At appropriate times and with sensitivity, share your faith experience. Tell others of times when God provided for you, answered a prayer, or opened a door.

Thought for the Day

Show me that you are redeemed,
and I will believe in your Redeemer.
Friedrich Nietzsche

Help us, L*ORD!*
Psalm 12:1

Using Arrow Prayers

An "arrow prayer" is a short prayer used in times of unusual need. Arrow prayers can be used, for example, when one is facing hostility, experiencing great pain, or feeling very sick. The Psalms are filled with such arrow prayers, including today's short reading.

The late minister and author Norman Vincent Peale often used arrow prayers. Dr. Peale tells of sitting at the head table in Houston, Texas, waiting to give a speech. Looking around at the crowd of faces, he noticed a man in the audience whose face was filled with hate—and he was glaring directly at Dr. Peale.

Although Dr. Peale did not recognize the man and felt they had never met, the individual was definitely hostile toward him. The anger being directed toward him was unsettling to Dr. Peale, so he offered this arrow prayer before rising to speak: "Lord, please help the man out there. Help me to love him."

Following the speech, the man came to Dr. Peale expressing appreciation for the talk. The man was transformed; his attitude and body language were both positive. The man explained that he did not like clergy because of an unfortunate experience earlier in his life. As he sat waiting for Dr. Peale to speak, the man admitted, he felt hostile. However, as Dr. Peale spoke, the man began to feel warmly toward him and started listening carefully to Dr. Peale's talk.

Whenever you experience an awkward, difficult, or troubling situation, try an arrow prayer.

-------- *Thought for the Day* --------

I am convinced that if you "shoot" prayers at people,
they will be profoundly affected.
Select a person who is a problem to you and shoot prayers at him,
asking God to help you reach out in love.

Norman Vincent Peale

The Lord is righteous and loves good deeds;
those who do them will live in his presence.
Psalm 11:7

Touching Others Through Our Lives

When Jerry, a corporate executive, died leaving behind a young wife and five children, hundreds of people came to the funeral home. His wife was not surprised by the large number of people who came, since Jerry had a way of making friends wherever he went, often with people who were forgotten by the rest of society. Jerry had once explained to his wife that everyone he met fulfilled a mission to bring God into his life. Jerry saw Christ in each individual.

Even though his wife knew that Jerry had a large circle of friends, she was unprepared for one visitor to the funeral home. While greeting the many people who were present, she noticed a woman who remained in the back of the room. She wasn't familiar and appeared lost in the sea of people.

Finally, the widow approached the older woman and noticed immediately that she carried a tattered canvas tote bag, a larger sack, and a shopping bag from a local department store. The bags was filled with the woman's belongings; obviously, she was homeless. As the widow introduced herself, the older woman began to weep, apologizing for her lack of control. "I should be consoling you," she said, "not the other way around."

The homeless woman explained that Jerry had been especially kind to her on many occasions. She was weeping in genuine grief at Jerry's death. "Your husband was the only person who ever loved me," she said to the widow.

That anecdote can prompt us to ask ourselves the following questions:

- Do we see Christ in other people, especially those on the fringes of society?
- Do we allow our lives to impact upon others through constant acts of kindness and compassion?
- Are we aware that God frequently walks into our lives in the shoes of other people?

Thought for the Day

Those who do not love their fellow beings live unfruitful lives.

Percy Bysshe Shelley

From the depths of my despair I call to you, Lord.
Psalm 130:1

Seven Reasons to Pray

Even though God knows all of our needs, Scripture stresses the necessity of prayer. Here are seven reasons we are urged to pray regularly.

- *Prayer connects us to God and God's power.* Changes take place when we pray. Sometimes the issue is transformed; other times we are the ones changed. Either way, God's power is at work.
- *Prayer is a way of sharing our burden.* Some problems are difficult to share with another human being. The issue may involve deep guilt or shame, making it impossible to confide in a friend. In such cases, prayer can help ease the burden.
- *Prayer puts into words what troubles us.* No difficulty can be resolved until it is identified and articulated.
- *Prayer reduces feelings of helplessness.* Rather than feeling as though life is out of control, when we pray, we take the first step in reclaiming our lives and putting order into chaos.
- *Prayer is a powerful reminder that we are not alone.* Life's troubles often leave us feeling isolated, lonely, and vulnerable. Prayer reminds us that we are not facing difficulty alone.
- *Prayer generates courage.* We become fortified, strengthened, and more confident as a result of prayer.
- *Prayer provides us with a sense of direction.* Rather than merely being tossed about on life's sea, we receive insight, guidance, and direction from prayer.

Thought for the Day

Whenever we address God in fervent prayer,
we change both soul and body for the better.
It could not happen
that any man or woman could pray
for a single moment
without some good result.

Alexis Carrel

You do...take notice of trouble and suffering.
Psalm 10:14

Love and Generosity Do Exist

In a world that often feels cold and calloused, it is always heartwarming to know that love and generosity do exist. Anne, the mother of three children, learned this during one Christmas season.

Although Christmas is a time of festivity, Anne and her husband were preoccupied with other thoughts. Their daughter, Lauren, had a form of cerebral palsy. With the help of state funding, they were able to send Lauren to an excellent school where she made great progress.

However, the funding was to end on Lauren's birthday in January. The little girl loved the school, so the parents wanted her to continue for another year. Unfortunately, they could not afford the expensive tuition.

Anne and her husband anguished over the issue through most of December. Then, two days before Christmas, the doorbell rang. A beautifully dressed woman stood on the front porch holding a brightly decorated Christmas present. The woman, whom Anne did not know, asked if Lauren lived there. When Anne said that she did, the woman handed her the package and walked away.

Anne called after the woman, asking her name or the name of the person who sent the gift. The beautifully dressed stranger answered, "My name is Nancy, and the gift is from someone who wants you to have it."

Anne closed the door and studied the package, which bore a card addressed to Lauren. She handed the gift to her daughter who opened the card. It read "A special present for your special needs." When Lauren tore open the package, she began pulling one-hundred-dollar bills out of the box. There were ten of them, enough to cover tuition for another year.

Of that experience, Anne says, "Love and generosity do exist in our world." Such a story should not only warm our hearts but nudge us to act with equal generosity and love whenever we are able. In that way, we demonstrate to others that God does "take notice of trouble and suffering."

Thought for the Day

We hand folks over to God's mercy
and show none ourselves.

George Eliot

He does not punish us as we deserve
or repay us according to our sins and wrongs.
Psalm 103:10

Nothing Can Separate Us From God

There are times when we act in ways that leave us feeling ashamed, guilty, and regretful. The danger in those moments is that we can be tempted to believe that God no longer loves or respects us.

Therefore, it is worth the psalmist's reminder that God's love for us is permanent and irrevocable. God's love remains true to us in spite of our weaknesses, failure to act, words, thoughts, indiscretions, shortcomings, blemishes, defects.

It reminds us that God's grace toward us does not waver, falter, oscillate, hesitate.

So when we behave in ways that bring us shame, guilt, and regret, let us rapidly express sorrow and seek God's forgiveness.

Thought for the Day

Our ground of hope
is that God does not weary of mankind.
Ralph Washington Sockman

The commands of the L*ORD are just....*
Psalm 19:8

The Need to Act When God Calls

For several years, Doug, a man in his mid thirties, had been homeless. An alcoholic whose home was the street and whose "bedroom" was a park bench, Doug drifted aimlessly. Missions provided him with a daily meal; he sold his own blood for money. Occasionally, he would question his lifestyle but just could not get motivated to make the necessary changes.

One sunny afternoon as Doug sat on a bench in San Francisco's China Park, an elderly Chinese man with a long, white beard and walking with a cane approached him. "I would like for you to come over," he said pointing to a nearby restaurant. "Come, have something to eat." The elderly man explained he owned the restaurant. "You're welcome anytime. Come now," he urged.

Doug followed the man into the restaurant. Not a word was exchanged between them until they got inside. There the man introduced Doug to his family who worked in the restaurant. Doug was seated at a table, and the restaurant owner's wife brought over a white candle and lit it. Together, Doug and the elderly man ate and ate. "The food just kept coming," Doug recalls.

Finally, when both were more than satisfied, the elderly man placed a one-hundred-dollar bill on the table, rose from his seat, and said, "Thank you for joining me." Then he went back into the kitchen. The waiter took the one-hundred-dollar bill and brought Doug back the change as he finished sipping tea. Doug was puzzled, but the waiter explained, "Father would like very much for you to accept the change for your journey home."

Because of that compassionate treatment, Doug did go home. He began to change his life that very day, thanks to the kindness of an elderly Chinese man and his family.

That true story raises an important question. What if the Chinese man had disregarded the call of his heart to help a homeless person? Possibly, a life would still be lost and drifting aimlessly. Let us remember to act when God calls us and when our heart nudges us to reach out.

Thought for the Day

If you treat an individual as he is,
he will stay that way;
but if you treat him
as if he were what he could be,
he will become what he could be.
Goethe

Even my best friend, the one I trusted most…
has turned against me.
Psalm 41:9

Six Truths for Relationship Happiness

Most of us have shared the psalmist's experience. A friend, a spouse, a child, someone we counted on, has disappointed and hurt us. Helpful advice in maintaining relationships comes from Howard Markman, a professor of psychology at the University of Denver and director of the Center for Marital and Family Studies. In the book, *We Can Work It Out: Making Sense of Marital Conflict*, coauthored by Clifford Notarius and Howard Markman, the authors summarize twenty years of research into six simple principles for happiness in a relationship. As you read them, ask God to help you use them to strengthen a relationship that is important to you.

- Each relationship contains a reservoir of hope. Even the most destructive conflicts start with good intentions—the basis of hope.
- One major act of cruelty will erase twenty acts of kindness.
- Little changes in you can lead to huge changes in the relationship.
- It's not the differences between people that cause problems but how the differences are managed once they arise.
- Men and women fight using different weapons but suffer similar wounds. Both men and women try to accomplish the same objectives: acceptance, support, affection.
- People need to practice relationship skills to become good at them.

Prayer for the Day

Loving God,
Help me let go of old, unhealthy habits.
Help me be forgiving and releasing.
Help me be willing to learn and grow.
Help me to have healthier, happier relationships.
VMP

I am like a lonely bird on a housetop.
Psalm 102:7

The Warmth of Friendship

When Laurie and her family moved to a new city where they had no extended family and no friends, they found themselves feeling lonely. Then the job that had brought them to the new city was abruptly terminated, and they found themselves unemployed and without medical insurance. Since the move took place while Laurie was expecting their third child, her spirits were as gray and bleak as the winter skies.

By chance, she learned of a young mother's prayer- and Bible-study group that met weekly during Lent. Uncertain that she, a stranger, would be welcomed, Laurie took the risk and joined the group. From the beginning, she was warmly welcomed.

As her pregnancy progressed, other women in the group offered to baby-sit for her two boys during Laurie's medical appointments. When she went into labor, several women called and offered any assistance she needed. When Laurie returned from the hospital with a new baby boy, each woman in the Bible-study group took turns bringing over the evening meal for an entire week.

"Each time I read or hear the Scripture passage 'I was a stranger and you received me...' (Matthew 25:35), I immediately think of that group of caring young mothers quietly doing God's work," Laurie says.

Let each of us be like the members of Laurie's group, quietly doing God's work through caring friendship. God's comforting presence, love, and grace can be conveyed and felt through friendship, so that no one need feel "like a lonely bird on a housetop."

Thought for the Day

What is life without a friend?
a dreary race to run,
a desert where no water is,
a world without a sun.
Henry Alford

My conduct will be faultless.
Psalm 101:2

Some Habits to Give Up

We should all do a spiritual inventory periodically. We need to take a close look at ourselves and our conduct, for we can adopt unhealthy attitudes without even realizing it. Here are some habits to give up:

- *Give up complaining.* Start to focus on positives in yourself, in others, in the world.
- *Give up criticism.* There is too much criticism in life. Most people are hurt by "constructive" criticism.
- *Give up unkind thoughts.* Only you know what you are truly thinking. If you harbor thoughts of jealously, ill-will, anger, or hatred, give them up.
- *Give up fear.* Don't hold yourself back because of fear. Take the risk. Plunge in. God wants you to grow and develop. That means letting go of fear.
- *Give up judging by appearances.* Refrain from judging others by what they wear, how they look or speak, the kind of car they drive. All these things can be deceiving.
- *Give up the standards of the world.* The most effective way to cut down on materialism is to stop measuring yourself by what others have. Before making that purchase ask yourself if it is something you need or something you just want.

Let us join with the psalmist's high goal: "My conduct will be faultless." Ask God to help you.

--------*Affirmations for the Day*--------

I am guided to good
by the power of God's love.
I am led to a higher consciousness
by the power of God's love.
I am directed to wisdom and insight
by the power of God's love.
VMP

I will advance
in purity of heart.
Psalm 101:3
(*The Jerusalem Bible*)

Some Habits to Take On

Yesterday we considered some habits to give up. Today let us think about habits to take on.

- *Take on more time to pray.* Add to your prayer life by rising fifteen minutes earlier, using ten minutes of your lunch hour, or retiring a few minutes earlier. Use the time to pray and meditate.
- *Take on more study of Scripture.* Give up some of the time you use reading newspapers and magazines and devote the time saved to studying a book of the Bible.
- *Take on the virtue of generosity.* Be extra generous with your money, time, and talents. Share with someone who has less than you and is in need of assistance.
- *Take on speaking words of encouragement.* The world is filled with bad news and sad news. People's lives are filled with harsh criticism and very little praise. Be the one who lifts spirits with words of encouragement.
- *Take on self-denial and sacrifice.* In a society where looking out for "number one" is fashionable, be the one who practices self-denial and sacrifice. Give yourself to do God's will.
- *Take on justice.* Don't follow the crowd. Where there is an injustice, be the one to speak out and act to help. Often it takes just one person to do so and thereby begin changing the situation.

Affirmations for the Day

God's love inspires me.
God's love energizes me.
God's love motivates me.
Through God's love
I will work and act
to benefit those around me.
VMP

Even if I go through the deepest darkness,
I will note be afraid, Lord....
Psalm 23:4

God Guides in Life and in Death

On December 6, 1991, Faye had an unusual dream. She saw herself standing alone in a small auditorium. From backstage came a familiar voice, that of a young man, reciting something she couldn't quite make out.

Then, suddenly and clearly, she heard that the young man was actually reciting a verse from the Twenty-third Psalm: "Yea, though I walk through the valley of the shadow of death...."

Faye recognized the voice of her nephew, who had also been one of her pupils. The auditorium was in the rural school where she taught him. In recent months, her nephew, now in his thirties, had been struggling against a terminal illness. The last time she visited him, Faye sensed he was frightened and feeling disconnected from God.

Faye prayed often that God would let her nephew know that he was close to God's heart and that God loved him and would look after him. After the dream, Faye again prayed for her nephew and then fell asleep.

The telephone awakened her early in the morning hours. It was Faye's sister calling to let her know that her son had died earlier that night at about the time Faye dreamed about him. She thought of her nephew's last words in the dream: "Yea, though I walk through the valley of the shadow of death..." and realized that God had indeed taken care of her nephew.

Let us use that story as a reminder that God guides us in life and in death. There is nowhere that God cannot be found.

Thought for the Day

When I die,
I should like to slip out of the room
without fuss;
for what matters
is not what I am leaving,
but where I am going.
William Barclay

Teach us how short our life is,
so that we may become wise.
Psalm 90:12

Responding to God's Call

God plants all sorts of ideas and dreams into our minds. Even if we neglect them and fail to act, it is never too late to follow God's call. Dreams can come true regardless of age.

For several decades, Richard Wood of Norfolk, Virginia, was a lawyer and superior court judge.

However, he had originally gone to medical school and was still interested in medicine. That interest was deepened when his son became a doctor. At age fifty-six, Wood gave up law and returned to medical school in Guadalajara, Mexico.

After graduating, Wood spent an eye-opening year as a village doctor in rural Mexico, caring for poor people with little access to modern medicine.

Wood is currently a pediatric resident at Children's Hospital of the King's Daughters in Norfolk, but his heart is with the Mexican poor. After completing his training, he plans to spend six months of each year among them. "I feel I owe them," he explains. "The Mexican people made it possible for me to fulfill my dream of becoming a doctor."

Take a moment to think about your dreams, hopes, and aspirations. Ask yourself if God is speaking to you through one of them. Pray about it. Speak to a trusted spiritual guide. Possibly, God is calling you to make a dream come true. Remember that life is short. The time to respond is now.

Thought for the Day

God wills the development of all men.
When from time to time
he makes them hear his call...
it is not for their impoverishment
but for their enrichment.
Paul Tournier

But I am in pain and despair;
lift me up, O God, and save me!
Psalm 69:29

The Light Does Return

Although the darkness of pain and despair enters every life, it does not become a permanent condition. God does send the light of rescue, recovery, and redemption. This certainly was the experience of Kathy, whose young husband died leaving her with two small children to raise.

"Nine years ago when my husband died, I barely made it through the necessary routines of the day," she recalls. She found it necessary to limit her grief just to function as a mother. However, Kathy did not deny the reality of her bereavement. "I let the grief run its course in all its variants: anger, sadness, raw fear."

There were days of deep depression and great anxiety. Those days were filled with fear that she would not be able to deal with the loss and the pain. With time, the intensity of those emotions diminished, little by little. At the same time, her inner resources grew, and her pleasure in life came back. "Somehow, the light returned," she says.

Kathy's light returned because God has promised to be with us in good times as well as bad. God can be relied upon to strengthen and support us so we do not fall apart but grow whole—physically, emotionally, and spiritually. That is why the psalmist calls out to God in times of distress.

"I am in pain and despair; lift me up, O God, and save me!" That prayer should flow easily from our lips whenever we face hard times. And behind that prayer should be the knowledge and faith that the light does return.

Thought for the Day

I saw a beautiful sunrise this morning....
Had the sky been clear and without clouds,
there would not have been such beauty.
Jim White

I am gripped by fear and trembling;
I am overcome with horror.
Psalm 55:5

Offering Half a Straw

A woman tells about an extremely despairing day in her life and how her teenage daughter helped her. The woman spent several hours touring nursing homes for her father who had Alzheimer's disease. Although her father could no longer remain alone safely, the woman found it difficult to consider placing him in a nursing home.

Already depressed by the day's events, the woman returned home to prepare dinner. The phone rang with the message that her son, who lived thousands of miles away, had been injured on the job and was hospitalized. Dinner did not taste good, nor did it sit well in her stomach. When the woman returned some dishes to the kitchen, she saw water on the floor. The dishwasher, on its last legs, had just broken, flooding the kitchen. The woman sat down and began to weep.

Her teenage daughter hurried from the dining room to see what had happened. Between sobs, the mother explained that the dishwasher was broken. Her daughter shook her head. "A dishwasher is not worth crying about." The mother responded, "It's the straw that broke the camel's back."

Interestingly, the teenager had never heard the phrase before. So the mother outlined the events of her day and concluded, "The dishwasher was the last straw." The teenager pulled out some towels and began soaking up the water on the floor. "I don't know if I can help you with a whole straw, but I can take half a straw," she said patting her mother's shoulder. "Come on, I'll help you clean up and we can do the dishes together."

The "half a straw" offered by her daughter was enough. The teenager's words and actions somehow made the problems smaller and left the mother feeling she would find the strength to handle them.

In the future, when family and friends seem overwhelmed by difficulties, rather than feeling helpless why not offer "half a straw"? Doing that often gives a person just enough support to survive a struggle or deal with suffering. Offering "half a straw" can ease the anxiety of those "gripped by fear and trembling."

Thought for the Day

Great works do not always lie in our way,
but every moment
we may do little ones excellently,
that is, with great love.
Saint Francis de Sales

God…cares for orphans and protects widows.
He gives the lonely a home…
and leads prisoners out into happy freedom…
Psalm 68:5-6

Expanding Our Prayers

It is always worth examining what we pray about and whom we pray for. We might ask ourselves:

- Am I praying only for myself and those closest to me?
- Do I intentionally include in my prayers people I may not know personally but whose needs are real?

Our prayer life should shift, grow, and mature over the years. We can expand our prayers by including:

- nations and people who suffer from civil strife and war
- the poor for whom daily living is a constant, unending struggle
- Third World countries with mounting debts and declining resources
- the very sick and terminally ill who are despondent and in great pain
- the lonely, found in every community and church, who think no one cares whether they live or die
- those grieving the loss of a loved one
- all those incarcerated in jails and prisons
- women and men who are unable to believe in God because a great cruelty was inflicted upon them earlier in life

So along with our own needs and the needs of our family and friends, let us expand our prayers to include those a little more removed from us but who are also in need of our prayers.

Thought for the Day

Pray only in a room with windows—
to remember the world outside.
The Talmud

Praise the Lord, *all living creatures.*
Psalm 150:6

Prayers of Gratitude

Yesterday we considered expanding our prayers to include those we may not know personally. Today let us think about the fact that a rich and full prayer life should include prayers of praise and thanks. Although prayers of need and intercession are valid, our prayer life will be lacking if we do not make room for prayers of gratitude.

Each of us has much to praise God for. Remember to thank God for these great blessings, which can be easily taken for granted.

- For daily examples of God's love, care, and support of us—let us give great thanks.
- For the loyalty and love of family, friends, and colleagues who stand by us—let us give great thanks.
- For food, shelter, and clothing—let us give great thanks.
- For a safe place to sleep at night, for comfortable homes—let us give great thanks.
- For the ability to see, speak, hear, walk, and run; for good health and life—let us give great thanks.
- For employment that contributes to the material support of ourselves and families—let us give great thanks.
- For God's unfailing presence with us in sunshine and rain—let us give great thanks.

To include praise and thanks in our prayers is to cleanse ourselves from ingratitude and selfishness. Prayers of praise show that we are not taking for granted God's many and diverse blessings upon us.

Thought for the Day

O for a thousand tongues to sing
my great Redeemer's praise!
Charles Wesley

You, O Lord, are a merciful and loving God,
always patient....
Psalm 86:15

Pursued by Mercy

An elderly man lived alone in a small rural community. Not much was known about him except that he was filled with bitterness and resentment. The few who knew his circumstances said his bitterness and resentment were justified.

When he was younger, his beloved wife died while giving birth to their only child. Shortly after the wife's death, his child died from complications related to the birth. "He has reason to be bitter," some justified.

After the two losses, the man became reclusive. He worked but had no known family or friends. He did not attend church and did not participate in any civic functions. In his mid seventies, when he was carried out of his small home to die in a hospital, no one visited. No flowers or cards were sent. He would die alone.

However, a student nurse in the hospital sensed the man's deep loneliness and spent time with him in spite of his protests with "Go away. Leave me alone." She came into his room and greeted him warmly every day. Sometimes she stepped quickly into the room, smiled at him, and departed. At night she tucked him in. All the while, however, he continued to protest her attention.

The student nurse remained faithful and pursued the elderly man with mercy. On the night of his death, she was at his bedside holding his gnarled old hand. Shortly before he died, tears formed in his eyes as he looked at the student nurse. For the first time in possibly forty or fifty years, he responded emotionally to another human being and said, "God bless you!"

It is worth remembering that our acts of mercy can penetrate the hardest shell. While our acts of mercy cannot undo life's cruelties, they can soften the blow and allow hope to emerge. It is through our actions that God's mercy, love, and patience become real to others.

Thought for the Day

We all have enough strength
to bear the misfortunes of others.

Francois La Rochefoucauld-Liancourt

Complete the work that you have begun.
Psalm 138:8

Seeing God at Work

When the daily news is filled with information about mass starvation, civil strife, looming war, violence in cities and homes, it can become difficult to see where God is working. Yet if we look carefully, there are many signs showing that God's kingdom is indeed emerging.

- God is working whenever acts of justice, kindness, and love are done.
- God is working whenever there are prophetic words of truth spoken to correct the abuse of power.
- God is working whenever quiet deeds of charity and mercy are done to those in need and pain.
- God is working whenever someone courageously stands for truth against popular approval.
- God is working whenever a person of power and prestige intentionally reaches out to help the less fortunate.
- God is working whenever an individual refuses to compromise on principles and morals.

In every community and in every church, women and men are quietly working to do good. It is through their efforts that God's presence and kingdom can be seen and felt. They are the answer to the psalmist's prayer: "Complete the work that you have begun."

Prayer for the Day

Eternal and glorious God,
I praise you for the gift of life.
Let me be included
with those whose daily living
makes your presence real in our world.
VMP

His name is greater than all others.
Psalm 148:13

What Forces Shape You?

A pastor teaching an adult religion class told of a friend who underwent a powerful religious conversion. It was so thorough a conversion that he sold all he had and moved his family to a remote area of the South to work with the poor.

After hearing the story, one man asked, "How old are his children?" The pastor said they were all teenagers.

"Well, then that was terrible," said the questioner. He went on to explain that, in his opinion, it was fine for the man to experience conversion and respond radically to God's call. However, it was unfair for him to inflict his religious zeal on his family. The questioner felt the father was sacrificing his children, and most members of the class agreed.

Ironically, the man who questioned the conversion and the family move to the South has a son who is in his second alcohol-treatment program. That same man has a daughter who has been sexually active since she was sixteen.

Behind that story is the reality that all of us are shaped and guided by forces. Thus the question is not whether or not we are affected but which powers will we allow to guide and shape us. Today's reading is a simple but powerful declaration: "His name is greater than all others." Let us be like the man who experienced a dramatic religious conversion and intentionally choose to serve the One who is "greater than all others."

Affirmations for the Day

I take responsibility for my choices.
I desire to follow God's guidance more closely.
I allow God to fill me with divine light.

VMP

He leads the humble in what is right....
Psalm 25:9
(New Revised Standard Version)

Spiritual Generosity

A naval officer who spent three years in the Pacific during World War II awakened at three o'clock one morning unable to sleep. He got out of his bunk, went to his locker, and took out a pen, writing paper, and his checkbook.

In those quiet, early-morning hours, he wrote a letter to his pastor and enclosed a check. He asked the pastor to cash it and give the money to a woman who had been his religious-education teacher when he was a boy. Because he often visited her when he was ashore, the officer knew that his former teacher was retired, bedridden, and living on a limited pension; and he included her in his prayers faithfully.

He mailed the letter the following morning and immediately had second thoughts. "What possessed me to get up in the middle of the night and do such a thing?" he wondered.

Six weeks later, he received a letter from his pastor, who wrote: "When I arrived at Mrs. B.'s house with the money, I learned it was the exact amount she needed for a new hearing aid she had ordered COD—but now couldn't afford. Without your gift, the post office would have returned it."

Immediately, the naval officer realized that it was God's spirit that had awakened him in the middle of the night and prompted him to send the money to his former teacher. His story is a good lesson for all of us. We should respond immediately when the urge to be generous strikes us. Let us have the humility necessary to be guided by God's spirit.

Thought for the Day

A gift with a kind countenance
is a double present.
Thomas Fuller

Happy are those who are concerned....
Psalm 41:1

Cultivating the Gift of Hospitality

An American Lutheran minister tells of an incident that happened while he was vacationing. On the way from Germany to Vienna, Austria, he took a wrong turn and became hopelessly lost in the Austrian countryside.

As the sun began to set, his sense of panic heightened; he could not find his location on any map and had no place to spend the night. Despite repeated attempts to secure lodging, he was unsuccessful.

Finally, in desperation, he stopped at a farmhouse and explained his situation, asking if the owner knew of a place he could find lodging. To the minister's surprise, the seventy-six- year-old farmer invited him to spend the night at his home. The minister gladly accepted the generous invitation.

The next morning, a Sunday, the farmer prepared a breakfast of farm-fresh eggs, cream, butter, and homemade rolls. Then he invited the minister to join him for worship at his Catholic church, where he introduced the American Lutheran to his parish priest. The minister was surprised a second time when the priest warmly welcomed him and asked him to help lead the service that morning and bring greetings.

What started off as a frustrating and disappointing experience ended in great delight and joy. The experience of getting lost was the highlight of his European trip. It was transformed because people exercised the gift of hospitality. The hosts' sympathy and kindness should inspire each of us to do likewise.

Thought for the Day

Hospitality is one form of worship.
Jewish Proverb

God is our shelter and strength....
Psalm 46:1

Using Faith to Face Problems Directly

A story from British naval history concerns a British destroyer lying in harbor in the West Indies. Five other ships from various nations were also anchored in the harbor.

Suddenly, a furious storm erupted, bringing with it destructive winds. Immediately, the British captain ordered his crew to weigh anchor and steam out to sea. He piloted his ship directly into the eye of the storm.

Two days later, he returned. The ship had been tossed about on giant waves but was otherwise fine. The other five ships that remained in the harbor were lying piled up and wrecked on the shore. Doing nothing and waiting for the storm to subside resulted in their ruin.

This story is a parable for dealing with problems and storms in our lives. Rather than avoid and ignore a problem, meet it directly with the faith and confidence that God will guide us safely through the storm.

Affirmations for the Day

Divine love brings order and harmony to my life.
Divine love sustains and upholds me.
Divine love guides me through the storm.
O God, I thank you for your presence in my life.
I trust you to help me
make good choices and live wisely.

VMP

I am weak and poor;
come to me quickly, O God.
Psalm 70:5

Finding God's Power in Our Pain

One of the strongest spiritual leaders of this century was Dr. Harry E. Fosdick, founding minister of the Riverside Church in New York City. This gifted man, whose ministry of preaching, counseling, and writing helped thousands of people, might never have carried such an impact had it not been for a devastating mental breakdown he experienced as a young man.

In his autobiography, *The Living of These Days*, Dr. Fosdick says that his nervous breakdown "was one of the most important factors in my preparation for the ministry." For the first time in his life, Fosdick faced a situation beyond his management and control. He dropped into the depths of emotional darkness and despair.

Yet it was there that he learned the power of prayer. "I learned to pray not because I had adequately argued out prayer's rationality but because I desperately needed help from a Power greater than my own," he writes.

From these depths Fosdick emerged stronger, healthier, more whole, and profoundly aware of God's power and presence. The time in the darkness powerfully shaped Fosdick's life and ministry, enabling him to help others experiencing despair.

Let us hold to the reality that God is present in the darkness of pain and suffering. God not only supports and sustains us but uses the experience to teach us important lessons.

Thought for the Day

The avoidance of legitimate suffering means
we also avoid the growth that problems afford us.
Charles R. Swindoll

Come and save me, L*ORD*;
in your mercy rescue me from death.
Psalm 6:4

A Mysterious Protector

In spite of his parents' repeated warnings that he never swim unattended, a nine-year-old boy decided to go swimming in a lake near his home in northern Wisconsin.

Unable to find swimming companions, the boy made his way to the lake alone and dived in. Halfway across the lake, however, he experienced a severe cramping in his leg. Although he struggled to remain afloat, he began to feel himself sinking beneath the waters.

Suddenly, another swimmer appeared from nowhere. He calmed the youth and gently brought him to shore. After the boy had calmed down, he rose from the shore wanting to thank his rescuer, but there was no one in sight. The mysterious person had disappeared as quickly and quietly as he had arrived.

Looking back on the incident, the young swimmer, now grown up, says of his rescuer, "I'm sure he was a guardian angel sent by God."

Whether we have had an angel encounter or not, all of us can be assured that God's power is there to protect us. Unfailing mercy drives God to seek our constant good.

------- *Affirmations for the Day* -------

God's power protects me;
I will fear no evil.
God's wisdom guides me;
I will live with confidence.
God's word leads me;
I will act boldly.
God's light floods my path;
I will walk courageously.
VMP

...they imagine the worst about me.
Psalm 41:7

Responding Creatively to Rejection

Actor Sylvester Stallone, who created one of film history's most memorable roles because he was being rejected, found a uniquely creative way to respond to rejection. Stallone was an out-of-work actor when he decided to create a hero for the "common" person.

His inspiration for the story came while watching Muhammad Ali beat a little-known fighter named Chuck Wepner. Ali won the fight with Wepner but not before the challenger went the full fifteen rounds, winning the respect of fans. That event gave Stallone his hero.

Stallone bought a book on screenwriting and wrote the story of Rocky Balboa, the "Italian Stallion," a small-time Philadelphia boxer who earns a long-shot chance to fight the champ. When it was complete, Stallone set out to sell the script. Producers were interested but wanted big-name stars such as Warren Beatty, Burt Reynolds, or James Caan to play Rocky.

However, Stallone knew Rocky could make him a star. Even though he and his pregnant wife were down to their last one hundred dollars, Stallone refused $265 thousand for the script from producers who wouldn't let him play the lead. The rest, of course, is history. *Rocky* was an enormous success, and Stallone became a star.

Stallone's success lay not only in his story but in his ability to reject rejection. He was secure enough and strong enough to pursue his dreams. It paid off. All of us can be inspired by his example. From people like Sylvester Stallone, we can learn to respond, not merely react, to rejection.

Today the psalmist laments the fact of rejection: "They imagine the worst about me." Whenever we experience negative perception, let us balance such thoughts and statements with the knowledge that God gives each of us great abilities and talents. We must not be unduly influenced by the opinions of others. To do so results in selling ourselves short and settling for second best. Let us use those talents and abilities to accomplish great things for ourselves and for God.

Thought for the Day

If you have a talent,
use it in every way possible.
Don't hoard it.
Don't dole it out like a miser.
Spend it lavishly,
like a millionaire intent on going broke.

Brendan Francis

Your love and loyalty will always keep me safe.
Psalm 40:11

Holding On and Moving Forward

Today Sally Jessy Raphael enjoys great popularity on television, having two Emmys, one for Best Talk Show Host and the other for Outstanding Talk Show. However, Raphael's rise has been painfully tortuous and slow. It has been a thirty-five year trek through show business.

As an actress and radio performer, she was fired eighteen times. She tried out for one hundred thirty-four commercial voiceovers—and was never chosen for a single one.

During the course of her career, she has lived in a car with her family when they couldn't afford a home, furnished an apartment (when she could afford one) from a thrift shop, and lived for three months on food stamps.

About her living-on-the-edge existence, Raphael says, "It was awful and wonderful in equal proportions. My life was not dull. I never needed to look for anything outside of it. It was wonderfully exciting, terribly defeating, very scary; but I loved the scariness."

Raphael's ability to hold on and continue moving forward is impressive. As we deal with life's setbacks and disappointments, let us be guided and encouraged by the psalmist's declaration: "Your love and loyalty will always keep me safe."

Affirmations for the Day

God has made me strong, energetic, and capable.
God works with me for my highest good.
God helps me respond positively to every situation.
Loving God, thank you for filling me
with talents and abilities.
Help me use them wisely for my good
and your glory.

VMP

Have reverence for the L*ORD*....
Psalm 33:8

Does Your Faith Make Any Difference?

An American executive while conducting business in Russia, made friends with a woman who had been a Communist from birth. She was born into atheism much the same way the businessman was born into his Baptist family faith.

As the American and the Russian came to know each other better, she surprised him one day by asking, "If you are a Christian, how have you lived differently from me today? When you got out of bed this morning, did you ask God what he wanted you to do and how you should live out this day? Did you spend your money differently yesterday because you believe God is real?"

The woman's honest and penetrating questions became a source of anxiety and guilt for the Baptist businessman. Traveling home on the plane, he reviewed her questions and concluded privately that there was not much difference between his lifestyle and hers.

Yet he knew that because he was a Christian, there should be a sharper contrast. He returned home determined to have his faith make more of a difference in the way he lived.

The questions raised by the Russian woman are ones which any of us could review to make our faith glow more strongly in our lives. Today's psalm challenges us to "have reverence for the Lord." A quick dictionary check of the word *reverence* shows it means "a feeling or attitude of deep respect, love, and veneration." The best reverence for God we can exhibit is a lifestyle in which our behavior matches our belief.

Thought for the Day

You are the light of the world,
but the switch must be turned on.

Austin Alexander Lewis

In the presence of your people
I will proclaim that you are good.
Psalm 52:9

You Are God's Representative

At times we may feel as though our lives have no real meaning. We simply function from day to day and from activity to activity, without sensing any purpose. Yet consider the sobering biblical thought that we are God's representatives at the office, at the kitchen counter, on the playground, in the grocery store, driving the carpool, in the neighborhood, on the campus, in the classroom, behind the counter, in the factory, at the garage, working at the keyboard, answering the phone, in the waiting room.

Today think about your life, the people with whom you come into contact, your sphere of influence. You are God's representative. For some people, you may be their only link to God. It is through your life that people see God's goodness.

Thought for the Day

Sometimes it may seem to us
that there is no purpose in our lives,
that going day after day for years
to this office or that school or factory
is nothing else but waste and weariness.
But it may be
that God has sent us there
because but for us
Christ would not be there.
If our being there
means that Christ is there,
that alone makes it worthwhile.

Caryll Houselander

...do good to those who are righteous.
Psalm 36:10

Showing Our Appreciation

A Florida musician has a special place in his home and heart for three coins: a dime, a nickel, and a penny.

As a professional organist, he was entertaining families during an Easter brunch at a private club. After he had worked for several hours, a boy of about seven came up to him and asked, "Please play 'Raindrops,' Mister."

The musician responded by playing "Raindrops Are Falling on My Head." As he looked over at the boy, it was obvious that he was pleased to hear his favorite song.

Later, as the youth and his family were leaving the club, the boy ran back and handed the organist three coins: a dime, a nickel, and a penny—still warm from being clutched in the child's hand. Then he ran from the club.

That incident took place more than a decade ago, but the organist has kept the coins and framed the caption "Please play 'Raindrops,' Mister." It is clear why the coins and caption hold a place in the organist's heart: the money, which represented the boy's entire fortune at the time, was given willingly as a token of appreciation for a favor requested.

Let us remember to be like that little boy. Whenever people do us a favor, extend us a kind act or word or deed, let us respond by expressing our sincere, heartfelt appreciation. That is one way for us to "do good to the righteous."

Thought for the Day

Gratitude is born in hearts
that take time to count up past mercies.
Charles Edward Jefferson

The LORD gives strength to his people.
Psalm 29:11

Strength for the Day

A magazine carried a remarkable story of great courage involving a mother who has a severely injured arm, and her three-year-old daughter. One morning the mother dressed the little girl in an orange dress and sent her out to play with other children.

Flowing through their backyard was a small but swift river. The mother had a great fear of water because she had nearly drowned as a child. Consequently, she never learned to swim. As she worked around the house that morning, the mother suddenly realized that three-year-old Margie had been out of the house longer than usual. She went outside and asked the other children, "Where's Margie?" One of them said, "Margie went to see the ducks in the river."

Terror immediately filled the mother's heart. The river was dangerous for a three-year-old, and the child had been instructed never to go near it without an adult. The woman ran to the riverbank and looked quickly up and down. Near the opposite bank, she saw something bright orange floating in the water. She ran to the street to seek help, but no one was in sight. Entirely alone, she acted quickly.

In spite of her fear of water and her injured arm, the woman plunged into ice-cold water up to her neck, waded to the opposite bank, and grabbed the orange object, which she knew was her child. Putting her injured arm under the child, she hurled her daughter onto the river bank and heard her land with a thud. Then the mother watched in horror as her daughter slid down the bank and back into the water. In spite of intense pain in her injured arm, she threw the child farther onto the riverbank. This time, her daughter landed safely. Later, mother and daughter were treated for minor injuries at a hospital and released.

Today's psalm is a reminder that God "gives strength to his people." One of God's blessings is special assistance when a great crisis emerges.

Thought for the Day

God gives the shoulder according to the burden.

German Proverb

...at night his song is with me....
Psalm 42:8
(New Revised Standard Version)

Singing in the Darkness

At fifty-nine, Mary Colburn of Norfolk, Virginia, developed post-polio syndrome as a result of the crippling disease she suffered as a child. Unable to walk, she must crawl from her bedroom to the bathroom. She is completely destitute and relies on modest government support for survival. In spite of her disability, Mary Colburn continues to sing in the darkness. On nights when the pain is so severe that she cannot sleep, Mary engages in an alphabet game to motivate herself and take her mind off the pain.

A) Accentuate the positive; eliminate the negative.

B) Balance your life.

C) Change; if you don't like something, then take some action.

D) Determination; resolve to remain steadfast in the present moment.

G) Gratitude; "I wake every morning and say I walk in gratitude," Mary declares in spite of the fact that she cannot walk.

H) Help someone else who is worse off than I am....

N) Never say never.

"I stop at N," Mary says emphatically.

Her example can inspire each of us. When our lives are darkened by difficulty, we can still find reasons to sing in the darkness.

-------- Thought for the Day --------

I would rather be able to appreciate things
I cannot have
than to have things
I am not able to appreciate.
Elbert Hubbard

He led his people through the desert.
Psalm 136:16

God Leads From Outpost to Outpost

Several centuries ago, a small regiment of soldiers was ordered to move from one desert outpost to another. They were led through the Algerian desert by an experienced guide, but due to swirling sandstorms, the journey took longer than expected. The men were on a limited water allowance and began to suffer extreme thirst.

Deceived by a mirage and believing they could see an oasis of water in the distance, the soldiers demanded that their guide take them there. In vain, the guide tried to tell them that there was no oasis. He refused to lose more precious time by wandering off the course.

The soldiers protested. Words led to blows, and the guide who was to lead them to safety was killed. Then the soldiers made a frantic dash in the direction of what they thought was water. Of course, they never reached it, and the entire company died on the burning desert sands.

Sometimes our lives are like a journey in the desert wilderness. We move "from outpost to outpost," from one safe place to another, and between each safe place lies great danger. Like the ancient people of Israel, we depend upon God to guide us safely through.

Affirmations for the Day

God's creative power is flowing through me.
God's creative power is leading me.
God's creative power is teaching me.
Through all of life's journey,
God's creative power is with me.
VMP

But destruction will catch them before they know it.
Psalm 35:8

Act on Your Good Intentions

The evening news aired a story about a man who ordered a headstone for his brother's grave. It was a life-size replica of a Mercedes-Benz, complete with windshield wipers and a TV antenna. In addition, it had every detail found in the most expensive model. The Mercedes was carved out of a fine stone from a quarry in Vermont. The sculptor spent a year working on it, and the total cost was $120 thousand.

Why would the brother have such an elaborate, expensive headstone created? He had promised to give his brother a car, but for years, he kept putting it off because he was too busy.

Then suddenly his brother died, and he was stricken with guilt. After the death, he found time to talk with a Mercedes dealer about models, to find a sculptor willing to do the work, to go to Vermont to pick out the stone, to meet with cemetery officials, to oversee the project. He found time.

The moral of this story, of course, is that we need to act promptly on our good intentions. Time can run out and opportunities can be missed.

-------- *Thought for the Day* --------

One of these days is none of these days.

Henry George Bohn

Give yourself to the LORD;
trust in him, and he will help you.
Psalm 37:5

Trust Is a Must

Earlier in this century, a shipping company advertised for a ship's radio operator. At the company headquarters, the employment office was crowded with applicants for the position. After completing the application form, each applicant was asked to be seated and wait to be called over the loudspeaker for an interview.

Midway through the morning, a man arrived at the employment office and was given an application form, which he quietly filled in. Then he sat down to await his turn.

After a few moments, however, he suddenly arose and walked into the office marked "private." A few minutes later, he came out with a broad grin on his face. He had been hired.

Upon learning what happened, one man in the group of waiting applicants protested: "We were here first. Why did you go in there ahead of us rather than wait your turn?"

The successful applicant replied, "Any one of you could have landed the job, but none of you were listening to the Morse code signals coming over the loudspeaker." He went on to explain that this message was being signaled out: "We desire to fill this position with someone who is constantly alert. If you are getting this message, come into the private office immediately."

Today's psalm urges us—not in code but in clear language—to give ourselves in trust to God; God will help us.

Thought for the Day

All that I have seen
teaches me to trust the Creator
for all I have not seen.
Ralph Waldo Emerson

I will always praise the L*ORD.*
Psalm 145:21

Mangoes for the Future

From India comes the delightful story of a very old man who was digging holes in his garden. Seeing him hard at work, a neighbor asked, "What are you doing?"

"Planting mango trees," he answered.

"Do you expect to eat from those trees?"

"No," replied the old man. "I won't live long enough for that but others will. The other day it occurred to me that all my life I have enjoyed mangoes planted by other people. This is my way of showing them gratitude."

That old man's example is instructive and shows us another way to apply today's psalm: "I will always praise the Lord." Can we consider ways to leave mangoes for the future as a way of showing our gratitude and praising God?

It is worth thinking and praying about. It is possible that someone reading this meditation today could leave mangoes for the future through

- a scholarship established for promising but needy students
- a contribution to a hospital that cares for children
- a donation to a hospice that provides for the terminally ill and their families
- money or property bequeathed to an organization or individual who could truly use the extra financial boost

Prayer for the Day

Loving and good God,
I praise you for your many blessings that flow over me.
In gratitude, I am willing to reach out with help.
In gratitude, I am willing to work at making life better
for those who come after me.
In gratitude, I am willing to share my talent,
time, and financial resources with others.

VMP

He lifts those who have fallen.
Psalm 146:8

Lifting Others Up in Prayer

This verse reminds us again that God lifts up those who have fallen upon hard times. Let us cooperate with this divine activity by including in our prayers today all those who stand in special need:

- those who routinely experience prejudice and discrimination
- those who are elderly, sick, and have no one to care for them or about them
- those who are physically or mentally challenged and their families
- those who speak out for truth and justice but feel unheard and misunderstood
- those who have recently learned they have a serious illness and are frightened
- those whose jobs have been eliminated due to downsizing or corporate mergers
- those who struggle in a difficult marriage relationship
- those recently separated and divorced
- those recently bereaved
- those recently convicted
- those recently paroled

When we pray for those who are burdened, we become partners with God, who replaces fear with faith and pain with peace.

Thought for the Day

Prayer is an all-efficient panoply,
a treasure undiminished,
a mine which is never exhausted,
a sky unobscured by clouds.
Saint John Chrysostom

My sins have caught up with me....
Psalm 40:12

Coping With Guilt

At one time or another, all of us experience feelings of guilt. When guilt is not managed properly, its impact can be damaging. Guilt feelings reduce self-confidence and the ability to feel good about ourselves. Following are some ways to cope with guilt in a healthy, mature manner.

- Remember that God always loves you and wants your life to be good. God does not want you to wallow in shame and self-hatred.
- Realize that guilt is a warning light alerting you that something is wrong. It is not a permanent state or a condition in which you must remain.
- Study your guilt. Ask yourself if your guilt is rational or irrational. Are your guilt feelings an appropriate response to a situation? Do you often feel guilty whether or not you have done something wrong? Are you surrounded by people who are skilled in making you feel guilty?
- If you determine that your guilt is irrational, find a more appropriate response. For example, if someone is manipulating you into feeling guilty, anger toward that person might very well be a healthy response.
- When you determine that your guilt is rational, act to resolve it. If you have done something or failed to do something for which you feel guilty, seek forgiveness from God and anyone else involved. If possible, make amends. Reassure yourself that God forgives, even if other people cannot.
- Remember that you are not perfect. God does not expect perfection from you, so don't demand it of yourself. Don't expend a great amount of energy in self-blame or self-hatred.
- Learn from the experiences that produced the guilt. There is no point in repeating the same mistakes. Review what went wrong, and resolve not to let it happen again. Seal your commitment with a prayer, asking for peace in the present and wisdom in the future.

Thought for the Day

How unhappy are those
who cannot forgive themselves!
Publilius Syrus

The LORD looks down from heaven;
he sees all humankind.
Psalm 33:13
(*New Revised Standard Version*)

God Knows When the Water Is Rising

In South America, an immense dam was constructed across a valley, forming one of the world's largest human-made lakes.

As the water gradually rose, it created many temporary islands, which grew smaller and smaller as the water level continued to climb.

Various jungle animals took refuge on those small pinnacles of land. However, their safety was in jeopardy because the water continued to rise. Kind people organized a small fleet of motorboats equipped with ropes, snares, nets, and cages and tried to save the endangered animals.

While some creatures were rescued, many resisted and fought against their rescuers. Unable to understand, the animals were afraid to trust the people who came to save them, and they perished.

God sometimes deals with us in a similar manner. We feel safe and secure on our small islands. When we are called to move off our comfortable, familiar islands, however, let us realize that it may be because the water is rising.

-------- *Affirmations for the Day* --------

I am guided to my good
by the power of God's love.
My life is abundantly blessed
by the power of God's love.
I live in peace and confidence
by the power of God's love.
VMP

I am weak from all my troubles. . . .
Psalm 31:10

Reducing Stress

Like the psalmist, we all experience the stresses and struggles of life. Without realizing it, we absorb great amounts of stress in merely meeting our daily responsibilities. Whether you are a homemaker, parent, corporate executive—or all three—life brings daily demands and stresses. The following suggestions are simple but effective and can help you reduce stress and enjoy God's world a little more.

- *Get physical.* Physicians strongly recommend that all of us do some type of aerobic workout for thirty minutes a day at least three times a week. Exercise is an effective way of working off anger and frustration.
- *Find a sympathetic ear.* Putting frustrations and fears into words helps ease them considerably.
- *Listen to another person's troubles.* Listening produces a double benefit. By listening, you take the focus off your own stresses while helping another person.
- *Practice "giving in" on some issues.* Whether you are parenting or managing, give in on some points. Always insisting on having your way is stressful.
- *Reject your problems for a while.* It is possible, and recommended, to turn your back on problems and stresses for a while—walk through a mall, take a ride in the country, read an entertaining book.
- *Ask God to help you lighten up.* Some of us take life far too seriously; the biblical virtue of joy is almost completely absent in our lives. Ask God to help you lighten up. Then intentionally look for reasons to smile, praise, and laugh during the day.

Thought for the Day

If your heart is troubled,
you are not living up to your belief.
Oswald Chambers

Sincerity and truth are what you require.
Psalm 51:6

Acting on Your Convictions

Former athletes, widely viewed as role models for today's youth, are in great demand in TV commercials promoting the sale of alcohol. At least one professional athlete, however, sees the moral implications of doing beer commercials.

Starting in the 1970s, Bubba Smith, who was a defensive end for Michigan State and the Baltimore Colts, appeared in various beer commercials. Then, in 1985, Smith served as a grand marshal of the homecoming parade at his alma mater in East Lansing, Michigan. While there, he was distressed to see many students at the pregame bonfire who were, in his words, "drunk out of their heads."

That night, Bubba Smith decided to stop making beer commercials. Although the sponsors insisted that the commercials were aimed at an older audience, Smith concluded that the ads were hitting impressionable youths. "I was selling to children," he says.

Bubba Smith's decision to quit appearing in beer commercials has cost him a considerable amount of endorsement money. But once he realized the detrimental impact those ads were having, he made the decision to quit.

Such integrity is commendable but all too rare. Often it feels easier to do and say nothing. Yet if more of us acted on our convictions, perhaps the world would indeed become a kinder and gentler place. Let us take heed of the psalmist's words to be sincere and stand for truth.

Thought for the Day

Never, for sake of peace and quiet,
deny your own experience or convictions.
Dag Hammarskjöld

Even in my suffering I was comforted....
Psalm 119:50

Turning Evil Into Good

We know that God can transform negatives into positives and evil into good, but do we realize that we are capable of doing so ourselves? *Newsweek* featured the story of John Penne, who learned in 1973 that both he and his wife, Wanda, had cancer. Subsequently, the Pennes sold the Milwaukee business they had run for twenty-six years and set out to make comfortable what remained of their lives.

As it turned out, John's cancer was treatable; but Wanda died after four years of chemotherapy. Grieving her death and wanting to honor her memory, John approached a local chapter of the American Cancer Society with an idea. During those final desperate days of taking Wanda to the hospital for treatment, John had been struck by the sight of all the sick people waiting for rides home from the hospital. He proposed that if the Cancer Society provided him with a car and a little gas money, he would drive patients to the hospital and back. Now in his seventies, John continues to chauffeur patients daily. "This is for Wanda," he reminds himself.

Not only does he provide a desperately needed service, John Penne has created good out of loss. Whenever we experience something negative in our lives, let us consider how we can cooperate with God to transform it into something positive and beneficial. This is one way to find comfort in our suffering.

-------- *Affirmations for the Day* --------

God's wisdom guides me unfailingly.
God's love gives me a clear vision.
Through God's wisdom and love,
I receive creative ideas and opportunities for good.
VMP

Happy are those who...
do not turn to idols....
Psalm 40:4

The Essence of Happiness

"Who are the happiest people on earth?" When the editors of a British newspaper asked readers that question, these were the four prize-winning answers:

- an artist or craftsman whistling over a job well done
- a little child building sandcastles on the beach
- a mother after a busy day bathing her baby
- a doctor who has finished a difficult, dangerous operation and saved a human life

Notably absent from the list were millionaires, royalty, people of fame and fortune. Those who responded to the question revealed great wisdom. The essential quality of happiness is not found in wealth and prestige, two widely worshiped "idols" in contemporary society.

Perhaps that survey can help you take a closer look at your own attitudes about what makes you happy. Honestly ask yourself:

- Am I thankful to God for what I have?
- Do I regularly express my gratitude to God?
- Am I envious of others for who they are and what they have?
- Are my goals, dreams, and aspirations consistent with God's values?
- Do I worship the one, true, holy God, or do I worship my own idols?

Thought for the Day

Idolatry is...
putting confidence in riches and power.
Martin Luther

I will praise you, LORD, with all my heart.
Psalm 9:1

Scrutinizing Our Attitudes Toward God

It is easy to mouth the words "I will praise you, Lord, with all my heart." More difficult is living that sentence daily.

Today conduct an examination of conscience regarding your attitudes toward God.

- Is God the most important person in my life?
- Do I give God my time through regular prayer, Bible reading, and worship?
- Am I self-centered, arrogant, egotistical?
- Is my schedule so filled that God gets squeezed out?
- Am I consumed by desires to have more, own more, and keep more?
- Am I driven by material successes and rewards?
- Do I respond when I see other people with needs and hurts?
- Am I a generous, giving person, or am I one who mainly takes and receives?

Do not be discouraged by your responses; we are all in need of improvement. Do continue to think about these questions and your responses. Then begin making the necessary adjustments. Remember that God always loves you.

Thought for the Day

The work of purging the soul
neither can nor should end
except with our life itself.
We must not be disturbed at our imperfections,
since for us
perfection consists in fighting against them.
How can we fight against them
unless we see them,
or overcome them
unless we face them?

Saint Francis de Sales

He fills my life with good things,
so that I stay young and strong like an eagle.
Psalm 103:5

Remaining Open and Receptive

For years, a mother duck led her new family of ducklings to the same pond. It was a place of safety and beauty. However, one year she found it dry and empty. Nothing remained but dried mud.

Yet she persisted in bringing her babies down to the pond, where she would walk about with flapping wings, anxiously quacking and trying to get her brood to enter.

The ducklings, however, with their fresh instincts, heard the far-off rippling of the water in a new dam being built farther upstream. The little ducklings refused to enter the dried mudhole. Instead, they left their mother quacking beside her empty pond and set out to find new water.

The mother duck had a closed mind. She could not accept the reality that the water was gone. She chose not to live in the real world so she remained in her little world because it was familiar.

Like the little ducklings, we must remain open to a new future, open to new ideas, open to others, open to learning new things—no matter what our age and experience. To do so is to maintain a childlike faith in God.

The only way to experience the truth of today's psalm—"He fills my life with good things, so that I stay young and strong like an eagle"—is to remain receptive to God through all of life's changes and chances. We must never become so certain that we leave no room in our minds and lives for God's added blessings.

Thought for the Day

Young people do the impossible
before they find out
it's impossible–
that's why God uses them so often.
Loren Cunningham

. . . you will restore my strength.
Psalm 71:20

Healthy Dependence

A Boston executive has been through so many personal and professional crises that she refers to herself as "Calamity Jane." "I've been spared nothing," she says. "Getting fired, running out of money, having my computer stolen, taking on work I could not handle."

Initially, when trouble came her way, the woman maintained a fierce independence and determination to manage her problems alone, refusing to let anyone know of her struggles. "I put a lot of energy into keeping up a facade of being in control and completely successful," she says. "Nobody ever knew I was in trouble."

Then one day she lost an important consulting contract and was devastated. The burden was so great, she finally allowed herself to confide in friends. Immediately, they organized a breakfast to brainstorm ways the executive could network and obtain new contracts. "That got me charged up again to take action," she recalls.

This woman's experience taught her the value of healthy dependence. At times, we must be willing to admit we have problems. When we confide in another person, we open ourselves to their insight, support, and assistance. It is often through the help of a friend that God restores our strength.

Thought for the Day

A friend should bear his friend's infirmities.

William Shakespeare

To you, O LORD, I offer my prayer;
in you, my God, I trust.
Psalm 25:1

Are You a Controlaholic?

Being a well-organized person is commendable. However, some people take organization a step further. These individuals need to be in complete and constant control. Being a controlaholic is unhealthy for at least three reasons.

First, the need to be in control at all times creates unnecessary stress. Second, when life takes an unexpected twist, those who are controlling find it difficult to cope. Finally, too much control implies a profound lack of trust in God.

Are you a controlaholic? You may be if you

- never do anything spontaneously
- fill your calendar months ahead with tightly scheduled activities and events
- become tense, upset, and irritable if your schedule is even modestly interrupted
- think you have to look perfect every time you leave your home
- think you have to look perfect even when you aren't leaving your home
- scream excessively at your children for messing up the house
- can't relax until "all the work is done"
- feel uncomfortable with spontaneity, mystery, and randomness
- expect too much from yourself, that everything has to be done perfectly to be acceptable
- are unable to see the distinction between being organized and being rigid

The first step in overcoming overcontrol is to acknowledge this compulsion. Then resolve, with God's help, to lighten up. Memorize the words of Psalm 25:1: "To you, O Lord, I offer my prayer; in you, my God, I trust."

Affirmations for the Day

Each day I release the old and make way for the new.
Each day God teaches me new things.
Each day I learn to trust the flowing of my life.
VMP

The Lord is…my strong fortress.
Psalm 18:1

When a Marriage Dies, God Does Not

A Kansas woman tells how her husband, one Sunday morning on the drive home from church, announced the end of their twenty-five-year marriage. He was involved with someone else and declared that their marriage was over and he wanted a divorce. "The storm broke in all its fury," she recalls. "It raged for months, battering and buffeting me from all sides."

During those months, she experienced an intensity of spiritual and emotional pain. The constant turmoil and the agony of rejection overpowered her at times. In addition, the uncertainty over her financial future and her fears about the impact the end of the marriage would have on the children were excruciating.

Looking back now, she now says, "I found that in the midst of extraordinary devastation, my firm anchor in the Lord held true. He calmed my storms, one by one, as they raged around me."

That true story is instructive for all of us. We should remember that even though

- a marriage dies, God does not
- a career ends, God does not
- health fails, God does not
- a friend betrays us, God does not

Affirmations for the Day

In all things,
through all storms,
within every crisis,
the Lord is my strong fortress!
VMP

All who see me make fun of me.
Psalm 22:7

The Signs of a Good Friend

The writer of today's verse has clearly found himself without the gift of friendship. He feels not only abandoned and alone but rejected by people.

All of us need and want to have good friends. And all of us should want to be a good friend to someone.

Who is a good friend? It is someone who

- listens carefully
- responds sensitively
- advises justly
- assists readily
- speaks compassionately
- defends boldly
- understands naturally
- shares generously
- praises loudly
- criticizes softly
- loves deeply

Affirmations for the Day

I now give and receive friendship freely.
I show love and appreciation to others.
I treat others the way I want to be treated.

VMP

Praise the LORD, my soul,
and do not forget how kind he is.
Psalm 103:2

Recalling God's Kindness in Unkind Moments

Have you ever been robbed? What was (or would be) your response to such an act?

Eighteenth-century Presbyterian Bible scholar Matthew Henry was once robbed of his wallet by a skilled pickpocket. This is what he wrote in his journal that evening:

> Let me be thankful....First, because I was never robbed before.
> Second, although he took my wallet, he did not take my life.
> Third, because, though he took my all, it was not much.
> Fourth, because it was I who was robbed, not I who robbed.

Matthew Henry displayed a remarkable attitude. In a moment of theft, clearly an unkind act, he was able to recall God's many kindnesses. Although his response did not bring back his wallet, such an attitude certainly softens the blow, brings perspective, and allows life to be viewed in a more balanced way.

Adopting an attitude of gratitude leads to great freedom. The hurts of life, which can rob us of joy, have a way of dissipating when we "do not forget how kind he is."

Thought for the Day

Leave sadness to those in the world.
We who work for God
should be lighthearted.
Leonard of Port Maurice

But God has indeed heard me;
he has listened to my prayer.
Psalm 66:19

Prayer Changes Us

Sometimes when we pray about a matter, the issue is not changed, but we are. Consider the pastor and congregation of Asbury Methodist Church in Springfield, Missouri. In 1990 someone broke into the church and stole sound equipment. The minister admits that both he and the members of his congregation were very angry about the burglary.

A year later, the intruder, an eighteen-year-old man, was arrested. It was his first arrest. He faced a certain jail term, and his wife and stepson resigned themselves to living on welfare.

As the minister and his congregation prayed about the matter, their initial anger softened. They also learned that under the county's victim-advocate program, church members had a voice in the sentencing.

The pastor invited the congregation to pray about and consider the burglar's fate. He prepared cards listing various options and asked parishioners to select one. Only six percent wanted the young man to serve jail time. Another six percent wanted the judge to decide. Eighty-two percent of the parishioners preferred a sentence of probation with community service. The judge concurred with the wishes of the eighty-two percent, and the young man was spared imprisonment.

Now the young man has a job, which he didn't have when he committed the crime. In addition, he and his family have attended services at Asbury Methodist Church.

The minister and his congregation are shining examples of people who know how to balance issues of justice and grace. They remind us that when we pray about a matter, sometimes the prayer changes us. Our hearts are softened and minds opened to a higher wisdom.

Affirmations for the Day

God's light directs my every step and each decision.
God's guidance helps me in each decision I need to make.
God's wisdom provides me with insight to make good choices.

VMP

Give praise to the LORD;
he has heard my cry for help.
Psalm 28:6

Ask for Help

We must never make the mistake of assuming that people know what we need and want. It is helpful to remember that no one is a mind reader. When we fall on hard times, we need to ask for help. A crisis is a legitimate time to let ourselves lean on friends.

Melinda is a therapist in the Midwest. When her marriage of fifteen years fell apart, a friend helped her keep on an even keel through the turmoil.

"I called Nancy and told her I was a wreck," Melinda recalls. Then she was very specific in asking for help. "I told Nancy I needed her to call me every day, to send me cards and presents, and to come over without waiting for me to ask. I never heard anyone make such demands. But for two or three weeks, my friend did exactly what I'd requested. It gave me tremendous comfort."

When Melinda's crisis subsided, Nancy thanked Melinda for being so direct. "As my friend, she wanted to help but wasn't sure how to do that," Melinda recalls.

Along with asking for help from a trusted friend, of course, we should also ask for God's assistance. As we make our needs and anxieties known to God through prayer, we will receive strength, insight, and guidance. Through prayer, we can make wiser decisions about our difficulty.

Thought for the Day

As the sea is subject to storm and tempest,
so is every man in the world.
John Donne

Strengthen me, as you have promised.
Psalm 119:28

It Is Courage That Counts

When the first locomotive was invented, several "experts" agreed that if a train went at the frightful speed of fifteen miles an hour, the passengers would suffer from nosebleed. They also cautioned that people could suffocate when the train went through a tunnel.

In 1881 the New York YWCA announced typing lessons for women. Protests were made on the grounds that the female constitution would break down under the strain.

Shortly after the telephone was invented, Joshua Coppersmith was arrested in Boston for trying to sell stock in the company that would produce telephones. Authorities said that all well-informed people knew it was impossible to transmit the human voice over a wire.

If you are struggling over an impossible-looking task, don't give up just because others say it cannot be done. Continue on. Act on your convictions. Exercise courage and persistence in the face of resistance and opposition. Ask God to deepen your determination.

Remember that almost every great idea or invention faced fierce resistance from authorities and experts who said it couldn't be done.

Thought for the Day

Success is never final.
Failure is never fatal.
It is courage that counts.
Tim Hansel

He promises peace to us…
if we do not go back to our foolish ways.
Psalm 85:8

Learning From Mistakes

Several years ago, Letitia Baldrige, author of numerous etiquette books, made a mistake that caused her great embarrassment and guilt. A friend who worked with the United Nations prepared a dinner in honor of Baldrige and her husband, Robert. The friend invited ambassadors from two countries.

"I would have been honored to attend," recalls Baldrige, "but I wrote the engagement on the wrong night in my appointment book. When the dinner was held, Bob and I were at the movies."

Baldrige was oblivious to the problem until the next morning when she heard the woman's hurt voice on the telephone. "At that instant I wanted to die," Baldrige says.

She apologized immediately over the phone, went to the woman's office to repent in person, then wrote a more formal four-page letter of remorse and sent it to the woman, along with two dozen roses.

Six months later, she sent flowers to commemorate the half-year anniversary of her blunder. Baldrige's friend had already excused her by this time but now called and repeated, "Letitia, you are forgiven."

Even though her friend has forgiven her, the experience left an indelible impression on Baldrige, and she has learned from it. Today Baldrige double-checks the date of every appointment while she is making it. No more jotting quick notes by the telephone with intentions of recording them in a datebook later.

When we truly try to learn from our mistakes, we transform them from "enemies" into allies. By learning from mistakes, we use them as life's golden opportunities to make ourselves wiser. Today's psalm tells us that we will experience peace when we learn from our mistakes and "do not go back to our foolish ways."

Affirmations for the Day

God blesses me with opportunities to learn.
God blesses me with second chances.
God blesses me with restoration and renewal.

VMP

The whole world stands in awe
of the great things that you have done.
Psalm 65:8

Five Spiritual Needs

Just as we have physical needs—food, shelter, water, air, clothing—we also have spiritual needs. Those spiritual needs appear in these five human issues.

- *The need for meaning.* "Why am I here? What is the purpose of my life? Do I make a difference?" These are the kinds of questions most people raise for themselves. Human beings long for a larger explanation for their existence.
- *The need for mystery.* Most individuals sense that there is more to life than what can be seen. A beautiful sunset, a rainbow after a rainstorm, the pattern of our galaxy—all can produce a sense of awe and wonder within us. Today's psalm is one expression of mystery, wonder, and awe.
- *The need for self-acceptance.* We are creatures who make mistakes, commit errors of judgment, violate rules and morals. Therefore, we need to come to terms with issues of overcoming failure, accepting ourselves, seeking forgiveness.
- *The need for a moral standard.* What is right? What is wrong? Where do we find guidance? Behind these questions is the realization that without some common standard of right and wrong, civilization is doomed.
- *The need for trust.* Life would be an unbearably lonely experience without the ability and desire to trust ourselves, others, and a higher power. Trust is the thread of life that connects us to other people and to God.

Although thinking about these issues can create anxiety, rest assured that raising them also reveals that we are spiritual persons seeking greater wisdom and knowledge in life. Often the questions are the way God calls us to a deeper spirituality.

Thought for the Day

The most beautiful thing we can experience is the mysterious.
It is the source of all true art and science.
He to whom this emotion is a stranger, who can no longer pause
to wonder and stand wrapped in awe, is as good as dead:
his eyes are closed.
Albert Einstein

Happy are the people whose
God is the LORD!
Psalm 144:15

What Is Your Viewpoint?

A grandmother invited her young granddaughter over for the day. Things were going well until the little girl fell and broke a large stick of peppermint candy. She began to weep as she looked at her broken candy stick.

As the grandmother gently wiped the tears away she said, "Look! Before you fell and dropped the candy, you had only one piece. Now you have two halves."

Almost instantly the girl stopped crying. Her face brightened as she absorbed the message, and she broke into a happy smile.

What is your perspective? Is your cup half empty or half full? Are you half happy or half sad? Are you half well or half sick?

Your viewpoint shows how you feel about yourself and reveals the nature of our relationship to God. Today's psalm is a simple reminder that the viewpoint of God's people is on the side of optimism and hope: "Happy are the people whose God is the Lord!"

Affirmations for the Day

I dissolve all negative, limiting beliefs.
I absolve myself for doubting God's goodness.
I resolve to welcome and enjoy God's abundance.
VMP

You give us great victories.
Psalm 89:17

The Strength to Apologize

George Washington, America's first president, was a tall man. Living in a day when the average American male was five-feet-six-inches tall (about three inches shorter than today), Washington was a full six-feet-three-inches. In addition, Washington had huge hands and took great pride in his physical strength.

When he was campaigning for election to the Virginia State Assembly in 1755, one of his speeches offended a man named Thomas Payne. The man grabbed a hickory branch and struck the much bigger Washington, knocking him to the ground.

The next day, Washington visited Payne's favorite tavern and demanded to see him. Payne thought he was going to be challenged to a duel. Instead, Washington apologized for any offensive comments contained in his speech and asked to shake hands in friendship.

Although Washington could easily have retaliated, and some believed he would have been justified, he chose to use his strength to unite rather than divide. Washington had both physical and moral strength. His actions moved an event from battleground to common ground.

Let us, like George Washington, exercise our moral and spiritual strength. Let us quickly extend an apology whenever we cause offense or hurt. In that way, we create harmony and unity rather than contribute to discord and division. God always gives us "great victories" when we act with moral and spiritual courage.

-------- *Thought for the Day* --------

As we grow in wisdom,
we pardon more freely.
Anne-Louise Germaine De Stael

...I am your servant.
Psalm 143:12

Being One of God's Servants

A fifty-year-old man tells of returning to work after a month's illness. Because his family needed the income, he returned to work twenty-four hours after being discharged from the hospital.

His employer immediately sent him on a one-hundred-fifty-mile business trip. Everything went well until he was returning home. Suddenly, he felt the car sway so he slowed to a stop. Getting out of the vehicle, he saw the rear tire was flat.

The man tried to change the tire but was too weak even to remove the spare tire from the trunk. Because the sun was beginning to set and because he was on a quiet country road, he became worried and prayed that God would help him.

Thirty minutes passed before he saw headlights coming his way. A red sports car approached and slowed to a stop, and a young man stepped out. Seeing the problem, the young man quickly and efficiently replaced the flat tire with the spare.

The older man offered money for the young man's assistance, but the latter refused. "Do unto others as you would have them do unto you," he said. "That's all the pay I need."

As his benefactor drove away the older man offered a prayer of thanks and asked God to be with his helper. When he returned home and told his family about the incident, he described the young man as one of God's servants.

In a society too often characterized by callousness and cruelty, let us soften life by being one of God's servants.

Thought for the Day

Those who mean well
are useless unless they do well.
Titus Plautus

The LORD makes me powerful and strong.
Psalm 118:14

Strengthen Your "I Can" Power

Michael Caine is one of the world's leading actors. However, had he taken the advice of Britain's chief casting director, he would never have succeeded. In his autobiography, *What It's All About?* Caine tells about his life before he became a famous star. Work in acting was scarce, the pay was modest, and he was deeply in debt.

Then he was given an opportunity to be interviewed by Britain's chief casting director, a very powerful man who could get him regular acting work. Caine was extremely excited and optimistic about the meeting.

On the day of the appointment, the young actor was ushered into a magnificent office. The casting director, obviously wanting to be helpful, began by telling Caine that acting was a very tough business. "My son is an accountant," he said, "and he has more chance of success in this business than you do."

Caine recalls he became numb as the man continued, "This may sound unkind, but you will thank me in the long run. I know this business well, and I can assure you that you have no future in it. Give it up, Michael."

Rather than giving up, Caine says he left the meeting more determined than ever to succeed in the world of film. Based on his own experience, Caine's advice to others is this: "If you want to do something with your life, never listen to anybody else, no matter how clever or expert he or she may appear. Keep your eyes open and your ears shut and go for it."

That's good advice. All of us should strengthen our "I can" power. Declarations such as "I can't do it," "I can't go on," "I can't face the future alone," reveal that we feel weak and timid. However, God wants us to be strong and is willing to help us. Whenever we find ourselves feeling and thinking "I can't" let us turn to the God who can empower us to declare "I can!"

Affirmations for the Day

God makes me stronger every day.
God makes me wiser every day.
I let go of fear and act courageously.
I let go of doubt and act with faith.

VMP

I kept on believing, even when I said,
"I am completely crushed."
Psalm 116:10

Learning to Fly With One Wing

"Ever since my husband died, I feel as if I'm trying to fly with one wing," said a depressed widow at her support group. She is not alone in her feeling. Every day, people are widowed, separated, or divorced; lose a job; or discover that they have a serious illness. Sooner or later, all of us have to learn to fly with one wing. Here are some suggestions to keep in mind when such a situation arises in your life:

- *Substitute a new way for the old way*. Things are no longer the same. You must learn to replace old ways of thinking, doing, and acting with new ways.
- *Forgive*. Every loss brings feelings of anger, guilt, regrets, and remorse. The way to let go is to forgive yourself and anyone who has hurt you.
- *Toughen up*. Life is not always smooth, clear sailing. When hard times come, get tough. Self-pity saps your strength and courage.
- *Face your own worst enemy*. Avoid the "Why me?" syndrome. If you don't, you will become your own worst enemy suffocating in self-pity.
- *Look for joy*. Biblical people faced great crises in their lives, yet Scripture is filled with the word *joy*. Like those people, look for reasons to laugh, sing, dance, and be joyful.
- *Concentrate on what you have*. Remember that few situations in life take everything away from you. Even after a great natural disaster, something is left. Take what remains, thank God for it, and ask God to bless it and expand it.

You can learn to fly with one wing if you make the remaining wing strong enough to keep you flying steadily. Keep believing in God and yourself even if you feel "completely crushed."

Prayer for the Day

Loving and good God,
I look to you for daily strength,
guidance, wisdom, perseverance, and patience.
VMP

Praise the LORD...
you servants of his, who do his will!
Psalm 103:21

Being God's Blessing

We talk and read a lot about God's blessings. However, we seldom consider the fact that we can be God's blessing to another person.

Consider how often in our daily lives we think about sending a card or letter to a special friend, making a phone call of encouragement, or stopping to visit someone, only to let the moment's inspiration slip away.

Such moments are often the Spirit of God nudging us to be a blessing. How often do we resist these opportunities to be God's blessing to another by

- putting them off for a more convenient time
- telling ourselves it wouldn't make any difference
- convincing ourselves we would look foolish

Learn to respond immediately whenever an impulse to act kindly comes to you. The truth is, we can never be too kind, too considerate, too encouraging.

A short note of encouragement, a few words of praise, a quick phone call to let someone know you care, can soothe the blows of a hard day for someone. Let us be God's servants doing his will in our world.

········ *Thought for the Day* ········

Some people are so heavenly minded,
they're no earthly good.
Susan Stafford

The LORD loves what is righteous and just.
Psalm 33:5

Tidying the World

Willis and Dorothy Pitkins of Dayton, Oregon, both in their eighties, refer to themselves as two "elderly ecologists." Their hobby is tidying the world. Willis and Dorothy began their unusual hobby several years ago while on their daily five-mile walk.

"We noticed while walking that there was a great deal of trash along the road," Mr. Pitkins explains. So, as a self-appointed litter crew, they started taking along large plastic bags to hold the trash and litter they picked up.

They are so diligent about their task that the Pitkins have become as familiar to the residents of Dayton, Oregon, as the letter carrier. Their philosophy is simple. According to Dorothy, "There are two kinds of people: the kind who make a mess and the kind who clean it up."

Not only are the Pitkins ecologically inspiring, their example might spur us to ask ourselves whether we are not all called by God to "tidy up" our part of the planet. Have not all of us been called to be a beacon of light and an oasis of hope?

Whenever the "untidiness" of fear, hate, darkness, injustice, oppression, and cruelty exist, it falls to all of us to work at "tidying" it up. Like the Pitkins, let us tidy the world as we walk along our path, remembering that the "Lord loves what is righteous and just."

Thought for the Day

If you aren't born beautiful,
it isn't your fault.
But if your surroundings are ugly,
that is your fault.
Dorothy Pitkins

How long will sorrow fill my heart day and night?
Psalm 13:2

Expressing Helpful Sympathy

Whenever someone experiences a crisis—death in the family, separation, divorce, job loss—that person welcomes support and encouragement from others. In their attempt to help, however, some people are clumsy and awkward, actually hurting rather than helping. The following ways to respond to someone who has experienced loss are practical, helpful, and comforting:

- *Respond immediately.* When you learn someone is hurting, promptly offer help. Don't delay, assuming the person is already receiving support.
- *Be specific.* Don't merely ask, "What can I do?" The person may hesitate to accept a vague offer. Ask if you can run errands, pick up people at the airport, prepare a meal, baby-sit, or perform other specific tasks.
- *Avoid platitudes.* Someone who is in pain is not helped by hearing "You will get over it" or "God has something better for you" or "Time will take care of things" or similar sentiments. Such statements minimize the hurting person's pain. It is better just to say "I'm sorry" or simply to embrace the person.
- *Respect personal wishes.* Some people want company in a time of pain and loss; others prefer to be alone. Respect the wishes and feelings of the hurting person, but let him or her know of your availability.
- *Resist giving advice.* A recently divorced man says, "I was overwhelmed with advice to take a trip, move out of the house, and join a singles' club. I really just needed time to be alone and decide what I felt would be best for me."

Thought for the Day

They are true disciples of Christ
not who know most,
but who love most.
Frederich Spanheim the Elder

...all night long the LORD protects me.
Psalm 3:5

Coincidence or Providence?

An Arizonan woman writes of an evening when a severe rainstorm erupted. From the second story of her home, she could see stalled cars caught in the flash flood.

A lone station wagon struggled through the water and headed up her street. The vehicle stopped for a moment in front of her house, then pulled into the driveway. The woman raced to the door and saw two teenage girls standing there. They were extremely frightened by the lightning, rain, and flooded roads.

One girl asked to use the woman's telephone, explaining that she wanted to call her father to let him know she was safe. Of course, the woman let them in and prepared hot cocoa while the girls made their calls.

Meanwhile, the woman's husband paced the kitchen floor nervously. The newspaper office where he worked was flooding, and he was waiting to hear from the facility manager. His anxiety was increasing because the man had not called.

The girls completed their calls and told the woman and her husband, "My dad told us to wait out the storm here, but he was a little worried about our being in a stranger's house. I gave him your number. I hope that was okay."

As the woman nodded, the phone rang. Her husband answered it and returned after a few seconds. "It was the facility manager, but he didn't want to talk about the newspaper office." A strange look came over the man's face. "He wanted to thank me for keeping his daughter and her friend safe!"

Was it mere coincidence or divine providence that the two teenager girls randomly selected a house in which they would be safely sheltered?

Thought for the Day

When I pray, coincidences happen,
and when I don't pray, they don't.
Sir William Temple

You are my God;
teach me to do your will.
Psalm 143:10

Maintaining Spiritual and Emotional Health

The American Medical Association recently issued a list of qualities that reflect emotional stability and maturity of character. According to the AMA, emotional stability and maturity are demonstrated by the ability to

- recover quickly from the stresses of life
- judge reality accurately
- love and sustain personal relationships
- work cheerfully and productively
- gratify hunger, thirst, and sexual needs in such a way as not to hurt others or oneself

That list is remarkably similar to what one would expect in a person who is spiritually healthy and mature. Why not review the list and ask yourself how you measure up? Make an honest assessment of yourself. If you feel you are deficient in some area, consider ways to improve.

You might find it useful to speak with a trusted spiritual guide or counselor or confide in a good friend. Like the psalmist who writes, "You are my God; teach me to do your will," ask God to guide you into greater spiritual and emotional maturity.

Affirmations for the Day

I am completely open to God's instruction.
I am completely open to God's guidance.
I am completely open to God's nurture.
Day by day and in every way,
I resolve to grow into spiritual and emotional maturity.

VMP

Your constant love is my guide.
Psalm 26:3

Some Jewish Saints

Saints come in all colors, sizes, and religious traditions. That observation was made by one woman whose family benefited greatly from a Jewish saint.

Nearly fifty years ago when she was a child, the woman's father died and the family was left destitute. In those days, there was almost no government assistance. Shortly after her father died, her mother became very ill.

Because the mother's temperature soared up to one-hundred-six degrees she was rushed to the nearest hospital. Of course, the family had no medical insurance of any kind. However, the doctors and nurses in the Jewish hospital labored for two weeks to save the mother's life.

After the mother was released, a representative from the hospital came to her home to see if the family could afford to make any payment, even a modest one. It took the hospital representative only a few minutes to determine that the family didn't have even pennies to spare.

The man concluded his visit with a gracious smile, thanked the family for receiving him, wished them all well, and left. The family was never asked again to make any payments.

"We had the good fortune of being helped by several Jewish saints," the woman now recalls.

Today's psalm reads simply, "Your constant love is my guide." True saints are those who are constantly guided by God's love. Let us be included in that godly company.

Thought for the Day

Self-sacrifice is never entirely unselfish,
for the giver never fails to receive.
Dolores E. McGuire

. . . I am content and at peace.
As a child lies quietly in its mother's arms. . . .
Psalm 131:2

A Day to Be a Child

Too often we forget that we are children of God. That means we should live and enjoy life like a child does. When was the last time you experienced the joyous spontaneity of a child? When was the last time you

- enjoyed poetry
- read a story to a child
- listened to a child read a story
- recited a nursery rhyme all the way through
- walked barefoot along a beach
- sang out loud
- harmonized with others around a piano
- threw a frisbee
- tossed a softball
- played a board game with a child
- picked flowers and gave them as a gift
- rested contentedly in the arms of God

Thought for the Day

Children have not mastered our fine art of deception.
They have not acquired
the obstructions to faith
that come with education;
they possess instead
unrefined wisdom,
a gift from God.
Gloria Gaither

I will be glad because you will rescue me.
Psalm 13:5

Creative Suffering

Here is a true story which should inspire all of us that we can be creative in our suffering. And if we can do that, then the suffering has some greater purpose.

Flu symptoms suffered at the age of two turned out to be spinal meningitis for Brian Berlinski of Clifton, New Jersey. The result was total deafness.

Thrust into a silent world, the frightened little boy screamed his frustration. The entire family entered therapy and early intervention. They all learned American sign language. As they relearned to communicate, little Brian relaxed and his tantrums ceased.

Then, his thirty-one-year-old mother, Diane, died of cancer. This time Brian withdrew deeply into himself. No matter how often it was explained that his mother had died, Brian continued to ask, "When is my mother coming home?"

Again, this remarkable and resilient family banded together around Brian's needs. More therapy reduced Brian's anxiety, and he began to emerge from his shell.

Over the next five years, Brian learned to speak clearly enough to communicate on the telephone. He writes exceptional short stories and has learned to play the piano and saxophone by feeling vibrations. Brian is also a very bright student. His father fought to keep Brian in the neighborhood school. Today he is the first auditorially handicapped child in his school's talented and gifted program. "I show hearing people that deaf is not deaf and *dumb*," he says proudly.

Whatever suffering comes our way, let us think of Brian and his response. Let us recall the words of today's psalm, "I will be glad because you will rescue me." The God who empowered Brian will empower us to respond creatively to our suffering.

Thought for the Day

Sorrow is one of the vibrations
that prove the fact of living.
Antoine de Saint-Exupery

Fill my mind with your wisdom.
Psalm 51:6

The Gift of a Quiet, Slow Day

Offer the gift of a quiet, slow day to yourself and to God. Our lives are far too busy, hectic, and frenzied, often squeezing out peace, tranquillity, and equilibrium.

Either today or one day within the next week, set aside twelve hours to turn off noisemakers such as TVs, radios, and stereos or CD players. Reduce or eliminate all external activity. Then make that day a quiet retreat day in your home. Use the time to

- daydream
- meditate
- pray at leisure throughout the day for your own needs and the needs of your family and friends, your community, and the world
- read the Psalms in a new version
- study a book of the Bible that you have always been curious about
- sing some hymns
- reflect on your own strengths and weaknesses and ask God to help you maximize your strengths and minimize your weaknesses

It is through the gift of a such quiet day that we come closer to God and allow our minds to be filled with God's wisdom.

Thought for the Day

A spiritual retreat
is medicine for soul starvation.
Through silence, solitary practice,
and simple living,
we begin to fill the empty reservoir.
This creates space within
for the feelings of forgiveness,
compassion, and loving kindness
that are so often blocked.

David A. Cooper

...I cry out all day
and at night I come before you.
Hear my prayer.
Psalm 88:1

Motivation for Prayer

Greg Burke is a news correspondent who files stories on the Vatican for *Time* magazine and Radio Free Europe. He often attends Pope John Paul II's private morning Mass and describes it as a moving experience.

Burke is always moved when he enters the small chapel at six-thirty in the morning and finds the pope already on his knees praying. The pope remains that way until the clock strikes seven, at which time he vests for Mass.

Of course, it may seem quite natural that the pope, as spiritual leader of Catholics worldwide, should be on his knees at prayer for half an hour. However, perspective can be added by recalling that the pope is in his seventies. He has been shot and wounded and has undergone several surgeries in the past couple of years.

"It isn't easy to pray like that when you're twenty-three, so you can imagine what it must be like fifty years later," Burke says. This seasoned news reporter is impressed by the pope's diligence in daily prayer on his knees. "Seeing him do it at his age makes it a little easier for us to try to join him in some way," he admits.

Today the psalmist declares, "I cry out all day and at night I come before you. Hear my prayer." We may not be able to pray all day and all night, but we can be inspired by the pope's example and set aside a few minutes each morning for prayer.

Thought for the Day

I love to pray at sunrise—
before the world becomes polluted
with vanity and hatred.
The Korester Rabbi

...I will not be silent;
I will sing praise to you.
Psalm 30:12

Making Prayer a Natural Part of Life

Praying can be challenging. Even the first disciples weren't sure how to do it. It was one the few direct questions they asked Jesus. "Lord," they said, "teach us to pray" (Luke 11:l). At that point, Jesus gave them and us the Lord's Prayer.

Families often find prayer to be especially challenging. Here are some ways for families to make prayer a natural part of daily life:

- *Attend church regularly.* Give your family the opportunity to join in public and private prayer. If children resist going, be strong and insist that this is an important family time of worship.
- *Pray before meals.* Mealtimes are ideal occasions for everyone to bow briefly and have someone offer a prayer of thanks for the food.
- *Pray at bedtime.* All children like to be tucked into bed. Make that time a ritual when brief prayers are offered.
- *Pray over crises and hurts.* Whenever a family member faces a crisis or has been hurt somehow, become comfortable with offering brief prayers asking for help, guidance, wisdom, courage—whatever is needed.
- *Respect the Church year.* While prayer is always an important spiritual discipline, try increasing prayer time during important seasons of the Church year, such as Advent and Lent.

The key to making prayer a natural part of life is to begin by beginning. Don't be concerned about getting it right or doing it perfectly. Just do it. In the process, everyone in the family will grow stronger spiritually.

Thought for the Day

I like to begin my day with prayer,
but, as I am not a bright-eyed morning person,
it is often a simple, sleepy prayer
committing the day to God.

Colleen Townsend Evans

I keep your teaching in my heart.
Psalm 40:8

Striking the Right Note

A newspaper headline proclaimed "Van Halen Strikes the Right Note." Eddie Van Halen, leader of a rock group that bears his name, responded graciously and compassionately to a group of hospitalized quadriplegics.

The newspaper story reported that a man approached the hospital promising to bring his "friend," Van Halen, to visit the New Start Homes in the Los Angeles suburb of Chatsworth.

The visit turned out to be a ruse, however. The man, who didn't know Van Halen, used the deception to steal a car from one of the home's nurses. When Eddie Van Halen heard about the hoax and crime, he volunteered to make the visit. His presence was doubly appreciated by both staff and patients.

Ask yourself:

- Does my living strike the right note?
- Do I bring harmony and concord to my small part of the world?
- Does my response to people and circumstances bring beauty and joy?
- Do I use my time and talent to make life a little better for others?

Affirmations for the Day

God gives me clarity of mind.
I will honor God by helping others.
God gives me purity of soul.
I will honor God by assisting others.
God gives me vitality of body.
I will honor God by empowering others.
VMP

I pray to you, O God, because you answer me.
Psalm 17:6

The Healing Power of Prayer

Intercessory prayer works. Patients who are prayed for experience more rapid healing and recovery than those who do not have the benefit of prayers.

This was the conclusion reported by Randolph Byrd, M.D., a cardiologist and faculty member at the University of California at San Francisco Medical School. In 1988, Dr. Byrd published the results of a study of nearly four hundred heart patients at San Francisco General Hospital. All of the patients received conventional medical treatment. In addition, half of the patients were prayed for by prayer groups in the community.

To ensure accuracy, neither doctors nor other hospital personnel knew which patients were being prayed for. In addition, none of the patients were aware that a "prayer experiment" was taking place.

When the data was analyzed, the patients who had been the subject of prayers looked as though they'd been given a miracle drug. Not one of them had to be placed on a mechanical ventilator, a drastic measure used to combat heart or lung failure. In contrast, twelve patients in the group that weren't prayed for had to be placed on the ventilators.

There is more. The prayed-for group required fewer potent medications, such as antibiotics and diuretics—and fewer of them died.

As you pray for yourself and others, factor the results of this study into your thoughts. It is another piece of evidence that prayer is a power that helps.

Thought for the Day

As a physician,
I have seen men, after all other therapy had failed,
lifted out of disease and melancholy
by the serene effort of prayer.
Alexis Carrel

You take notice of trouble and suffering
and are always ready to help.
Psalm 10:14

Another Look at the Healing Power of Prayer

Yesterday we considered the healing power of prayer based upon a scientific experiment. Today we take a second look at the relationship between healing and prayer.

One week before her son's wedding, Joan discovered a lump in her abdomen. Thinking it was simply a hernia, Joan was shocked when her physician told her she had a malignant tumor.

Surgery was immediately scheduled. Although the doctors removed a cancerous tumor the size of a grapefruit, other cancerous tissues were discovered which could not be removed. Joan was told she had ovarian cancer and that most women in her condition died within twenty-four months.

Despairing, Joan turned to Scripture for comfort and began reading those passages that encourage all troubled people to trust God and pray. "I began to truly believe that my life was in God's loving hands and that he would take care of me," she says.

Family members and friends from her church committed themselves to visit Joan once a week in order to pray for her. In spite of the prayer support, however; there were times when Joan found it hard to hope because her doctors were convinced it was only a question of months before the cancer would end her life.

Family and friends continued to pray while Joan followed through with various medical procedures. Her story has a happy ending. Two years after surgery and chemotherapy, a liver scan revealed no sign of cancer. Today, fourteen years later, Joan is still cancer-free and living a healthy, happy life.

Thought for the Day

On all my expeditions,
prayer made me stronger,
morally and mentally,
than any of my nonpraying companions.
Henry Stanley

Some trust in their war chariots
and others in their horses,
but we trust in the power of the L*ORD* *our God.*
Psalm 20:7

A Physician at Prayer

Over the last two days we have looked at scientific evidence establishing the link between prayer and healing. Today let us add this testimonial from Larry Dossey, M.D., former chief of staff of medicine at Dallas City Hospital and author of several books, including *Healing Words: The Power of Prayer and the Practice of Medicine.*

Dr. Dossey has practiced medicine for more than twenty years and has always been interested in anything that could further help his patients. He came to be interested in scientific studies supporting the connection between prayer and healing. As he reviewed the academic studies, he discovered that there were over one-hundred-thirty studies done on the topic, with more than half clearly concluding that prayer could influence a variety of living organisms, from human beings to bacteria.

"I came to feel that I could no more ignore this information than I could withhold from my patients a drug or surgical procedure that had been shown to be effective," he says.

As a result, Dr. Dossey now incorporates prayer into his medical practice. Each morning he comes into his office a little early and prays for the patients he will be seeing that day.

Let us, too, continue to trust "in the power of the Lord our God."

Thought for the Day

More things are wrought by prayer
than this world dreams of.
Alfred, Lord Tennyson

Bow down before the Holy One....
Psalm 96:9

Turning News Into Prayers

Most of us read a daily newspaper or weekly news magazine. Both can serve to inform our daily prayer. For example, a quick review of today's local newspaper reveals the following people and issues that can use prayer support:

- A *mother's eight-year-old son struggles with epileptic seizures*. Because of the seizures, the child cannot ride a bicycle or be left unattended at a beach or swimming pool. Drug therapy leaves him lethargic and dizzy. His family is desperately seeking alternative treatment. This is a family in need of patience, trust, and guidance.
- *The end of Ramadan, the ninth month of the Islamic lunar calendar and the month in which the angel Gabriel came to the prophet Mohammed some fourteen hundred years ago to reveal the Koran:* This news can be used to spur prayer for people of another faith who are often misunderstood and discriminated against in our country.
- YMCA *associations celebrate one-hundred-fifty years of service*. There are more than two thousand YMCA associations in the country providing shelter, exercise facilities, and classes for thousands of people. This news provides an opportunity to thank God for their work.

Of course, the media are also filled with news of wars, conflicts, and violence worldwide, as well as locally, disturbing reminders to pray for international, national, and local political leaders. By turning the news into prayers, we "bow down before the Holy One" and ask continuously for divine aid.

-------- *Thought for the Day* --------

Far from turning us away from the world,
Christ directs us to it.
He awakens within us
an altogether new concern for it.
Paul Tournier

In your constant love and goodness,
remember me, LORD!
Psalm 25:7

Constant Love

In September 1943, Edward Cheskovich Konenko was born in a Nazi labor camp in Lumpertheim, Germany. His mother was Ukrainian and his father Polish. Both were prisoners working in the camp.

After nine months, the little boy was ripped from his mother's arms and sent to a German orphanage. His mother was sent to Ravensbruck concentration camp, and his father died in the camps. When the war was over and the mother, Stephanie Konenko, was liberated, she tried to find her son. But the orphanage had been destroyed during the war. Unable to locate her son, she returned to her native Ukraine.

What Stephanie didn't know was that Edward had been adopted by an American family when he was six. He grew up in California under the name Ed Determan. Although his birth mother remarried and had a daughter and two more sons, she never gave up looking for Edward. In 1992, using the American Red Cross' Holocaust victim-tracking system, she was able to trace her son to the Fort Lauderdale, Florida, area. By now a father and grandfather, Determan had assumed that his mother was dead.

Finally, fifty years after she last saw her son, the two were able to have a forty-minute telephone conversation. Speaking through an interpreter, the seventy-one-year-old Stephanie Konenko said, "I cry every night, I pray every night for this day. I am suffering for my son." She continued, "I have been searching for you for fifty years...I need to see you. I am worried that I am going to die." Her son promised to visit her in the spring.

That is a powerful story of a love that would not give up. Through half a decade of imprisonment, war, and separation by different continents, cultures, and language, Stephanie Konenko continued to love and seek for her son.

God's love is like that mother's—persistent, pervasive, constantly seeking us. God loves us permanently and unconditionally. When we go astray or do wrong, we need only ask forgiveness and respond to God's love.

Thought for the Day

O love of God, how deep and great.
Far deeper than man's deepest hate.
Corrie Ten Boom

You are my God, and I give you thanks.
Psalm 118:28

Thanking God for the Gift of a Friend

A study conducted over a nine-year period in California showed that people without a good network of friendships have more health problems and a mortality rate two to five times higher than others.

Stress-related health problems increased as people have fewer friends and relatives to help them cope. In line with that research other studies reveal that:

- Pregnant women under stress, without supportive relationships, have three times more complications than those with a support network.
- Unemployed men who have strong support from family and friends report less depression, fewer illnesses, and lower levels of cholesterol.
- Women who have a close friend to confide in are less prone to depression.

Today let us thank God for the gift of friends. Friendship meets several deep human needs, including the desire to be known, to give, to receive encouragement.

If you feel lacking in solid friendships, ask God to send good people your way. Try reciting the following affirmations to better prepare yourself for the gift of a new friend.

Affirmations for the Day

God is working with me to create new friendships.
God's love is guiding me to good people.
God is sending wonderful new people my way.

VMP

I sing a hymn of thanksgiving....
Psalm 26:7

Guidelines for Deepening Friendships

As we meet people, some easily and naturally become more than acquaintances and colleagues; they become good friends. For those friendships to grow and deepen, they need attention and nurturing. The acronym FRIEND is a good way to think about the ingredients that grow a friendship.

F is for *fellowship* and *fun*. Friends spend time together and know how to enjoy that time. They celebrate one another's special days and commiserate when days are not so good.

R is for *readiness to listen*. When friends experience problems—personal or professional—they lend one another a sympathetic ear.

I is for *interesting*. Friends will stimulate one another. They can talk about books, politics, religion, and movies and grow as a result of the conversations.

E is for *encouraging*. Not only are good friends good listeners in tough times, good friends are also solid sources of praise and encouragement.

N is for *nourishing*. Good friends nurture their friendship by celebrating birthdays, graduations, promotions, and other achievements.

D is for *dependable*. True friends are loyal and reliable. Good friends see one another at their best and at their worst and still remain friends.

Over the course of a lifetime, we will meet thousands of people. Only a few will become good friends. For those few, we must always express thanks to God. When we have good friends, we can more easily "sing a hymn of thanksgiving" to God.

Thought for the Day

Friendship is a strong and habitual inclination in two persons to promote the good and happiness of one another.
Eustace Budgell

Search your hearts and be silent.
Psalm 4:4
(New International Version)

Taking Time Out

At times it is wise to interrupt our living by taking some time out. That is what performer Neil Diamond did when he was at the height of his popularity.

Even though he admits to being a driven workaholic, in 1972 he chose to take a four-year break from his work as a singer, composer, and lyricist.

"I had gone through one marriage and was into my second with two kids when I told myself I'd better step back and take a look at what I'm doing and where I'm going," he explains.

So for forty-eight months he stopped performing and stayed home. He also went into analysis. "I took fours years to get to know my children, my wife, and myself. It's probably the most important period of my life," he now says.

Those four years were not wasted. Diamond emerged a new person. He declares he was more relaxed, happier, freer onstage, easier to live with, and easier on himself.

Psalm 4:4 advises, "Search your hearts and be silent." Sometimes the best thing we can do for ourselves is to slow down the pace of life, take a hard look, make the necessary adjustments, and reemerge to a new life.

Affirmations for the Day

God gives me wisdom to reflect and understand.
I gladly risk exploring my inner nature.
God helps me listen to my heart.
As I listen,
the right response comes to me.
VMP

God remembers those who suffer;
he does not forget their cry.
Psalm 9:12

Lonely People

Just weeks before his death, Elvis Presley, was asked by a reporter, "Elvis, when you started playing music, you said you wanted three things in life. You wanted to be rich; you wanted to be famous; and you wanted to be happy. Are you happy, Elvis?" The singer replied, "No, I'm as lonely as hell."

How ironic and how sad. Elvis Presley was rich, famous, and surrounded by all sorts of people. Yet he was lonely. At a first reading, Elvis' comment could be viewed as offensive, but he actually defined his issue accurately. Hell is a lonely place.

There are many people just like Elvis. Though they live in crowded cities and apartment buildings they feel alone.

The note left behind by a Chicago woman who jumped off the fourteenth floor of her apartment building explained that she killed herself because of loneliness. A reporter at the scene interviewed a neighbor who said, "I wish I'd known she was lonesome. I'm lonesome myself."

Loneliness is a burden, even for psychologists. The *Portland Oregonian* published a story about a prominent clinical psychologist who took his own life. In a note left for his staff, he said, "Tonight I feel tired, alone, and suddenly very old. The full understanding of these feelings will come only when you, too, are tired, alone, and old."

The truth is that all of us experience feelings of loneliness. There may be times when we go an entire day without speaking to anyone or having someone speak to us. There may be times when we wonder if anyone really cares whether we live or die. In those moments of loneliness, we should turn to prayer and not despair. We should turn our loneliness over to God and ask him for special grace.

Prayer for the Day

Loving God,
Remember me when I am lonely.
Into my darkness bring your light,
to my weakness bring your strength.
VMP

...I am content and at peace.
Psalm 131:2

Are You Addicted to Work?

According to a recent Harris poll, the amount of leisure time enjoyed by the average worker has fallen nearly forty percent in the last two decades. More people are spending more time working. Are you a work addict? The following questions can help you decide.

- Do I truly enjoy working? Are work and recreation nearly the same for me?
- Do I frequently take work home, to family gatherings, kids sports functions? Do I even take work on vacations?
- Do I often do more than two things at once (typing and talking on the phone, driving and dictating)?
- Do I work to the exclusion of other things, including family time and socializing with friends?
- Do I actively maintain a long list of job-related "Things to Do"?
- Do I work until late at night and start again early in the morning after only a few hours sleep?
- Do I find it difficult to relax, watch TV, take weekends off, or go on a vacation?

If you answered yes to most of these questions, you may be addicted to work. For your own emotional and spiritual health, and for the sake of your family and friends, you need to find ways of freeing yourself from work addiction.

Seek counsel from someone you trust or a counselor skilled in addiction issues. Pray and ask for God's guidance as well. In the end, you will enjoy life and work better. Like the psalmist, you will be able to declare, "I am content and at peace."

Thought for the Day

The really efficient laborer
will be found not to crowd his day with work,
but will saunter to his task
surrounded by a wide halo of ease and leisure.
Henry David Thoreau

He trains me for battle....
Psalm 18:34

The Gift of Determination

Two-year-old Serena woke up one morning and couldn't move. Panic stricken, her parents rushed her to the hospital in Taiwan, where she was diagnosed with polio. Death was a frightening possibility. Serena survived the polio, but was left with withered legs.

Seeking better medical help for Serena, the family emigrated to the United States where Serena could undergo further therapy at a Los Angeles hospital. After years of treatment, Serena was finally able to walk with the aid of a brace and crutches.

The little girl eventually wondered how God might help her use her experience with polio. She volunteered at the orthopedic hospital where she had learned to walk. Her experience there led to a determination to study medicine in the hope of helping others like herself.

With the support of her husband and family, and despite the concern of many who didn't believe she could cope with the rigors of medical training, Serena persevered. Today Dr. Serena Young is an orthopedic surgeon who performs surgery while leaning on her crutches.

When tough times come our way, sheer determination can be a gift that helps us get through and achieve our goals. Ask God to train you "for battle."

-------- *Thought for the Day* --------

Determination digs a shelter in your heart,
a warm, replenishing place you can come to
whenever discouragement has you wondering,
"Why should I go on?"

Paul Coleman

"He does not turn away from them,
but answers when they call for help."
Psalm 22:24

Examining the Possible

When life deals us a harsh blow, we often feel boxed in, trapped, out of control, and despairing. Yet despair itself can be dashed if we take the time to examine what is possible. The next time you face a crisis, ask yourself,

- Isn't it possible that time will change things, bringing me relief, reconciliation, healing?
- Isn't it possible that my suffering is not a permanent condition, that this, too, shall pass?
- Isn't it possible that something positive and good will emerge from this?
- Isn't it possible that I can take this and make something meaningful come out of it?
- Isn't it possible that new, life-affirming ideas will come to me in spite of my suffering?
- Isn't it possible that day by day God will give me strength, wisdom, insight, and support?
- Isn't it possible that God will not turn?

Prayer for the Day

Eternal and good God,
Renew my mind and my body
so that I can see light, not just darkness,
hope, not just despair.
VMP

Happy are those who are concerned for the poor.
Psalm 41:1

Being a Kindly Soul

Tom recalls being deeply impressed by a quiet act of compassion that took place when he was a little boy in the 1930s during the Great Depression. Many people were unemployed, but Tom's father had the good fortune of working periodically as a postal clerk. Because the work was not steady, however, the family struggled financially.

Eventually, the lack of steady work caught up with the family. Tom's father did not have enough money to keep up his life-insurance premium. A colleague in the post office who learned of the dilemma was moved with compassion because the family had seven children. The colleague quietly paid the insurance premiums.

Later that year, Tom's father died. All that stood between the family and complete disaster was the insurance settlement. "To this day I regard that person as a kindly soul sent our way by God," Tom comments.

The world needs a liberal sprinkling of more such kindly persons. All of us should accept the challenge and joy of being angels of mercy who show up just in the nick of time to help someone in need.

Unfortunately, some Christians believe that worshiping regularly and being connected to a faith community is what brings them blessings. The words of today's psalm are a corrective for that self-serving view. According to the psalmist, the people who truly enjoy God's blessing are those with compassion for the needy: "Happy are those who are concerned for the poor."

Thought for the Day

Strive unceasingly to be pleasing to God,
and ask that God's will
may be accomplished in you.
Love God with all your might,
for you owe the Lord a great deal.

Saint John of the Cross

You have always helped the needy.
Psalm 10:14

God Gives Coping Power

When Lisamaria Martinez was five years old, a strange rash erupted all over her body. The rash was followed by blisters. Her temperature soared to one-hundred-five degrees, causing her eyes to swell shut. Her parents rushed her to a hospital, where an alarmed emergency-room physician told the terrified parents that their little girl could die.

Over the next few weeks, Lisamaria's blisters broke open, her skin slithered off, and clumps of her hair fell out. She couldn't bear to open her eyes because the light hurt too much. As the girl's world darkened, doctors diagnosed the mysterious illness as Stevens-Johnson syndrome, a rare skin condition.

Then Lisamaria's parents learned the worst: their daughter was permanently blind. Although devastated, the parents also experienced hope through the realization that their daughter had returned from the brink of death. Surely, they could all find a way to cope with the blindness.

During the next five years, little Lisamaria inspired those around her. In second grade, she entered the annual "Braille Readers Are Leaders Contest," declaring her determination to win. And win she did, by reading sixty-two books in three months. By third grade, she was in Brownies, pushing her cane ahead of her as she hiked trails with friends. While in Brownies, she also found an outlet for what her father calls a "natural desire to help people." She began to collect canned goods for homeless shelters and visited the elderly in hospitals.

In 1990, Lisamaria was nominated for the national Kiwanis Hope of America Award and received California's prestigious Jefferson Award for Students. She and her mother were flown to Washington, D.C., for the presentation and had their picture taken with First Lady Barbara Bush.

Often when a great crisis strikes us, we feel weak and powerless. Yet God is present day by day to help us and give us coping power.

-------- *Affirmations for the Day* --------

God is my unfailing source of power.
God is my unlimited source of strength.
God is my unending source of creativity.

VMP

Let me hear the sounds of joy and gladness.
Psalm 51:8

Choose Your Reaction

No matter what happens in life, there is always one option left for us: we can choose how we react to what has happened. For example, we can

- visualize a positive outcome rather than imagine the worst
- celebrate what we have left rather than mourn what has been lost
- recommit ourselves and our energies to overcoming the hard time
- act with dignity like a survivor rather than a victim
- take charge of things over which we do have control and accept what is not in our control
- work to make something positive come out of every tragedy
- accept the truth that no crisis is permanent, that things and feelings change for the better
- seek support from others who have suffered in similar ways and take comfort that we are not alone
- ask God to help us "hear the sounds of joy and gladness"

-------- *Prayer for the Day* --------

Eternal and loving God,
Teach me the art of patience when things go well
and help me to use it
when my life is in turmoil.
Help me choose my reactions wisely
when trials and troubles come.
VMP

Wash away all my evil
and make me clean from my sin!
Psalm 51:2

God's Cleansing Power

Entertainer Glen Campbell appears as a clean-cut American singer with a guitar, an exceptional voice, and a lifestyle similar to the song he popularized, "Gentle on My Mind." However, in his candid autobiography, *Rhinestone Cowboy*, Campbell describes a lifestyle out of control to liquor, pills, and drugs.

He writes of four wives and eight children and of falling asleep in bathtubs so thoroughly drunk that his fourth (and present) wife regularly checked to be sure he wasn't drowning. Campbell's destructive pattern was similar to that of Elvis Presley's. The miracle is that Campbell did not die in agony, crawling around on the bathroom floor.

The difference, Campbell says, was God's intervention in his life. It was not a dramatic event; he simply realized that he was in a self-destruct mode and regularly thumbed through the Bible seeking help. "God took it all away," he says referring to his addiction to liquor, pills, and drugs.

Campbell's experience is echoed in the ancient psalmist's cry: "Wash away all my evil and make me clean from my sin!" God's grace redeems and cleanses us.

-------- *Thought for the Day* --------

Man is born broken.
He lives by mending.
The grace of God is the glue.
Eugene O'Neill

My sacrifice is a humble spirit, O God;
you will not reject a humble and repentant heart.
Psalm 51:17

Making the Choice to Suffer

Believe it or not, we probably choose to suffer more often than we may be aware. We generally make that decision when we see that our suffering has value and purpose. For example, we choose to suffer a little whenever we

- place someone else's needs ahead of our own—a spouse, children, friends, even a stranger
- donate portions of our hard-earned income to a charity or needy individual
- take the time to listen and show compassion toward a hurting friend
- honestly assess ourselves, see our strengths and weaknesses, and act to correct our weak parts
- see injustice and act to correct it
- try to heal hurting relationships
- forgive someone who has hurt us deeply
- apologize and ask forgiveness when we have been wrong and caused hurt

Let us recognize our vicarious suffering and acknowledge it as a sign of our ever growing spiritual maturity. "Sacrifice is a humble spirit" spoken by the psalmist today.

Prayer for the Day

Loving and glorious God,
In ways large and small,
help me to be a healing,
comforting, strengthening person
for others.
VMP

I am weak and poor, O Lord,
but you have not forgotten me.
Psalm 40:17

A Lesson in Compassion From Children

Eleven-year-old Ian O'Gorman, a fifth-grade student in Oceanside, California, had a malignant tumor removed from his small intestine. Physicians also recommended chemotherapy to further treat his cancer.

Because Ian could not bear to see his hair fall out in clumps as a result of the treatment, he decided to have his head shaved. However, he was concerned about being ridiculed at school.

To his astonishment and surprise, his classmates chose to join him by having their heads shaved. "If everybody has their head shaved, people don't know who has cancer and who doesn't," explained one of Ian's classmates.

Consequently, thirteen boys in Mr. Alter's fifth-grade class shaved their heads so one sick classmate would not feel out of place.

Such a response from fifth-grade students is not only commendable but reflects great maturity and deep compassion. In reflecting upon that action, let us examine our own attitudes and responses when issues emerge.

- Do we see and sense the fears, concerns, or anxieties that other people have from time to time in their lives?
- Do we actively try to respond with compassion and kindness, or do we delay in acting or not act at all?
- Do we realize that we are God's representatives and that, like God, we must not forget about the weak and the poor?

Prayer for the Day

Loving God,
Once again I offer you
my hands to touch others with your love,
my feet to walk in your ways,
my eyes to see how you see,
my tongue to speak your words of love.
VMP

Because I have been foolish....
I am bent over, I am crushed.
Psalm 38:5-6

Don't Sabotage Yourself

A quick dictionary check of the word *sabotage* reveals the definition "deliberate destruction." The term originally referred to deliberate damage done to machinery by wooden shoes. Several centuries ago, French workers wore crude wooden shoes called sabot. Whenever the workers felt that they had been excessively abused by factory owners, they retaliated by throwing their sabots, their wooden shoes, into the machinery, hence "sabotaging" it.

We can sabotage our own lives just as easily by throwing messages of negativism and defeat into our minds.

We can sabotage our own lives by convincing ourselves that we are incapable, lacking in talent and will power.

We can sabotage our own lives by entering into relationships that are unhealthy.

We can so effectively sabotage our lives that we stop the flow of creativity and productivity. We become unable to grow, flourish and live victoriously as God intends for us to live.

In today's reading the psalmist declares he has been foolish and now feels "bent over...crushed." Let us not be foolish and sabotage our lives. Let us live as triumphant, honorable, confident children of a good God.

-------- *Prayer for the Day* --------

Loving God,
strengthen my every weakness
and protect me against my own carelessness,
negligence, and foolishness.
Day by day and year by year,
let me grow into greater maturity.
VMP

Beautiful words fill my mind. . . .
Psalm 45:1

You Are What You Think

Carol Hazel writes in *Cathedral* magazine that she was pregnant with her first child at thirteen, her second at sixteen, the third at nineteen, and the fourth at twenty-one. She managed to hold on to a job until she became sick. Then she was forced to accept welfare.

Seeing that government assistance was a dead-end street, Hazel talked her way into a twelve-week course in construction work. Upon graduating, she found herself in an unusual job as an apprentice stonemason in New York City carving stones that would become a tiny part of the Cathedral of Saint John the Divine. When the church is completed, it will be the largest gothic cathedral in the world.

Hazel describes her transformation this way: "The stone got me. It fascinated me the first time I saw it. I saw the men working there and thought, *I can do that!* And before I knew it, I was sitting in front of this stone."

Notice the order in Hazel's transformation. "I saw the men working there and thought, *I can do that.*" We are what we think. If at the very core of our consciousness we receive messages of beauty, hope, humor, faith, and possibility, then we will be filled with life and opportunities.

-------- Thought for the Day --------

In every life,
we each find ourselves, at one time or another,
faced with a test and a trial.
I tell you
that the outcome
will be greatly determined
by attitude, by our mental disposition.
Edward Paul Cohn

That man never thought of being kind.
Psalm 109:16

Giving More Praise

The Duke of Wellington, the British military leader who defeated Napoleon at Waterloo, was a difficult man to serve under. Although he was a brilliant tactician, he was not one to shower his junior officers and staff with compliments.

Yet even Wellington realized that his leadership style was deficient. When he was older and had retired from military service, a young woman asked him what, if anything, he would do differently if he had his life to live over. Pausing briefly, Wellington replied: "I'd give more praise."

Wellington's comment is probably appropriate for most of us. We could all increase our "praise quotient" considerably. Today, think about the various people you will come in contact with—your spouse, your children, a friend, a colleague, a store clerk, a postal official, a receptionist. Then prepare yourself to find something good in each of them or in what they do, and praise them for it. It will lift their spirits and brighten your day.

Unlike the person described in today's psalm, be a person who thinks about being kind.

.... *Thought for the Day* ....

The sweetest of all sounds is praise.

Xenophon

Lord, will you hide yourself forever?
Psalm 89:46

Keeping the Faith Anyway

A woman wrote to a well-known spiritual leader about a faith dilemma. She explained that God had powerfully and miraculously answered a prayer for her eight-year-old son. The boy needed open-heart surgery and, against all odds, survived without any permanent problem.

Yet, three years earlier, this woman's husband, despite the best medical attention and earnest prayer support, had died.

"I just can't understand why God heard my prayers for our son but allowed my husband to die," she wrote tearfully. "Is God there or isn't he?" Long before that woman, the psalmist experienced a similar faith dilemma: "Lord, will you hide yourself forever?"

There are two responses for the distraught woman. On the one hand, her life experience is a reminder of God's sovereignty. God is always the final determiner of what will and will not happen. We may not like the outcome nor understand it, but that is life.

On the other hand, the woman (and all of us) should be reassured that God has not lost track of her circumstances, even though her life seems to be swirling out of control. God is there.

God knows when we struggle with faith, hurt from wounds, experience life's blows. In the midst of unanswered questions, we must hold to our faith in God and in God's ultimate goodness.

Thought for the Day

If I stoop into the dark,
it is but for a time:
I press God's lamp close to my breast;
its splendor soon or late
will pierce the gloom:
I shall emerge one day.

Robert Browning

But I trust in you, O L*ORD.*
Psalm 38:15

Three Ingredients for Coping

In recent years, stress researcher Richard Lazarus and his colleagues at the University of California at Berkeley have consistently found that positive emotions, such as hope, trust, and love, have a beneficial impact on coping with stress. They cite three positive aspects.

First, emotions act as time-out periods in which people take a break from the demands of coping.

Second, those same emotions help people sustain and persist in problem-solving and coping efforts.

Third, Lazarus and his research team suggest that positive emotions help people renew and restore their depleted resource pool.

Today's psalm verse begins with the word *But*. Evidently, the writer was suffering. Earlier in the psalm, he says, "I am in great pain; / my whole body is diseased" (38:3). Yet he holds to his hope in God: "But, I trust in you, O Lord."

The writer is exercising the positive emotions of hope, trust, and love. Not only are these emotions important coping mechanisms, they keep him connected to God. When we face difficult and stressful times, let us remember the three ingredients for good coping: hope, trust, and love.

Affirmations for the Day

I trust God naturally and easily.
I exercise hope, trust, and love.
I am a creative, resourceful person.
VMP

O LORD, you give me light;
you dispel my darkness.
Psalm 18:28

Doing It First

Some people crave the satisfaction of being the first at something. For example:

- Thomas Power was the first to spend two weeks in a fallout shelter in 1959.
- Eva Shain was the first woman to judge a world heavyweight championship bout—Muhammad Ali versus Ernie Shavers in 1977.
- Steve Newman was the first man to walk solo around the world, completing his four-year trek in 1986.
- Frank McNamara and Ralph Schneider established the first credit card, Diner's Club, in 1950.
- Sister Carolyn Farrell, a Sister of Charity, was the first nun to become mayor of an American city, Dubuque, Iowa, in 1980.

Consider being the first in your neighborhood, community, office, or church to

- respond promptly to a need
- comfort a grieving family
- give generously to a world relief collection
- visit someone who is hospitalized or homebound
- encourage a person who has been recently separated

Those firsts may not get your name entered in a record book, but they will make a big difference to some people. Through these firsts, you will be God's agent, giving light and dispelling darkness.

Thought for the Day

A saint is simply a human being
whose soul has grown up to its full stature
by full response to its environment, God.
Evelyn Underhill

He did not forget us when we were defeated.
Psalm 136:23

Organizing for Kindness

A woman wrote to a friend sharing her surprising good news in the midst of a personal loss. Her seventy-eight-year-old husband had died suddenly. The day of his death, he was in the process of painting the exterior of their home. Of course, the painting was left undone, and she had no idea about what to do or how to complete the work.

Then a few days after the funeral, she received a phone call from a young man who explained that he knew her husband from the YMCA, where they both swam laps in the pool. After offering his condolences, the young man went on to say, "Don't worry about the painting job that was left undone. My friends and I will come by and finish the painting this weekend."

Sure enough, six young gentlemen who knew her husband from the pool at the YMCA arrived the next Saturday and painted the entire house.

The recent widow's spirits soared. "I will never forget such generosity, nor will I ever again doubt that there are still some kindhearted folks left in this world," she told her friend.

There are times when we can perform an act of kindness by ourselves. At other times, such an act requires the effort of a group. When we see a need too large for one, let us consider organizing for kindness. When we do, people who may feel defeated by life will know they are not forgotten.

Thought for the Day

When I think of those
who have influenced my life the most,
I think not of the great
but of the good.
John Knox

Let us be happy, let us celebrate!
Psalm 118:24

Four Tips for Life Enhancement

Everyone knows that life is a mixture of sunshine and rain, joy and sorrow, great hopes and deep despairs. Here are four tips for greater life enhancement:

- *Laugh a little.* Most of us are guilty of taking ourselves too seriously. Learn to laugh at yourself. Doing so will ease the stress and pressure of life. Laughter is good medicine for the soul.
- *Cry a little.* Rejection and rebuke are part of living. Included in the package of life will be some disappointments and defeats. It's okay to cry. Tears are a gift of God. Crying heals the heart, so let tears flow. Remember that suffering just comes into life. Often we have no control over the events that produce it. However, self-pity is an option. Avoid it.
- *Play a little.* Once in a while, take off your shoes and walk barefoot in the grass or on the sand. Remember that life is meant to be enjoyed. Don't curl up in a corner and be a timid spectator. Get into life with gusto and energy. Act like a child occasionally.
- *Pray a little.* Every day, make the decision to live a life that pleases God. Speak with God through prayer many times during the day. Begin and end each day with short prayers. During the course of the day, ask God for guidance, praise God for the good you see, and bring to God the needs of others around you.

Applying these four tips often will help take the sting out of life's pains while deepening life's joys.

Prayer for the Day

Loving God,
I thank you for the gift of my life.
Let my actions and my words
be helpful to others
and pleasing to you.
VMP

Even I go through the deepest darkness,
...you are with me.
Psalm 23:4

Being Open to Bear Burdens

We are usually open to and aware of the needs of family and friends. But we also need to be open to bearing the burdens of people we meet through chance encounters.

Carolyn, a young mother from Memphis, was shopping in an office-supply store when she noticed that the young man waiting on her appeared to be weary. Although Carolyn was in a hurry, a voice inside her said, "Linger a moment and wait." She paused and said to the young man, "You must have had a difficult day. You look tired."

"Yes," the young man replied. He was very tired. After a pause, he explained, "I have cancer. Tomorrow I check into the hospital to prepare for a bone-marrow transplant. Fortunately, my sister is a perfect match."

Initially, Carolyn felt uncomfortable having a stranger share such personal information with her. But the young man continued, saying that time was critical. He would be in isolation for one hundred days. If the treatment was successful, he would be fine. If not... He did not finish the sentence. The young man also told Carolyn that he had a wife and a five-year-old child, and he was extremely concerned about both of them.

As the young man continued to speak, Carolyn suddenly felt great compassion for him. Gently touching his arm in reassurance, she spoke of the excellent doctors at his cancer center and the new techniques currently being used. She reminded him of God's promise to walk with all of us through the dark valleys of life.

Three months later, the newspaper carried the young man's obituary; he had died from his cancer.

In that chance encounter, there was benefit for both Carolyn and the young store clerk. He needed someone just to listen, and she needed the reminder to be open to bearing the burden of a stranger.

Thought for the Day

If you want to help the soul of your neighbor,
you should approach God first
with all your heart.
Ask him simply to fill you with charity,
the greatest of all virtues;
with it you can accomplish what you desire.
Saint Vincent Ferrer

Even though you are so high above,
you care for the lowly....
Psalm 138:6

Making Adversity Work for You

Disappointments and troubles come into every life. The key, therefore, is not avoiding adversity, but making it work for you. The following is an A-B-C-D-E-approach for making adversity your partner.

- *Accept* the fact that a problem exists, that perhaps your world has even turned upside down.
- *Believe* that God is active in your life, creating new opportunities for your personal and professional growth.
- *Confidence* is crucial. Have confidence in yourself and your ability to manage whatever comes. Also have confidence in God to guide you safely. Repeat the words of Psalm 138: "Even though you are so high above, you care for the lowly."
- *Develop* an openness to change. A difficulty can open us to new ways of thinking, feeling, acting, and working.
- *Energy* is important. In spite of energy-sapping trouble and trial, do everything you can to maintain a high-energy level. Proper diet, rest, and exercise will help you tackle the issue at hand with energy and enthusiasm.

-------- *Affirmations for the Day* --------

With God's help, I act assertively.
With God's help, I face challenges creatively.
With God's help, I risk exploring new opportunities.

VMP

Yet you left us helpless among wild animals;
you abandoned us in deepest darkness.
Psalm 44:19

Maintaining Perspective

The writer of today's psalm verse is experiencing moments of anger and bitterness. These negative feelings are so pervasive that he has completely lost perspective and is blaming God for his dilemma. All of us need to be cautious that in the midst of difficulty we do not lose perspective and balance like the man in the following story.

Several decades ago someone asked a mortician at a California cemetery, "What was the most expensive funeral you ever observed here?" The mortician did not hesitate or search his memory.

He told of a man embittered over a marriage separation. Although he was extremely wealthy, he left nothing to his children or his estranged wife. Instead he provided bountifully for his own final ostentatious farewell. Prior to his death, he earmarked $200 thousand for his funeral expenses. Factoring inflation into that amount, it would be nearly a million dollars today.

First, a bronze casket was purchased costing nearly $20 thousand. Then a beautiful rose window was created in the mausoleum for $25 thousand. After other funeral expenses were paid, the mortuary still had about $100 thousand left. The man had stipulated that any money left over was to be used for orchids, so the mortuary ordered $100 thousand worth of flowers.

Sadly—but hardly surprising—only three people attended this extravagant funeral.

While that story is extreme, it serves as a reminder that we must not allow anger, bitterness, and hostility to rule our lives. No matter what happens to us, we must always maintain balance and perspective. This is something that God can help us do.

Prayer for the Day

Loving and glorious God,
Forgive me if I squander time,
misuse opportunities, blur loyalties,
resist growth, or lose perspective.
Inspire me to be more thoughtful,
generous, wise, compassionate,
kind, and loving.
VMP

The Lord saved me from death.
Psalm 116:8

God Is Amazing

One night a Montana woman tucked her four children and two visiting nieces into bed. She offered a prayer asking God to watch over each drowsy child through the night. Then she retired for the evening.

At four-thirty the next morning, the woman was abruptly awakened by a sound. Suddenly, she found herself running down the hallway into her children's bedroom on the other side of the house. She stood in their doorway, hearing her heart pounding in her ears. Something bad was about to happen. Seconds ticked by. The children went on sleeping peacefully in their bunk beds. Everything was quiet, and the woman wondered, *Why am I here? Am I just dreaming?*

Then before her eyes, the upper half of the bunk bed came apart. She dashed forward to catch the heavy mattress-board and mattress before they crashed down onto her youngest child, a two-year-old who was sleeping in the bottom bunk.

She shouted for her husband, and together they adjusted and secured the beds. They worked so efficiently that the children were not even aroused from sleep. When her husband asked how she happened to be in the room at just the right time, the woman did not know how to answer. However, they both thanked God for saving their child from injury or death.

Thought for the Day

Lord, I shall be very busy this day.
I may forget you,
but do you not forget me.

Sir Jacob Astley

Give yourself to the LORD;
trust in him, and he will help you.
Psalm 37:5

Commitment Is Costly

Joni Erickson Tada is a best-selling author and gifted artist. She is also paralyzed from the neck down, the result of a diving accident in 1967. Since 1982 she has been married to Ken, a California high school teacher. In a recent article, she wrote that "the most ordinary of husband-and-wife routines can be a challenge when a disability is involved."

By way of illustration, she described a recent evening when she collapsed into bed with a cold. Unable to use her hands, she cannot blow her nose; nor can she cough, since she has no chest muscles. She knew it would be a rough night for her, but even rougher for Ken.

At three o'clock in the morning, she groaned and asked Ken to help her sit up so she could try coughing. Ken rose, sat her up, and tapped her back gently. He also held a tissue to her nose as she coughed and sputtered. That routine was repeated an hour and a half later.

When morning came, both were exhausted, but Ken had to go to work. While there is great love between Joni and Ken, she says that their marriage vows and commitments are tested daily because she is paralyzed and bound to a wheelchair. Each day she and Ken "grab hold of God's grace for dear life, hanging onto his help as though our lives depended on it."

In reality, the way Ken and Joni live is the way each one of us should live daily. When we make commitments and promises, they must be kept. When it becomes inconvenient and difficult to keep them, we must "grab hold of God's grace."

Prayer for the Day

Loving and glorious God,
I ask you to help me rise to every challenge,
accept every responsibility,
fulfill every commitment,
keep every promise,
overcome every temptation.
VMP

"Stop fighting," he says, "and know that I am God...."
Psalm 46:10

Don't Major in Minors

After his wife was diagnosed with cancer, a man realized that small disagreements and tensions no longer seemed to matter. When the cancer went into remission, however, small issues began to be magnified again. The man developed a reality check for himself:

- Am I overreacting?
- Am I making a big deal out of something small?
- Is this really worth the tension it is causing?
- What would happen if I kept quiet?
- Is there not some value in our difference of opinion?
- How important will this issue be tomorrow? next week?
- What would God think about his argument?

There is wisdom in the man's approach to issues. His questions are ones that all of us should raise whenever a difference of opinion begins to emerge.

Obviously, couples, family members, and friends need to resolve issues. Often, however, the level of unhappiness is not consistent with the importance of the disagreement. Let us seriously ask ourselves if we are guilty of majoring in minors.

Thought for the Day

People seem to fight about things
very unsuitable for fighting.
They make a frightful noise
in support of very quiet things.
They knock each other about
in the name of very fragile things.

G. K. Chesterton

Worship the L*ORD* *with gladness.*
Psalm 100:2
(New Revised Standard Version)

Serving God With Gladness

There can never be enough joy in our daily lives and in our service to God. As a way of increasing joy and serving the Lord with gladness, begin each day with prayer, asking God to fill you with love and joy. Ask God that the love and joy you experience flow freely from you to others throughout the day. Then, live joyfully throughout the day. Be open to opportunities to bring joy into the life of another person. For example:

- Prepare a meal and deliver it to someone who is sick or recently home from the hospital.
- Invite a lonely child to come to your home and play with your children.
- Have a lonely person join you for dinner in your home or at a restaurant as your guest.
- Offer a day of childcare to give a busy, exhausted mother some time for herself.
- Buy gift certificates at a restaurant and give them to the next homeless person you encounter.

The most effective way to deepen our joy and serve God with a glad heart is through helping others.

-------- *Prayer for the Day* --------

Holy and loving God,
Enable me to be
kind to those in difficulty,
strong for those who feel weak,
helpful to those whose burdens are heavy,
sympathetic to those whose hearts are breaking.
VMP

At sunrise I offer my prayer
and wait for your answer.
Psalm 5:3

Making Time for Yourself

An earlier generation counted every nickel. Our generation counts every minute. Most people know exactly how long it takes to drive to work or school, how much time will be spent there, how long it will take to return home, and how much time is needed to prepare and eat the evening meal before going on to the next activity. Even though we live life at full throttle, we must make time for ourselves. Here are six ways to do that:

- *Be flexible.* Learn the difference between what must be done (arriving at work on time, keeping medical appointments) and what can wait for a convenient time (laundry, cutting the lawn).
- *Simplify.* Clear the physical and emotional clutter from your life. Maybe you can live in a smaller house or apartment that needs less care. Are there some civic activities and committees you really don't need to be involved in?
- *Plan rest periods.* Unless you build some "breathing space" into your life, it simply won't happen. Give yourself the gift of solitude. Begin by planning one afternoon a month. The psalmist tells of rising at dawn to pray and meditate and enjoy the sunrise.
- *Learn to say no.* By saying no to some of the time demands on you, you maintain control of your life.
- *Accept limitations.* You can't do everything. If you take on too many activities, some will get short-changed and you will be unhappy.
- *Be free.* When you exercise your right to say no or when you give yourself an afternoon off, don't feel guilty. Remind yourself that everyone must have time to rest and recuperate.

Affirmations for the Day

God leads me to create the highest good
for myself and others.
God guides me to manage my time
honorably and wisely.
God is with me when I am busy,
when I am resting,
and at all moments in between.
VMP

You love what is right and hate what is evil.
That is why God, your God, has chosen you.
Psalm 45:7

The Christian Task

A woman discovered that one of the men who collected her trash every week could not read. Moved with concern and compassion, she gently offered to teach him. For a year, the man came to her home once a week for a two-hour tutorial. Together they struggled to make him literate. The progress was slow and limited, but by the end of the year, he was beginning to read at a second-grade level.

On the last night of his lessons, the man brought his "teacher" a gift-basket of fruit and said, "I'm sorry I can't read better yet, but I want to thank you very much. No one has ever taken this much interest in me." The woman was moved to tears by his remark.

The tasks for all of us are

- to be useful
- to build faith
- to inspire others
- to encourage people
- to be a source of light
- to bring hope into despair
- to convey God's compassion and love

Thought for the Day

We are not criticized for being Christians
but for not being Christian enough.
Cardinal Leon Joseph Suenens

You crowned him with glory and honor.
Psalm 8:5

We Are Cracked Cathedrals

Psychologists emphasize the importance of healthy self-esteem. It is the key to happiness, the door to success, the road to vitality, an essential component of personal fulfillment, the path to healthy relationships, and the ingredient for eliminating toxic ones.

Yet all of us have experiences from time to time that dent our self-esteem. There are life events that leave us feeling depressed about our ability and worth. The next time you feel badly about yourself, replace those negative feelings with the image of yourself as a "cracked cathedral."

In some of Europe's ancient cathedrals, the windows are falling out, stones are loose, and a tower may be leaning. On the surface, the structure is nothing more than an ancient ruin—but it is still a cathedral.

In moments when we are tempted to think too little of ourselves, we must remind ourselves we are like cracked cathedrals.

- We are created in the image of God.
- We are called children of God.
- We are crowned "with glory and honor" by God.

When events pound at our self-esteem, we can maintain emotional and spiritual balance by recalling that God views us as unique and gives us love, respect, and honor.

Affirmations for the Day

I thank God for the way I am made.
I was not made from a common mold.
I am special, distinct, and unique.
VMP

Proud men have set a trap for me;
they have laid their snares,
and along the path they have set traps to catch me.
Psalm 140:5

God Can Turn on the Lights

A group of tourists was being shown through Carlsbad Caverns in New Mexico, an underground wonderland of connecting passageways. When the group reached the deepest part of the cave, all the lights were turned out so that the group might experience the deep, dense darkness of the cave.

The darkness was so overpowering that a seven-year-old girl began to cry. Her eleven-year-old brother placed his arm around her and whispered, "Don't cry. There is a man down here who can turn the lights on."

That is also true of God. Whenever we are in darkness, our God can turn on the lights. No matter

- how complicated the problem
- how dreary the journey
- how stormy the weather
- how treacherous the path
- how confusing the events
- how disturbing the issue

our God sees, hears, and answers prayers.

Thought for the Day

It is but right that our hearts should be on God,
when the heart of God is so much on us.
Richard Baxter

Why am I so sad?
Why am I so troubled?
I will put my hope in God,
and once again I will praise him....
Psalm 42:11

The Right Attitude Makes a Difference

The humorous story is told of a small town that had a bar at one end of Main Street and a cemetery at the other. One night, a man who had been drinking heavily left the bar and headed home. While taking a shortcut through the cemetery, he fell into an open grave. He felt the walls around him and tried to climb out, but he just couldn't do it. So he sat down and decided to wait until morning when the cemetery workers would come and help him out.

A few moments later, another man who had too much to drink at the same bar came by. As he walked through the cemetery, he fell into the same open grave. He, too, felt around the walls and tried unsuccessfully to climb out.

Suddenly, from behind him and out of the darkness of the grave, he heard a voice say, "You can't get out of here!"

Frantically, the man leaped out of the grave.

That fictional story points to this truth: there are times when we think we cannot do something. Yet with the right motivation, it can be done.

The next time we face an "impossible" or "insurmountable" problem, let us examine our own attitudes toward it, asking if it is really as hopeless as we think. Notice that today's psalm writer made an attitude adjustment: "Why am I so sad? Why am I so troubled? I will put my hope in God."

The right attitude can make a big difference.

Thought for the Day

Attitudes are capable
of making the same experience
either pleasant or painful.
John Powell

Don't let my enemies gloat over me.
Psalm 35:24

Winning Over an Enemy

When Steven Spielberg, director of *E.T.*, *Jurassic Park*, and other screen hits, was a thirteen-year-old making movies at home and school, he was tormented for months by a bully. "This was somebody I feared," he recalls. "He was my nemesis. I dreamed about him."

Wisely, young Spielberg decided that since he had no interest in beating the bully, he would win him over. So he invited the bully to help him with a movie. Spielberg explained that the plot involved fighting Nazis, and he asked the bully to play the hero.

At first, the bully laughed. When he realized Spielberg was serious, however, he agreed and appeared in the film complete with helmet, fatigues, and backpack. "After that he became my friend," Spielberg says.

Acceptance is a power that can transform an enemy into a friend. It is quite likely that the young man became a bully because it was the only way he could gain attention. Spielberg showed him a better way.

Thought for the Day

He who lives by fighting with an enemy
has an interest in the preservation
of the enemy's life.
Friedrich Nietzsche

The power of the wicked will be broken....
Psalm 37:17
(*New International Version*)

Reversing Hate

Only four days after a black family moved into their new home in Liverpool, New York, they became victims of a racial crime. The mother backed out of the garage early one morning. As she watched the automatic door shut, she saw in foot-high, blazing hot-pink letters the words KK. DIE NIGGER.

The scrawled words sent a wave of fear and panic through the woman and her fourteen-year-old son. Her other two children, ages eleven and six, did not understand and were confused by the words. The family called the police, who reassured them that the perpetrators of this serious racial crime would be pursued aggressively.

Meanwhile, as word of the racial slur spread, the community responded to the new family. A young man and woman dressed in work clothes and carrying a paint can, a bucket, and various cleaning tools came and asked the family if they could remove the words from the garage door. Soapy water, sandpaper, and paint soon obliterated the hate-filled words from the garage door, and a spirit of friendship blossomed.

Throughout the day, a steady stream of well-wishers came by. One family brought fresh flowers. A smiling woman brought a homemade layer cake. "We all marveled," the mother says. "Our day had ended so differently from the way it started."

By the community's immediate bold and compassionate response, "the power of the wicked" was broken. They took something ugly and made it beautiful.

-------- *Thought for the Day* --------

Prejudice is the child of ignorance.

William Hazlitt

The Lord *takes care of those who obey him.*
Psalm 37:18

Play Out the Hand Dealt You

When Dwight Eisenhower was president he was asked, "Who is the greatest man you ever met?"

He responded immediately, saying the greatest person he had met was not a man but a woman—his mother. Although she had little formal education, she had great wisdom.

Specifically, President Eisenhower recalled this important lesson taught by his mother. He and his brothers were playing a card game with their mother. Little Dwight was dealt one hand of cards that was utterly impossible, and he began to complain about it.

His mother immediately asked all the boys to put down their cards because she wanted to tell them something—especially, Dwight. She explained to her children that they were playing a game in their home with their mother under loving circumstances. Even though she loved them all, she had managed to deal a bad hand to Dwight.

"Now, when you get out in life where they don't love you so much, you are going to be dealt many bad hands," she explained. "What are you to do? You are to pray to God. You are to trust God, and like a man, you are to play out the hand that is dealt you."

That, the president told his interviewer, was one of the wisest lessons he learned while still in his youth. Indeed, it is useful advice for all of us. When life deals us a bad hand, we are to pray, trust God, and then, like mature adults, play out the hand that has been dealt us.

Affirmations for the Day

God makes me serene and peaceful.
God places perfect wisdom in my heart.
God gives me courage to accept and face challenges.

VMP

He gives me help and makes me glad.
Psalm 28:7

Choose to Be Challenged

So much emotional and spiritual energy is consumed by negative images and thoughts. Yet negative images and thoughts can be transformed if you choose to be challenged by life's changes and chances. The next time you experience a negative emotion, remember that

- fear can give way to courage
- anger can give way to energy
- loneliness can give way to partnership
- confusion can give way to insight
- detachment can give way to involvement
- anxiety can give way to serenity
- resentment can give way to appreciation
- hostility can give way to hospitality
- resistance can give way to acceptance

Remember that you are not a soloist in life; there is a higher power, God, who provides help and offers joy.

-------- *Thought for the Day* --------

People who believe
in a power greater than their own
that operates in the world for good
are always a step ahead
in the process of self-empowerment.
Kathryn D. Cramer

I praise you, for I am fearfully and wonderfully made.
Psalm 139:14
(New Revised Standard Version)

An Exercise for Renewing Strength

Today's psalm declares that God has carefully created us and has given us all the tools we need to manage our lives with creativity and dignity. Using the words of the psalm, try practicing the following exercise for renewing strength the next time you feel overwhelmed and underequipped. Say to yourself:

- I have stamina.
- I think creatively.
- I am emotionally powerful and stable.
- I have high energy.
- I reach out for help when I need it.
- I am proud of myself.
- I have people I can count on.
- I feel healthy and capable.
- I face problems optimistically.
- I feel committed and connected to God.
- I can channel anger into power.
- I manage my responsibilities well.
- I can take a risk and face a challenge.
- I am self-confident.
- I can regain control.

-------- *Thought for the Day* --------

Jesus did not say,
"You will never have a rough passage,
you will never be overstrained,
you will never feel uncomfortable."
But he did say,
"You will never be overcome."
Julian of Norwich

He trains my hands for war,
so that my arms can bend a bow of bronze.
Psalm 18:34
(New Revised Standard Version)

The Importance of Physical Exercise

We can often handle emotional problems better if we are physically fit. An increasing number of scientific studies come to the same conclusion, namely, that regular exercise has a powerful effect on our emotional state.

In his book *The Exercise Prescription for Depression and Anxiety*, psychologist Keith Johnsgard evaluates various studies and concludes that regular aerobic exercise (at least three or four times a week for twenty to thirty minutes each time) produces the following benefits:

- It reduces symptoms of major depression, sometimes as effectively as psychotherapy or antidepressant medication.
- It helps prevent serious depression from occurring or at least diminishes the intensity and duration of its symptoms.
- It reliably and consistently reduces hostility.
- It makes a person calmer and less emotionally reactive.
- It impacts immediately and positively on anxiety. The more intense the anxiety, the more vigorous a workout may be required to bring about a noticeable effect.

The point Dr. Johnsgard and others make is that being physically fit improves our resistance to stress. Today's psalm is a reminder that sometimes life is a battle. If we are to "bend a bow of bronze" in our own defense, we must be in good physical condition.

Thought for the Day

A sedentary life
is the real sin
against the Holy Spirit.
Friedrich Nietzsche

So we will not be afraid, even if the earth is shaken....
Psalm 46:2

Letting Go of Fear

Too many people hold themselves back because of fear. They find themselves trapped in one place and unable to find peace, forgiveness, and serenity because of their fear.

Some people fear trying a new love because they were betrayed in the past. Some fear forgiveness, choosing to cling to the false belief that they are unworthy and unlovable. Some fear seeking therapy for depression because it means trusting someone else. Some fear leaving an oppressive work situation because it means the risk of a new job. Some fear closeness because they believe they will become overly dependent. Some fear taking on a new challenge, thinking they will fail. Some fear terminating an abusive relationship because the unknown future is frightening.

Whatever it is that intimidates you and threatens to hold you back, make a conscious attempt to let go of fear. Replace human fear with divine trust in God. It is possible to "not be afraid, even if the earth is shaken."

Thought for the Day

God incarnate is the end of fear;
and the heart that realizes
that he is in the midst...
will be quiet in the midst of alarm.

Frederick B. Meyer

Those who wept as they went out…
will come back singing for joy….
Psalm 126:6

The Quiet Good

Helen Hayes, the First Lady of the American Theater, faced a great challenge in 1949. Her only daughter, Mary MacArthur, aged nineteen, caught a cold. After that, she complained of aches and pains. When the symptoms did not ease, Mary was sent to New York City for a more complete medical examination. Her condition was diagnosed as infantile paralysis—polio. At that time, polio vaccines were not available. Consequently, Mary MacArthur died.

The weeks and months that followed were extremely difficult. Light appeared in Helen Hayes' darkness when the National Foundation for Infantile Paralysis asked for her help in raising money for other polio victims. Hayes responded positively and met many people who also suffered from polio. Some had children who were very sick, others had lost children to the disease. But all were quietly helping.

Helen Hayes began to think of them as the "Quiet Good." She explained, "We see evil as noisy and good as mostly always quiet. Evil gets the big headlines. Good hardly ever does."

The courage of those women and men engaged in the "Quiet Good" in the face of great personal suffering from polio inspired in Helen Hayes a determination to face her loss and deal with the suffering. As she returned to work on the stage and contributed her time to the Foundation for Infantile Paralysis, Helen Hayes experienced the truth of today's psalm: "Those who wept as they went out… will come back singing."

Small acts of kindness and compassion have a great impact. They should never be underestimated or devalued. Let us strive always to be part of the "Quiet Good."

Thought for the Day

Do all the good you can
to all the people you can,
in all the ways you can,
as often as you can,
as long as you can.
Charles Haddon Spurgeon

Don't give in to worry or anger;
it only leads to trouble.
Psalm 37:8

Seeing the Opportunity in Adversity

The apocryphal tale is told of a chicken farmer who suffered every spring because his land flooded. Because the farm had been in his family for several generations, however, he did not want to leave it.

The flooding became more and more serious with each spring. It was a major challenge to move the chickens to safety on higher ground. One year the waters rose especially rapidly, and the farmer could not save all the chickens. Hundreds died in the flood.

That was the last straw for the frustrated farmer. He came into the farmhouse and in a voice filled with despair told his wife, "I've had it, but I'm trapped. We can't afford to buy another farm, and we couldn't sell this one anyway because of the yearly floods. I don't know what to do."

His wife saw an opportunity in their adversity. "Raise ducks," she recommended.

Because troubles come into every life and because no one can escape them, the key is to take adversity and turn it into advantage, a burden and turn it into a blessing. Those are better options than giving into worry or anger.

Affirmations for the Day

The light of God within
creates miracles in my life
here and now.
The light of God within
produces perfect results
in every phase of my life.
The light of God within
leads me to the right place
at the right time.
VMP

You girded me with strength….
Psalm 18:40
(*The New American Bible*)

Taking Inventory of Your Strengths

Often a crisis point becomes such a time of upheaval that you can forget you have many strengths with which to cope. For example, a woman who loses her job may forget that she still has excellent physical health and a strong emotional disposition, both of which are powerful strengths for moving forward and obtaining a new position.

If you are facing a stressful period in your life, take the time to take an inventory of your strengths. Ask yourself, *What do I have going for me?* Write your answers. Perhaps your list will look similar to this one:

- Excellent physical health
- Mental stability
- Ability to persevere
- Good friends
- Supportive family
- A university degree or trade skill
- Some money in the bank for a "rainy" day
- No major financial obligations
- A deep faith in God
- Connection to a church
- A sensitive and compassionate pastor

Today the psalmist acknowledges, "You girded me with strength…." God created you with inborn strengths. As you grow, God continues to have your strengths develop, mature, and expand so that when tough times come, you can tap into those strengths.

Prayer for the Day

Loving God, I thank you
for creating me rich in imagination,
for creating me rich in creativity,
for creating me rich in strength.
Now, empower me to use your good gifts
to shape, manage, and direct my crisis
to a successful outcome.
VMP

How long will sorrow fill my heart day and night?
How long will my enemies triumph over me?
Psalm 13:2

Defeating Growth Versus Nourishing Growth

There are two types of people: those who defeat their own growth and development and those who nourish and expand their growth. When faced with a personal crisis, those who defeat growth engage in the following kind of self-talk:

- I'm sunk.
- It's hopeless. I'll never be able to change and adapt.
- I'll never come out of this.
- There aren't any jobs in my field.
- Everybody is downsizing. I'll never find work.
- I can't recover from this. What's the use of trying?

People who nourish growth and take advantage of adversity think:

- Change is hard, but I can do it.
- It looks bleak, but I'll find a way.
- Job opportunities are tight, but there are positions out there.
- My situation is difficult, but I have the ability to overcome it.
- My career field is flooded, but I will continue searching for work while looking at other options.
- I have overcome past traumas, I will overcome future traumas.

We all have times when, we take a negative view of life. We need to remind ourselves at those times to move from growth-defeating statements to statements that nourish growth. The psalmist begins pessimistically but concludes positively by declaring, "I rely on your constant love;/ I will be glad, because you will rescue me" (v. 5).

Prayer for the Day

Loving and kind God,
Bless this day and all that takes place in it.
Let my thoughts and my words
reflect my faith and not my fears.
VMP

"Yes, so mighty is God,
our God who leads us always!"
Psalm 48:15
(*The New American Bible*)

God Does Not Make Mistakes

During the oppressive noonday heat, a weary farmer with a philosophical mind took a break by sitting under a walnut tree. As he relaxed, he looked at the pumpkins growing in front of him and thought, *How strange that God puts such large, heavy pumpkins on a frail vine that has so little strength it has to trail on the ground!*

Then looking up into the cool branches of the tree above him, he thought, *How strange that God puts small walnuts on such a big tree with branches so strong they could hold a man!*

Just then, a gentle breeze dislodged a walnut from the tree, and it dropped on the farmer's head. As he rubbed his head, he reflected on the experience and thought, *God makes no mistakes. It's a good thing there was a walnut growing on the tree instead of a pumpkin.*

God, who is great and wise, makes no mistakes. So when the breezes of life blow, let us remember the farmer and his reflection: God makes no mistakes. "God…leads us always!"

Thought for the Day

Events of all sorts
creep or fly
exactly as God pleases.
William Cowper

Commit your way to the LORD;
trust that God will act.....
Psalm 37:5
(*The New American Bible*)

Rejecting Rejection

G. Campbell Morgan, a prominent and popular English clergyman, served large churches where massive crowds came each Sunday to hear him preach. Morgan's literary output of sermons and books was immense.

However, before he began his ministry, he was twice rejected as unfit for the ministry by ecclesiastical authorities. One rejection was particularly difficult for him. In 1888, he was one of one-hundred-fifty young men who sought ordination. Although he passed the doctrinal examinations, he had to preach a trial sermon. In a huge auditorium that seated more than a thousand, three ministers and seven hundred fifty-six others came to listen to the candidates. Two weeks later, Morgan's name appeared among the one hundred five rejected for the ministry.

Jill Morgan, his daughter-in-law, wrote in her book *A Man of the Word*, "He wired to his father the one word, 'Rejected' and sat down to write in his diary: 'Very dark everything seems. Still, He knoweth best.'"

After taking time to recover from the rejection, Morgan rejected the verdict, reapplied for ordination, and was accepted. He went on to become one of England's most outstanding clergymen.

Let us not be defeated by rejection. Rather let us, like Morgan, reject rejection. Let us trust in God to help us move forward and closer to our dreams.

Thought for the Day

God governs the world,
and we have only to do our duty wisely
and leave the issue to him.
John Jay Chapman

You have made many wonderful plans for us.
Psalm 40:5

Trusting God and Taking a Risk

There are times in our lives when all of us hold back, fearing to take a risk. Yet psychologists often point out that the very areas we resist are often those in which we can experience the greatest opportunity and growth.

Look over your life today and ask yourself how you might benefit by trusting God and taking risks in the following areas:

- sharing what you want, feel, think, or need with a spouse or partner
- sharing feelings and dealing with unresolved conflicts with a friend
- seeking a promotion, changing jobs, or starting your own business
- investing, buying property, or setting up a retirement program
- returning to school, completing a degree, or taking classes outside your field
- starting an exercise program or making a commitment to a more physically invigorating life
- entering into therapy to look at unresolved personal issues
- enlarging your circle of friends by reaching out to new people and making them part of your life
- opening yourself up to people of other faiths or other countries
- making a religious commitment, attending a weekend retreat, or seeking a spiritual director

Thought for the Day

The absurd man is he who never changes.

Auguste Barthélemy

It is well with those who deal generously....
Psalm 112:5
(*New Revised Standard Version*)

The Importance of Giving Generously

There is a spiritual law of cause and effect. As we give generously to others we, in turn, receive unusual and unexpected benefits. This law is reflected in today's psalm, as well as in the words of Jesus recorded in Luke 6:38: "Give to others, and God will give to you." This spiritual law works something like this:

- Give and it will be given to you to extend your own horizons.
- Give and it will be given to you to broaden your interests.
- Give and it will be given to you to live in a larger and more rewarding world.
- Give and it will be given to you to rise above your private griefs and disappointments.
- Give and it will be given to you to overcome fear, worry, and anxiety.
- Give and it will be given to you to live with faith, optimism, and hope.
- Give and it will be given to you to enjoy life in great abundance.
- Give and it will be given to you to enjoy the company of great souls from all ages.
- Give and it will be given to you to live a life filled with meaning.
- Give and it will be given to you to experience friendship, loyalty, and love.

-------- *Thought for the Day* --------

Giving is not a debt you owe;
giving is a seed you sow.
VMP

Give thanks to him and praise him.
Psalm 100:4

The Gracious Art of Receiving—and Giving

During the Vietnam War, two Marines were taking a lunch break on the steps of an improvised medical clinic being set up for Vietnamese civilians. When the two soldiers had almost finished their rations, they noticed a small frail boy among the patients who were milling about. He was about eleven years old and was obviously being treated for malnutrition. The Marines knew he was hungry. He was not begging, however, but curiously regarding them with friendly eyes.

The two Marines looked at each other, then offered the child their only remaining food, one of the round chocolate disks that fits in the bottom of a C ration can. The boy accepted the gift wordlessly, cautiously. Then, carefully, the youngster broke the disk into three equal pieces, he placed one piece in each Marine's hand, bowed in impeccable, gracious Vietnamese style, and slipped away.

That youth reveals a wisdom beyond his years. He knows the gentle art of receiving and giving. Such a charming and gracious response is one way to praise God who ultimately sends all good gifts our way.

-------- *Prayer for the Day* --------

Loving God,
I confess it is easier for me
to give than to receive.
Help me learn the art
of being a gracious receiver,
as well as a generous giver.
VMP

Happy is the person who is generous....
Psalm 112:5

Generosity Is the Path to Happiness

Hetty Green was the wealthiest woman in America around the turn of the century, accumulating a million dollars through shrewd investments. She managed her own money, unusual for a woman at that time, and had large interests in nearly every major corporation in the world. Yet Hetty Green was an unhappy woman and a notorious miser. She went to ludicrous lengths to save pennies.

For example, after she had read the morning paper, she would send her son downtown to sell it. When she was told that the bottle for a prescription she was having filled would cost an extra nickel, she returned home and brought her own bottle to the druggist.

One of the saddest examples of Hetty's extreme miserliness occurred when her son's leg was dislocated in an accident. She tried to nurse him at home to avoid medical expenses. When the injury worsened, she put ragged clothing on before taking him for treatment in the hope that the doctor would think her poor and reduce his fee. Because of the delay in getting medical attention for her son, the child's leg had to be amputated.

When Hetty Green died, she left an estate of more than $100 million. Yet she spent her life rooming in the cheapest hotels and eating in dingy restaurants.

How sad that this gifted financial wizard was unable to enjoy her money and share her wealth. None of her money ever benefited others or contributed to her own happiness. She lived in misery because she was a miser.

Today's psalm reminds us that it is generosity that leads to personal happiness in life.

Thought for the Day

A man there was, and they called him mad;
the more he gave, the more he had.
John Bunyan

The LORD gives strength to his people....
Psalm 29:11

Responding to Life's Demands

A priest was sent to do mission work on an island in the Pacific. While walking to the church on his first Sunday there, the man encountered a professional beggar. The beggar knew the priest would be walking that path and deliberately waited for him.

"Give me a coin," the beggar pleaded. The priest did so. Pleased by his success, the beggar waited for the priest the following Sunday and several after that, receiving a coin each day.

However, one Sunday the priest saw the beggar and spoke. "Give me an offering for the church." Startled and confused, the beggar reached into his clothing and came up with a coin.

On the next Sunday, the same exchange took place, except this time the priest said, "Bring your coin to the church and give it yourself." The beggar did. At the church, people took an interest in the beggar and helped him find a job. Soon he became a convert and an active leader in the Church.

When it came time for the priest to leave for another assignment, the beggar thanked him, "I never knew I had anything to give until you asked me for a coin."

In a sense, we are all like the beggar—uncertain of our own resources—until a person or an event demands something from us: we discover that we have a terminal illness, we learn that one of our children is very sick, we experience the death of someone we love deeply. Life makes the demand that we give a "coin"—the coin of courage, hope, sacrifice—and we respond positively and are surprised that we have more resources than we ever assumed we had. "The Lord gives strength to his people," declares the psalmist.

Prayer for the Day

Loving and eternal God,
Whenever I face darkness in my life,
let me remember that you give me
strength, courage, and resourcefulness.

VMP

Those who obey the LORD
will learn from him the path they should follow.
Psalm 25:12

Look for the Learning Opportunity

God uses many opportunities to help us learn, grow, and mature. We can find learning opportunities in experiences such as

- having a child
- experiencing serious injury or illness
- getting a divorce
- losing a friendship
- filing for bankruptcy
- experiencing kindness from an adversary
- being passed over for a promotion
- getting fired or demoted
- moving to a new city
- changing careers
- feeling the sting of failure

Today's psalm is a reminder that in difficult moments we need to be open to new learning and seek out God's new direction for life.

Thought for the Day

Life is not an exact science;
it is an art.
Samuel Butler

I will...protect those who acknowledge me as LORD.
Psalm 91:14

God's Protecting Power

A Wisconsin woman bears testimony to the reality of God's protecting power. Tuesday was chicken night at the restaurant where Debbie worked as a waitress, but few customers ordered chicken on one particular evening. As a result, the manager invited Debbie to take some chicken home, and she put several pieces into a paper bag.

Because the last customers lingered, the restaurant was late in closing, and Debbie missed her bus. Unable to afford a cab, she began walking home on the dark Milwaukee streets, praying and singing a hymn to relieve her fears.

Suddenly, a man with a knife leaped out of the shadows and pushed and dragged her down a dark side street. As she was being dragged, the woman heard four words come from out of nowhere. It was an odd message but very clear and very firm: "Debbie, eat your chicken."

The woman thought she was losing her mind to hear a message like that in such a desperate, dangerous moment. As she was being dragged farther into the darkness, however, she struggled to pull a piece of chicken from the bag. Just as she had managed to get a hold of a piece to bring to her mouth, her attacker stopped. Suddenly, two large dogs that were rummaging in spilled trash cans perked up their ears, sniffed the air, and began growling. With teeth bared, they approached the two and began to charge. The attacker fled, but the dogs did not chase him. Nor did they lunge at Debbie. They merely fixed their eyes on the chicken that she still held in her hand. Debbie tore a piece of meat off and threw it down, where they fought hungrily for it. Dropping pieces every few yards, Debbie got the stray dogs to follow her home. By the time she was safely inside, she understood the message: "Debbie, eat the chicken." It was God's protecting power.

Thought for the Day

The Lord my pasture shall prepare,
And feed me with a shepherd's care;
His presence shall my wants supply,
And guard me with a watchful eye.

Joseph Addison

Give us success in all we do!
Psalm 90:17

True Success

In her book *First Lady From Plains*, former First Lady Rosalynn Carter explains why her husband, Jimmy, left a promising career in the United States Navy just when he had been selected by Admiral Hyman Rickover to work on development of the country's first nuclear submarines. Jimmy's decision, she says, came after he attended his father's funeral.

Although Jimmy knew his father was well liked and extremely active in the community, he was surprised to learn of his quiet generosity. At the funeral home, families told Jimmy how his father had purchased graduation clothing for children because their parents couldn't afford it. Jimmy learned that his father loaned money to farmers when crops failed.

One widow told Jimmy that his father had helped support her financially for several years so she could provide for her children, a generosity that was completely private. No member of the Carter family had been aware of it.

Those revelations gave Jimmy Carter a whole new perspective on life in a small Georgia town and made his glamorous success in the Navy seem insignificant.

Thought for the Day

The measure of our success
will be the measure of our ability
to help others.
Frederick B. Meyer

You have always helped the needy.
Psalm 10:14

A Small First Step

An African-American mother and her teenage son were in church one Sunday when the priest spoke about the importance of loving neighbors and enemies. Following his homily, the priest invited parishioners to respond with their thoughts or questions.

"I find it hard to love my neighbors because of racism," declared the usually quiet young man. The emotion in his words surprised his mother.

The youth explained that whenever he walked down the street, people clutched their purses or crossed the street to avoid him. He hated going to the store for his family because the store personnel watched him, thinking he was going to steal something.

Although the mother understood, she was sad that her son was already experiencing such harsh racial judgments. She realized that as a black male, her son did not enjoy the privilege of mutual respect.

Following the sermon, several parishioners talked together and discovered that their sons had similar experiences. "What can we do?" asked one. They agreed to take this one small step: whenever they saw a young black male, they would intentionally look at him, smile, and say hello.

A few weeks later, the parishioners found that their approach was working. At first the youths were surprised, but then they began to smile back and greet their neighbors by name.

Obviously, that action does not clear the neighborhood of racism, but positive transformation is beginning to take place. Taking that first small step is the start of correcting every problem and every social issue. God needs our partnership to help the needy.

Thought for the Day

A loving person lives in a loving world.
A hostile person lives in a hostile world.
Everyone you meet is your mirror.

Ken Keyes, Jr.

...people will sing and shout for joy.
Psalm 132:16

Making Time for Simple Pleasures

What do the following three people have in common?

It is seven o'clock in the morning, and Cheryl, still in her bathrobe and clutching a cup of coffee in one hand, is pulling weeds from her Maryland garden with her free hand. She grins broadly in spite of the fact that last summer while gardening she slipped on wet grass and broke her leg in three places. "It still makes me happy just being out here," she says.

In Minnesota, a couple is taking their children to a country lake where the children, armed with small loaves of bread, will feed ducks and ducklings. This is hardly a major event except that the couple have five children, ages two through seven. Even the most minor outing requires considerable preplanning. "These outings bring all of us great joy and bring our family even closer together," the father explains.

In Chicago, Illinois, Barbara returns from her day job and whips up dinner for the family. Immediately after the meal, she departs for her welding class at a community college. Using torch and goggles, she is excited about the trade she is learning and the thrill she receives from transforming a sheet of steel into something artistic.

What does each of the above individuals have in common? The ability to enjoy simple pleasures. In a very serious world, they are having fun. For many people there is not enough "singing and shouting for joy."

To maintain emotional and spiritual balance in life, all of us need to consider opening ourselves up to simple pleasures. Those simple pleasures become not only interesting diversions but brief respites, points of fulfillment, or simply satisfying endeavors.

Thought for the Day

Love your life, poor as it is.
You may have pleasant, thrilling, glorious hours, even in a poorhouse.
The setting sun is reflected from the windows of the almshouse
as bright as from the rich man's abode.

Henry David Thoreau

With your strength you strengthened me.
Psalm 138:3

Breaking the Procrastination Habit

God expects you to follow through on your commitments whether made to others, to yourself, or to God. Too often, a delay results in a denial of the act. Here are some tips to break the procrastination habit:

- Begin with a prayer, asking God to help you stop procrastinating.
- Believe in God's power to answer your prayer.
- Repeat today's psalm: "With your strength you strengthened me."
- Believe in yourself. Don't tell yourself you can't do it; self-criticism is reinforcing. Tell yourself that you can and will break the procrastination habit.
- Contract with someone to do a certain task. Such an agreement can provide the motivation you need to complete it on time.
- Ask for support from your spouse or a trusted friend. When you feel discouraged, that person can boost your spirits.
- Promise yourself a reward. Identify a gift you will give yourself at each completion point. This is an effective way of nurturing and rewarding yourself.
- Keep in mind that a project is often less difficult than you may first believe.
- Be patient with yourself. Not every problem has a quick-fix solution. Reforming a lifelong pattern of procrastination may take some time, but it can be done.

Thought for the Day

Defer not till tomorrow to be wise,
Tomorrow's sun to thee may never rise.
William Congreve

Praise his supreme greatness.
Psalm 150:2

More Reasons to Thank God

While there may be many things wrong in our society, there are some that are quite right and bordering on perfect. We often take for granted things that work properly more than ninety-nine percent of the time.

Jerry Fritz of the Management Institute at the University of Wisconsin-Madison School of Business reports that if some workers settled for a less-than-perfect success rate, we'd have some major problems:

- Some two hundred thousand people would receive the wrong drug prescription each year.
- Our drinking water would be unsafe to drink three and one-half days of the year.
- Our homes would be without electricity seven hours a month.
- Twenty-two thousand checks would be deducted from the wrong bank accounts every hour.
- Twelve babies would be given to the wrong parents each day.
- One hundred fourteen thousand five hundred mismatched pairs of shoes would be shipped per year.

So the next time you are tempted to feel that things are bad, remember that there are some things that work very, very well.

Prayer for the Day

Loving and glorious God,
Today I thank you
for the many things I often take for granted:
the air I breathe,
the water I drink,
supermarkets filled to overflowing;
the ability to walk, talk, see, and hear,
to work and earn a living.
For all these and more,
I thank you.
VMP

I am a worm,
despised and scorned by everyone!
Psalm 22:6

Practicing Self-Healing

Many days bring small hurts, rejections, and slights our way. Some are intentional; others are not. Nevertheless, they still sting and can leave emotional bruises. Here are six ways to provide self-healing:

- *Acknowledge the reality of hurt.* The first step toward healing is to admit we have experienced a hurt. Psychologists know that hidden hurts can escalate until they become impossible to resolve. Face your feelings, experience the pain, and move on.
- *Express anger in healthy, acceptable ways.* When we are hurt, we usually become angry as well. A good way to give vent to anger is to share the hurt with a trusted friend.
- *Build self-esteem.* When someone offends us, it can impact negatively on our self-esteem. The psalmist may be suffering from a bout of low self-esteem when he writes, "I am a worm, despised and scorned by everyone!" An effective way to balance negative thoughts is to recall our good qualities.
- *Try to get into the mind of the offender.* How does the situation look from the other person's viewpoint? Was the one who did the wrong lacking in sensitivity or judgment? Did he or she know this would cause pain? Considering such questions can prevent us from overreacting.
- *Make a cost-benefit analysis.* When any of us harbor unforgiving, angry thoughts toward another who has hurt us, we can become miserable. Holding back forgiveness usually heightens and expands our pain. Extending forgiveness often breaks the gloom and reduces hostile feelings.
- *Seek clarification and reconciliation.* This will take courage, but it is often helpful to approach the offending person and say, "Something has gone wrong between us, and I want to clear it up. I value your friendship and can't have something in the way. Can you help me understand why you said that? May I share how it felt for me to hear that comment?"

Thought for the Day

The weak can never forgive.
Forgiveness is an attribute of the strong.
Mahatma Gandhi

Just so will they be blessed
who fear the LORD*.*
Psalm 128:4
(*The New American Bible*)

Noticing and Responding

Many negative stories are reported about New York City, but the following lovely gesture, unfortunately, went unreported in the media. A rider on the New York subway system described the incident, which took place one bitterly cold winter night.

Very few people were riding the subway at that hour, but at one stop a woman who was obviously very poor, and just as obviously very drunk, boarded the car. As soon as she sat down, she fell sound asleep. As the train swayed and screamed along the tracks, she continued sleeping.

On the woman's hands were two tattered, worn-out gloves, so full of holes that it was difficult to believe they provided any warmth from the cold. The other passengers could hardly keep their eyes off the woman. Perhaps they were wondering, *Why do people allow themselves to get like that?*

Then, a young Puerto Rican youth rose to get off the train as it slowed down. He could have gone out a closer door, but he chose to walk by the sleeping woman. As he did so, he paused briefly and removed his gloves, laid them on the woman's lap, and got off the train. When she awakened, she had warm gloves to wear.

God expects us to be kind. God expects us to notice the needs of others and respond. Today's psalm is a simple reminder that "they will be blessed who fear the Lord."

Thought for the Day

You must be holy in the way God asks you to be holy.
God does not ask you
to be a Trappist monk or a hermit,
but wants you to sanctify the world
and your everyday life.
Saint Vincent Pallotti

God is our shelter and strength,
always ready to heal in times of trouble.
So we will not be afraid....
Psalm 46:1-2

God Is Able

This verse is a clear declaration that God is capable of anything, is able to meet all of our needs, and is willing to do so. Therefore, we should not be afraid.

God is able to give us

- strength for our weakness
- wisdom for our foolishness
- direction for our drifting
- grace for our trials
- love for our hate
- peace for our anxiety
- plenty for our poverty
- clarity for our confusion
- hope for our despair
- light for our darkness
- healing for our pain

Always remember that the God of Moses and Miriam, of Jesus and Mary, of Paul and Martha, is able to do for us what he did for them.

.... *Thought for the Day* ....

The world is filled,
filled with the Absolute.
To see this
is to be made free.
Teilhard de Chardin

The LORD is my shepherd.
Psalm 23:1

The Faith Factor

Greater scientific evidence is emerging regarding the effectiveness of a "faith factor" in healing and reducing medical problems. One researcher who has studied the impact of the faith factor is Harvard Medical School cardiologist Dr. Herbert Benson. He notes that patients who prayed were successful at lowering metabolic rates, slowing the heart rate, and reducing other symptoms of stress.

Among the prayers that had a positive impact were the Jesus Prayer ("Lord Jesus, have mercy on me...") and the Twenty-third Psalm ("The Lord is my shepherd...").

In addition, some psychiatrists are recognizing the power of prayer in emotional healing. Arthur Kornhaber, a nationally known child psychiatrist, often includes prayer in his sessions with troubled children. "To exclude God from psychiatric consultation can be a form of malpractice when treating some patients," he says. "Spirituality is wonder and joy and shouldn't be left in the clinical closet."

Today's psalm points to the reality that we all have a shepherd in our life. We can turn to God our Shepherd for guidance, insight, support, strength, and healing.

Thought for the Day

The goodness of God
knows how to use our disordered wishes and actions,
often lovingly turning them
to our advantage
while always preserving
the beauty of his order.
Saint Bernard of Clairvaux

To you, O Lord, I offer my prayer,
in you, my God, I trust.
Psalm 25:1

Seven Different Types of Prayer

Every prayer is valid. But there are different kinds of prayer depending upon our mood, purpose, and state in life. Sometimes our praying incorporates several different prayers into one.

Consider shaping your devotional time around one of the following types of prayer:

- *The prayer of praise.* Here you simply exalt God for being God. You focus on God's beauty, holiness, love, mercy, and faithfulness.
- *The prayer of thanksgiving.* This is a prayer of thanks for God's salvation, care, help, insight, and guidance.
- *The prayer of confession.* In this prayer, you confess your sins, shortcomings, and unkind acts. You ask forgiveness and seek help not to repeat past mistakes and sins.
- *The prayer of intercession.* Here you pray for others who have needs and hurts. You ask God to continue blessing your family members, friends, and colleagues.
- *The prayer of petition.* You pray for yourself in this prayer, asking that God grant you various blessings and opportunities.

Prayer for the Day

Give us a pure heart
that we may see thee.
A humble heart
that we may hear thee.
A heart of love
that we may serve thee.
A heart of faith
that we may live thee.
Dag Hammarskjöld

The righteous will praise you indeed;
they will live in your presence.
Psalm 140:13

Spiritual Etiquette

Since prayer is talking with God, we should apply the social rules of etiquette to our conversations with God just as we do when conversing with people. Here are some ways to practice good spiritual etiquette:

- *Don't talk too much about yourself.* Constant use of the words *I*, *me*, and *my* is boring and overly self-centered. Of course, there are times when you need to unburden and share your personal hurts, but allow God to reveal himself to you as well.
- *Vary the topics of conversation.* Variety is the spice of prayer life. Remember yesterday's reflection on the various types of prayer. Try some of them.
- *Don't monopolize the conversation.* Practice some times of silence. This allows God to speak to you. If you fill your prayer time completely with your own talking, God may not be able to get through as effectively.
- *Say "please" and "thank you."* Good manners apply to prayer and God. Exercise your imagination when thanking God by offering thanks for things often taken for granted: beautiful flowers and plants in the spring, colorful leaves in the fall.
- *Compliment God.* God may not need your praise, but your prayer life is deepened and made more joyful when you compliment God through your praise and adoration.
- *Acknowledge God's presence.* Just as you say hello to people you meet during the day, acknowledge God's presence whenever you encounter him. When you witness a lovely act say "Thank you, God." When a friend or stranger unexpectedly brightens your day, say "Thank you, God, for that gift." Remember that you live in God's constant presence.

Prayer for the Day

God, of your goodness give me Yourself, for you are sufficient for me.
I cannot properly ask anything less, to be worthy of You.
If I were to ask anything less, I should always be in want.
In You alone do I have all.

Julian of Norwich

I walk in the presence of God....
Psalm 56:13

The Parable of the Monarch

There was once a monarch who was extremely insecure. Consequently, he demanded and received complete loyalty from his subjects except in one area: the people continued to put their ancient god above their monarch.

In an effort to discourage worship of this god, the monarch summoned three of his wisest advisers and asked, "Where might the people's god be hidden, and thus eliminated from the people's lives?"

The first adviser suggested that the god be hidden in the sky. "No," said the monarch after a moment's reflection. "The people might learn to fly one day, and then they would find their god again."

The second adviser suggested hiding the people's god at the bottom of the ocean. The king thought about this and said, "No. One day the people might probe the ocean depths and find their god again."

Finally, the monarch called on the third and wisest adviser, who said: "You should hide the people's god in the everyday lives of the people." And that is exactly what was done.

The parable reminds us that God is found in ordinary things and places, that we should look for God less in the great events of the world and more in the dull routines and gentle moments of life. In biblical times, God was found in a manger and in the life of a carpenter's son.

As we go through our daily tasks, let us become more aware that God may be found at our place of work, in a nursing home, at our school, among our children. Like the psalmist, we "walk in the presence of God."

Thought for the Day

We may ignore,
but we can nowhere evade
the presence of God.
The world is crowded with him.
He walks everywhere incognito.
C. S. Lewis

With God on our side we will win.
Psalm 108:13

Ample Resources

One of the country's great pastors and preachers was Harry Emerson Fosdick, founding minister of the Riverside Church in New York City. Dr. Fosdick had two daughters, the oldest of which was Elinor, who graduated from Johns Hopkins Medical School in 1937.

In 1939, Elinor married another physician, Dr. Roger Sherman Downs, and the couple had two children. With the outbreak of World War II, Roger Downs entered the Navy and was assigned overseas. He and his wife were separated for several years. Finally in 1945, Lieutenant Downs was assigned to the Port of New York, and the family was thrilled to be reunited.

On a visit to his in-laws, Lieutenant Downs retired early one evening. When he did not appear from the guest room the next morning, the family checked on him to find that he had died during the night. Dr. Fosdick had to break the cruel news to his daughter. "That was the hardest thing I ever had to do in my life," the clergyman confided to a friend. And later to another friend he wrote, "The blow that has fallen on our household is very heavy, but you may be sure that the resources are ample to meet it."

The fact is that his daughter, widowed so young, emerged from her grief. She built a splendid career for herself in medicine, working with the World Health Organization in Geneva, with Arab refugee children in Lebanon, and later at Columbia University Medical School.

Today's psalm reminds us that no matter what darkness falls into our lives, "with God on our side we will win." God provides us with ample resources to manage every aspect of life, good and bad.

Thought for the Day

This was the strength of the first Christians,
that they lived not in one world only,
but in two,
and found in consequence
not tension alone,
but power,
the vision of a world unshaken
and unshakable.

Harry Emerson Fosdick

They must thank him with sacrifices,
and with songs of joy....
Psalm 107:22

An Example of Commitment

Two clergymen were touring mission sites in Korea, led by a guide-interpreter. One day, they saw a boy pulling a crude plow in a field by the side of the road while an old man held the handles and directed. One of the clergymen commented to the guide, "I suppose they are very poor and can't afford an animal to do the plowing."

"Yes," replied the guide. "They are poor, but that is the family of Chi Noui. When the church was being built, they were eager to donate something but had no money, so they sold their only ox and gave the money to the church. That is why this spring they are pulling the plow themselves."

Touched by this act, the two clergymen remained silent for some moments. Then one of them responded, "That must have been a real sacrifice."

This time, the guide was quiet before answering. "They did not call it that," he said finally. "They thought it was fortunate they had an ox to sell."

That story might sharply evoke the following self-examination:

- How do I use my resources to further the work of God?
- Am I generous in supporting spiritual ministries?
- Do I feel fortunate that I have discretionary funds to share?
- Do I give out of a grateful heart, or do I give reluctantly?
- Do I honestly try to honor God "with sacrifices, and with songs of joy"?

Thought for the Day

If you are not generous with a meager income,
you will never be generous with abundance.
Harold Nye

My life is disappearing like smoke;
my body is burning like fire.
Psalm 102:3

Uncomplicating Life

Life can be confusing. However, much clutter and confusion in life can be eliminated when we act decisively. There are times when we move forward only if we

- face what needs to be faced, honestly and directly
- deal with what must be dealt with
- accept what must be accepted
- change what needs to be changed
- build what needs building
- drop what must be dropped
- pick up what needs to be picked up
- eliminate what needs to be eliminated
- give what needs to be given
- take what needs to be taken
- share what must be shared—generously
- let go of what must be released
- hold on to what must be held—tightly
- incorporate what must be incorporated
- stop what must be stopped—promptly and permanently

When we feel like today's psalm writer—that life is disappearing "like smoke"—we can do a quick review and see what decisive action we need to take. God will help.

Affirmations for the Day

God illumines my mind.
God places perfect wisdom in my heart.
God's love within
produces perfect results in my life.
VMP

I am weak from all my troubles.
Psalm 31:10

Seeing the Need Behind the Smiles

A young widower asked a high school student from his church to baby-sit for his children one evening. When the young woman arrived, she found the house clean but sparsely furnished. She also noted that the children's clothes were faded from many washings and the dishtowels were thin from many rounds of drying plates and silverware.

When it came time for the evening meal, the sitter remembered the children's father telling her that she would recognize supper in the refrigerator. She found inside, however, a quart of milk, half a loaf of bread, margarine, and some liver sausage. She was stunned. The girl made sandwiches and poured milk for the children. They declined second helpings, but it was obvious the children were still hungry. They seemed to know, however, what the limits of their meal should be. No amount of encouragement could convince the children to eat more.

Silently, the sitter wiped up the crumbs from the table and washed the few dishes. When the children were asleep, she called her mother and explained what she had found. She asked her mother to shop for groceries and bring them to the young widower's home. "I'll pay for those groceries from my earnings," she assured her mother. The mother soon arrived and together they stocked the refrigerator.

When the children's father returned home, the sitter tried to tell him that she was happy to stay with the children for free, but he insisted on paying her. She sensed it was a point of personal pride for him to pay for her services.

After that, the young woman occasionally saw the family at church and lamented that their neat appearance and polite smiles kept her and others from seeing their true needs.

As we come into contact with people, let us ask God to make us sensitive to their needs, hurts, and disappointments. Let us ask God to guide us to respond with compassion and with wisdom. Sometimes behind smiles and neat appearances are people like the psalmist, who declares, "I am weak from all my troubles."

Prayer for the Day

Loving God,
Do not let the blessings of my life
cloud my awareness
of those whose lives are difficult
and whose needs are desperate.
VMP

Don't give in to worry…
it only leads to trouble.
Psalm 37:8

Worry Is Useless

Worry is a crippling emotion. It sheds no light, emits no creative energy, and changes nothing. The next time you find yourself worrying about not having enough money, your weight, your health, your job, your spouse or children, your appearance, or any other matter, ask yourself the following questions:

- Will worrying bring me more money?
- Will worrying change my weight?
- Will worrying improve my health?
- Will worrying make my job more pleasant or secure?
- Will worrying strengthen my relationship with my spouse or children?
- Will worrying enhance my appearance?
- Will worrying solve any other problem or challenge?

Today's psalm reflects the wisdom that worry is useless in situations of small concerns and is equally useless in circumstances of great concern.

-------- *Thought for the Day* --------

A day of worry is more exhausting
than a day of work.
Sir John Lubbock

I will sing with joy because of you.
Psalm 9:2

Maintaining a Sense of Humor

There is no specific command in Scripture ordering us to maintain a sense of humor or to employ the therapy of laughter. However, the Book of Proverbs notes: "Being cheerful keeps you healthy. It is slow death to be gloomy all the time" (17:22).

Humor and laughter are important elements in our lives. With them, we can truly "sing with joy" because of our God. According to various theologians and psychologists, a sense of humor

- smoothes out life's rough spots by helping us keep things in balance and perspective
- enhances physical, emotional, and spiritual health
- eases tension in social and professional situations
- helps mend a wounded spirit
- provides a safety valve for times of emotional stress
- softens the impact of our own mistakes and blunders
- encourages optimism in times of trial
- generates courage in the face of difficulty

Let us enjoy and employ laughter in our daily lives.

Thought for the Day

Laugh and grow strong.
Saint Ignatius of Loyola

There is no one who does what is right.
Psalm 14:1

Praying for Those Who Serve Others

Today's psalm excerpt expresses an all-to-common cynicism: "There is no one who does what is right." To offset that cynicism, we must recall the many people who *are* doing what is right, often at great personal and professional sacrifice.

From time to time (and perhaps even more often), we should include in our thoughts all those who serve others. Often that service is done for a small salary and little recognition.

Let us remember all who serve the marginalized, neglected people; those who

- distribute food in countries ravaged by famine and wars
- minister in jails, penitentiaries, and prisons
- defend the defenseless in courtrooms across the country
- practice medicine amid the dangers and challenges of the inner city
- teach the physically and mentally challenged
- nurse the injured and the deformed

Let us pray fervently for such courageous women and men because they do what we cannot do or are unable or unwilling to do. Let us pray that they will offer their services with joy and compassion and that they will radiate hope and reflect the great love of God for all people.

Thought for the Day

Virtue demands courage, constant effort,
and, above all,
help from on high.
Saint John Vianney

The danger of death was all around me....
In my trouble I called to the LORD.
Psalm 18:5-6

Prayer Is the Only Way to Survive

Syndicated columnist Jack Anderson reported on two brothers who put all their faith in prayer, even though there seemed to be no God in the concentration camp at Auschwitz. The Bash brothers, Samuel and Mordecai, believe their faith got them through the horrors of the Holocaust.

Imprisoned and facing certain death, the brothers ripped some cloth from the uniforms they wore. Then, with thread and pieces of wire, they fashioned the cloth into crude Yarmulke, or skullcaps, that devout Jews wear for prayer. "We were not allowed to have them," says Samuel, "so we hid them and prayed."

When a guard caught them wearing the caps, they were beat unmercifully. "But even after that," says Samuel "we continued to pray because we believed it was the only way to survive the terrible ordeal."

Today they wear their handmade skullcaps proudly, and they still continue to pray for those who died, for those who survived, and for those who carry on.

Although none of us faces the extreme situation of the Bash brothers—or even that of the psalmist who wrote, "The danger of death was all around me"—we can learn from them. Whenever we face any problem, we should pray and ask God to help us. The witness and promise of Scripture is that God can come through in the most surprising, unexpected ways.

Thought for the Day

Build yourself a cell in your heart
and retire there to pray.
Saint Catherine of Siena

My God, my God, why have you abandoned me?
Psalm 22:1

What to Do During God's Absence

Like the psalmist, there are times when we feel desperately that God is absent from our lives. In those moments, we must remember that God's absence is not abandonment. Sometimes we are given "space" in which to reflect and act.

Consider the example of Leland Stanford, a California lawyer who was elected governor of his state in the late nineteenth century. Later, Stanford amassed a fortune as a builder and became president of the country's first transcontinental railroad.

Sadly, however, Stanford's only son died at the age of fifteen. Both parents were devastated. They could not feel the comforting presence of God in their lives at that time. In fact, Stanford declared, "I have nothing to live for."

Shortly after that declaration, Stanford had a life-changing dream. His son appeared to him saying, "Father, never say again you have nothing to live for. Live for other people's children."

Soon Stanford made plans to build a great university. He invested $21 million and established Leland Stanford, Jr., University in Palo Alto, California. In addition, he and his wife became the devoted servants of their wealth, generously contributing to a variety of worthwhile causes.

During a time when God's absence seems a painful experience, there is something we can all do: we can do good—after which, the pain eases and the light returns.

Thought for the Day

God is the friend of silence.
Trees, flowers, grass, grow in silence.
See the stars, moon and sun,
how they move in silence.

Mother Teresa of Calcutta

"He does not neglect the poor or ignore their suffering;
...but answers when they call for help."
Psalm 22:24

Moving From "Why me?" to "What next?"

The *Chicago Tribune* reported an incident that happened late one night in Florida. Ricky Hosea was victimized by two drivers: one hit-and-run and one drunk. His massive injuries included fractured shoulders and collarbone and broken arms, legs, and most ribs. His pelvis was shattered, and most of his teeth were knocked out.

In spite of such extensive injuries, Hosea lived. However, he was unconscious for more than four months, during which time a respirator kept him alive. Even the most seasoned professionals around Hosea did not believe he would ever walk again. Yet two years after his accident, Hosea walked out of Chicago's Rehabilitation Institute with only the aid of leg braces and two wooden canes. He expects to walk without any aids some day. "They are just steppingstones," he declares confidently.

Hosea has rented an apartment near the hospital so he can continue his own therapy and continue returning to visit, comfort, console, and inspire other patients who are just beginning their treatment.

Hosea is a great source of hope to staff and patients. He became that way when a transformation in his thinking took place. After the tragedy, he spent many nights wondering *Why me?* Now he says, "I wonder why I got a second chance. I would like to do something with it!"

The key to transforming adversity into advantage, for ourselves and for others, lies in moving from the question "Why me?" to the question "What next?" "Why me?" is unanswerable and leads to a dead end. "What next?" permits God to help us see other possibilities and open new opportunities.

Thought for the Day

If God has let you suffer,
it is because he sees something good in it.
Pope John Paul II

How wonderful are the good things
you keep for those who honor you!
Psalm 31:19

Conducting an In-Home Retreat

For many people, taking a week or even a weekend for a spiritual retreat is difficult, if not impossible. However, it is possible to take a busy week at home and turn it into a spiritual retreat. Here are some suggestions:

- *Add spiritual music to your day.* Rather than turning on the television or radio, play religious music as you do your daily tasks. Both the words and the melodies can create a spiritual atmosphere.
- *Read a spiritual book.* If time is an issue, refrain from reading the newspaper or secular magazines for the week. Substitute a spiritual book, perhaps a biography of a holy person, such as Mother Teresa or another spiritual giant.
- *Do some spiritual homework.* Use the week to catch up on spiritual chores, things you have neglected due to lack of time. For example, write letters to three or four people who would be cheered by hearing from you. This is a kind act and a way of welcoming more people to your inner circle.
- *Take time for soul-searching.* Several times during the week, think about your life and conduct an examination of your conscience. Ask yourself if the path you are on is the right one. Ask yourself where you want to be spiritually in the next month and the next year.
- *Fast and pray.* Skip a meal or two and use that time to pray and meditate. The spiritual discipline of not eating will be good, and you will appreciate the next meal more.

Making a private retreat in your home may take some planning and may force you to reorganize your week. However, it will be a wonderful gift to yourself. You will experience the truth of the psalmist's words: "How wonderful are the good things you keep for those who honor you!"

Thought for the Day

If our spiritual life does not grow where we are,
it will grow nowhere.

Oswald Chambers

No one cares for me.
Psalm 142:4

Healing Family Conflict

Every family experiences conflict at one time or another. Those conflicts can leave family members feeling like the psalmist, who writes, "No one cares for me." The following guidelines can help heal family rifts:

- *Appreciate individual differences.* Some people need support after a conflict, while others need time alone to think and reflect. Responding appropriately to these different styles is a good step toward restoring harmony.
- *Separate the behavior from the person.* Rather than "You're completely immature and unreliable" try saying, "I'm upset because you did not honor the curfew and came home two hours late."
- *Recognize that objectionable behavior may be only temporary.* Try to roll with some issues. Children and teenagers often outgrow behavior that is currently causing tension.
- *Be age-appropriate in your expectations.* A great deal of family tension is eased when parents don't allow their children to act, think, and behave in age-appropriate ways.
- *Accept issues that have no resolution.* Maybe you dreamed that your daughter would graduate from college, but she has chosen another path. Mourn your loss and move on.
- *Look for resources outside the family.* Confiding in a good friend or a pastor or joining a support group can provide important resources.

Thought for the Day

Govern a family as you
would cook a small fish
very gently.
Chinese Proverb

I come to you for safety.
Psalm 25:20

A Class Act

Thirteen-year-old Ann describes a time when her oldest brother, then eighteen, underwent heart surgery. Ann knew it would be a serious operation and was very concerned. She cried a great deal the night before her brother, Walt, was to have surgery.

Ann's parents accompanied Walt to the hospital, and a grandmother came to stay with the other children. "The day of his surgery was the worst day of my life," the young teenager recalls. She looked at her watch constantly, counting down the hours and minutes until the time of her brother's surgery.

At school, she was constantly in tears. Unable to eat lunch, she left the lunchroom and made her way to the chapel of her private Christian school. There, she began to cry softly and pray for her brother.

As she prayed, Ann heard a noise from behind her. Turning around, she saw the entire class walking toward her. They all knelt down, and the teacher led the class in prayers for Walt's safety through surgery.

"I knew God sent them to pray with me," she said. "That many people praying together can sure change someone's life. It changed mine." Walt came through the surgery safely and is fine today.

That action by a group of children reminds all of us of the importance of prayer support. Whenever we learn of illness, tragedy, or loss of any kind, let us be quick to join people in prayer, asking for God's protection and provision.

Prayer for the Day

Lord, help me live from day to day
In such a self-forgetful way,
That even when I kneel to pray
My prayer shall be for—others.

Charles Delucena Meigs

Sin speaks to the wicked man....
he no longer does what is wise and good.
He makes evil plans....
Psalm 36:1,3-4

Life Means Choosing

Today's psalm speaks of people who make decisions and choices. The "wicked" person has chosen: "He no longer does what is wise and good. He makes evil plans."

Wise choices balance life and bring beauty to the world. As people of God, let us choose

- love over hate
- prayer over despair
- giving over taking
- building and creating rather than destroying
- praising rather than criticizing and judging
- persevering rather than quitting
- acting rather than delaying
- forgiving rather than revenge
- smiling rather than frowning
- faith rather than fear
- community rather than isolation

-------- *Thought for the Day* --------

Be strong! It matters not
how deep entrenched the wrong,
How hard the battle goes,
the day how long;
Faint not—fight on!
Tomorrow comes the song.
Maltbie D. Babcock

The LORD protects and defends me;
I trust in him.
Psalm 28:7

Don't Be Afraid

The next time you face a situation that is frightening or even terrifying, consider the following story about a sixteen-year-old girl.

Cancer had ravaged her body, and she lay close to death in a Phoenix hospital. A friend who was a priest called upon her regularly. His pain and anguish over her diminishing life was clearly visible to her each time he visited. Quietly and softly, the girl sought to comfort him by saying, "Father, don't be afraid." The priest was touched by her comment. It was a profound expression of Christian theology in the face of death: "Father, don't be afraid."

"Father, don't be afraid." Behind those four small words is a large faith. Behind the statement is a profound awareness that the Lord "protects and defends," that God can be trusted in death and in life.

Affirmations for the Day

God's will and love for me are perfect.
Therefore, I don't have to hang on.
I can let go and let God guide.
I can go with the flow of life.
VMP

Put your hope in the LORD....
Psalm 37:34

Safe in the Love of God

Kathryn Koob, a member of the United States embassy staff in Tehran, Iran, was held hostage for four hundred forty-four days. She credits her faith for sustaining her during that harrowing time.

Even though she was isolated in a tiny bedroom with the curtains closed, the memories of the faith that had been passed on to her came flooding back. To strengthen herself, she recalled hymns, psalms, and biblical stories.

After five months of isolation, Koob was given a roommate, fellow hostage, Ann Swift. Soon the two of them began to have devotional times together, and soon a small community of faith emerged.

Looking back, Koob shares the following insight: "Our captivity was long and difficult. But I found my days filled with the spirit and power of the Lord. Those four hundred forty-four days became a time of spiritual growth. When the mobs in the streets by the embassy were screaming 'Death! Death!' I knew I was safe in the love of our Lord."

We may not be hostages surrounded by people screaming for our death, but whenever we feel threatened, frightened, vulnerable, and alone, let us recall Koob's experience as well as the words of today's psalm: "Put your hope in the Lord." Like Koob, we can feel safe in the love of our Lord.

Thought for the Day

Life isn't logical or sensible or orderly.
Life is a mess most of the time.
And theology must be lived
in the midst of that mess.

Charles Colson

...I offer you daily what I have promised.
Psalm 61:8

Making Ourselves Available to God

If it were not for the fact of God and our faith, the world could look extremely depressing. Just consider that in our world there are so many who are sick, starving, sad, deprived, wounded, bitter, fearful, hurting, angry, and hostile.

Thus it is crucial that we, who are the people of God, make ourselves available to God daily. It is through us that God can

- reduce the world's pain
- increase love and compassion
- feed the hungry
- clothe the naked
- minister to those in prisons

-------- *Thought for the Day* --------

Let us bring what is our own,
God will supply the rest.
Saint John Chrysostom

They succeed in everything they do.
Psalm 1:3

Take Charge of Your Life

He was born in Columbus, Ohio, in 1890, the third of eight children. At age eleven, he left school to help with family expenses. His first full-time job brought $3.50 a week. At fifteen he became interested in the automobile, a recent introduction to American life. He got a job in a garage at $4.50 a week.

The young man knew he needed more education and training, so he enrolled in a correspondence course. He worked all day in the garage and spent his evenings studying by the light of a kerosene lamp. With more education and confidence, he planned his next move: a job with the Frayer-Miller Automobile Company of Columbus.

One day he walked into the plant where owner Lee Frayer was bent over the hood of a car. Frayer asked him what he wanted, and the youth boldly replied, "I just thought I'd tell you I'm coming to work here tomorrow morning." When the owner asked who hired him, the young man replied, "Nobody yet, but I'll be on the job in the morning. If I'm not worth anything, you can fire me."

Early the next morning, the young man arrived for work. Frayer was not yet there. The youth noticed that the floor was thick with metal shavings, grease, and dirt, so he began to clean it.

The rest of the young man's future was predictable. He went on to achieve a national reputation as a race-car driver and automotive expert. In World War I, he was America's leading flying ace. He later founded Eastern Airlines. The young man was Eddie Rickenbacker.

Some people drift with the current, letting it take them wherever it flows. Others paddle in the waters of life, charting their own course and destiny. God expects us to paddle and not to drift. When the waters become too rough, we are to ask for God's guidance and help.

Thought for the Day

The world is a ladder for some to go up
and some to go down.
Italian Proverb

May the LORD answer you when you are in trouble!
Psalm 20:1

Now Is the Time to Try God

A young man wrote to an advice columnist, "I must share what I feel with someone who won't tell me I am a Jesus-freak."

Twice in his life, the young man had turned to prayer for help. Not knowing how to address God properly, he simply said what was in his heart, "Please, God, help me find a way out of this mess." Both times, a solution came to him clearly and convincingly.

He told the advice columnist that since he is not an especially religious person, he is mystified why and how his tangled life suddenly seemed to straighten out. Some suggested he was just lucky, but he rejects that view saying, "I honestly believe someone up there heard my prayers, moved things around, provided an exit, and allowed me to walk out of a tangled maze into the bright sunlight of reason."

The advice columnist responded by affirming her awareness of prayer's power. She concluded the column by urging others to pray saying, "Maybe now is the time to try God."

Thought for the Day

God excludes none,
if they do not exclude themselves.
William Guthrie

...we will shout for joy over your victory.
Psalm 20:5

The Power of Affirmation

A teacher agreed to take over a class that other teachers found impossible. The third-grade group of children consisted of hyperactive and unresponsive youths.

The teacher's opening comment on his first day included this litany of affirmation, "I'm happy you are all here, and I want you in my class." Then he gave three reasons why he welcomed the opportunity to teach them.

First, he said, they were the brightest and smartest children he had ever taught. Second, he told them they were the most sensitive and caring youths in the school. Third, he said their ability to study independently of others would be a delight for him to experience.

Each day he repeated his litany of affirmations. By the end of the semester, his class of "impossibles" tested an entire grade point average higher than the other third-grade classes.

Because of him, the children had an unbelievably good year. In fact, they proved to be one of the most successful third-grade groups in the school's history. Such is the power of affirmation.

Ask yourself, *Who do I know that could use the extra boost of daily affirmation?* "Adopt" that person and affirm his or her talents, abilities, and gifts as often as possible. Pray that God greatly bless that life. Then, watch and see what wonders emerge and what victories over which you can, like the psalmist, "shout for joy."

Prayer for the Day

Loving and glorious God,
Let me be a source of inspiration,
hope, and confidence for someone else.
Toward that end, direct my energies,
instruct my mind, shape my words, and sustain my will.

VMP

A gang of evil men is around me;
like a pack of dogs they close in on me;
they tear at my hands and feet.
Psalm 22:16

The Paralysis of Analysis

The story is told of legendary publisher, William Randolph Hearst. One day he walked into the offices of the *San Francisco Examiner* and heard a group of reporters talking about a man who was stranded on a rock in San Francisco Bay. The tide was rising and would soon overwhelm the man, and the reporters were debating with one another about how he had managed to get himself into such a precarious position in the first place.

Finally, Hearst broke in saying, "What difference does it make how he got there? Charter a boat, recruit volunteers, and save the man! That's the important thing!"

Are you guilty of the paralysis of analysis? Have you ever said or thought "How could you let this happen?" "How did you get yourself into this mess?" "What were you thinking when you let this take place?"

Statements and thoughts like this do not offer solutions. They only add to the burden already being carried. Resolve today to eliminate the paralysis of analysis and to commit yourself to action. Where there is a problem, work toward a solution. Where there is a burden, act to lift the load. And where there is danger, assist in creating safety.

That way you can make certain the person who is struggling will not feel like today's psalm writer who felt that "a gang of evil men" was all around.

Thought for the Day

We judge ourselves by our motives
and others by their actions.

Dwight Whitney Morrow

Give thanks to the God of heaven,
his love is eternal.
Psalm 136:26

The Ripple Effect of Kindness

Forty years ago a couple were living overseas while the husband served in the Air Force. When a telegram arrived telling them their youngest son had died. The Air Force granted them emergency leave.

Only the man, his wife, and some other wives from their B-29 flight crew were in attendance. It was a very difficult time for the couple, emotionally and financially. Like most Air Force families at the time, money was tight and they lived from check to check. Besides dealing with their own grief, the couple was worried about covering funeral costs.

Several days after the funeral Western Union delivered a telegram to the grieving parents. The couple assumed it was a note of sympathy from the squadron overseas. To their absolute surprise, the telegram was a money order for $500. The members of the squadron had organized a collection and were donating this sizable amount from their own meager paychecks.

Today, more than forty years after the fact, the couple still talk and think about that gracious, generous act of kindness.

Love is a power that moves people to be kind—and kindness has a ripple effect upon the receiver. It continues to be felt long, long after the actual act of kindness.

Today, let us remember to be kind, very kind. Our acts of kindness may be the most effective way of giving "thanks to the God of heaven."

Thought for the Day

Do not chase after all kinds of knowledge,
enlightenment and understanding
in the hope of gaining the hearts of others.
You will gain those hearts more surely
by showing openness and graciousness to them.

Saint John Chrysostom

They go from strength to strength.
Psalm 84:7
(New International Version)

Living With God's Strength

When faced with an overwhelming challenge, problem, issue, or crisis, don't forget that God has promised to give you

- strength beyond your strength
- power beyond your power
- hope beyond your hopes
- love beyond your own love
- wisdom beyond your wisdom
- energy beyond your energies
- courage beyond your courage
- faith beyond your faith
- endurance beyond your endurance
- ability beyond your abilities

Remember today's psalm when you feel helpless or hopeless. God's people "go from strength to strength."

-------- *Affirmations for the Day* --------

With God's help
I now transcend
all feelings and thoughts of weakness.
Because of God's help
I am strong and courageous.
Because of God's help
I am bold and willing
to take risks and accept challenges.
VMP

Your presence fills me with joy.
Psalm 16:11

How to Feel More Joy

Life can be a painfully serious affair. Perhaps that is why the word "joy" appears so often in Scripture. Although Christians are expected to make the world a better place, they are also expected to do that with joy. Here are five ways to experience more joy in daily life:

- *Train your eye to see beauty*. Of course, there is much in the world which is ugly: war, famine, crime, violence. Yet there is much that is beautiful: a child at play, lovers walking hand in hand, blooming flowers and green grass. Train your eye to see and appreciate beauty.
- *Recall happy times*. Balance what is in your mind with thoughts of happy times. Look back and ask yourself, *What gave me great pleasure?* Perhaps it was a childhood memory, a family gathering, a special celebration. Relive that time frequently.
- *Praise God for all blessings*. Rather than waste time cursing the darkness, thank God for the light that is present. Review your life making a mental note of all the good things you have. Then thank God for them. Carry the list with you, reviewing it and praising God for all blessings.
- *Nourish yourself spiritually*. Don't provide for family, friends, and strangers at the expense of your own inner life. Make the time to nourish yourself spiritually. Read a spiritual book, attend a retreat, gather with others for Bible study.
- *Cultivate friendships with positive people*. Surround yourself with people who live joyfully. Their joy will be contagious.

Thought for the Day

God works continually,
a thousand joys
he would pour into you at once,
if suffer it you could.

Angelus Silesius

The laws of the LORD are right,
and those who obey them are happy.
Psalm 19:8

God Is Good for You

When David Larson was training for a career in psychiatry, faculty advisers cautioned him against combining his Christian faith with the practice of psychiatry. "Religion hurts people," they warned.

That advice deepened Larson's curiosity and led him on a fifteen-year quest. Over the years Larson was surprised, even shocked, to learn that God *is* good for people. His review of various studies reveals the following:

- Regular church attenders live longer, have fewer heart attacks, and experience a lower incidence of arteriosclerosis, high blood pressure, and hypertension.
- Religious people are less likely to abuse alcohol and are far less likely to use illicit drugs.
- Prison inmates who make a religious commitment are less likely than their counterparts to return to jail.
- Marital satisfaction and overall well-being tend to increase with church attendance.
- People who attend church regularly are more than twice as likely to remain married.

In short, Larson believes that there is ample evidence to show that religious commitment, far from causing problems, has a definite impact upon reducing them.

Thought for the Day

Those who follow biblical values
live longer,
enjoy life more,
and are less diseased.
David Larson

Let me hear the sounds of joy and gladness.
Psalm 51:8

The Gift of Perspective

Paul was recently involved in a car accident. An uninsured motorist, failing to stop for a red light, struck Paul's vehicle. Paul's car was totaled and he was rushed to the hospital in an ambulance.

Initially, Paul lost the use of his left leg because of great swelling. For months he had to use crutches to walk and found the entire matter extremely frustrating and depressing. Although physicians told him he would recover completely, his spirits were broken.

One day while walking with his crutches and feeling very sorry for himself, Paul was greeted from behind with a loud, friendly "Hello."

Looking back, his eyes met the eyes of a complete stranger. He could not figure out why a stranger would greet him so warmly until he noticed that the man was using crutches as well, not because he had a broken leg, but because he had no leg. Full of life, the man zipped past Paul.

The man's cheerfulness had an immediate impact upon Paul. While he had been moping over the accident and his *injured* leg, this stranger was full of life with his *missing* leg. That chance encounter made the rest of Paul's recovery easier. Now, whenever Paul begins to feel sorry for himself, he recalls that man and his cheerful greeting.

When we are losing our sense of balance and perspective, God will often send us a gift in the form of another person who has accepted a circumstance in life far more difficult than our own. This person may even exhibit joy in life and provide us with the gift of perspective. In this way, God lets us hear, once again, "the sounds of joy and gladness."

Prayer for the Day

Loving God and good God,
Help me to maintain balance and perspective
so that nothing robs me
of joy or peace.
VMP

I look to the LORD for help at all times.
Psalm 25:15

Praying Together

Prayer is a very intimate aspect of spirituality. Couples who would like to pray together often hesitate and feel awkward about couple prayer. Yet the rewards of praying together are worth the effort. Here are some ways two people can become more comfortable praying together:

- *Begin gently*. Start with brief prayers that include just a few sentences. Short prayers allow both partners to feel more comfortable.
- *Be patient*. Sometimes one partner is more eager than the other to begin family devotions. Make the suggestion, but give your partner time to think and warm up to the idea. Perhaps beginning with just one prayer a week is enough.
- *Pray over meals*. Offering a prayer of thanks for a meal is a natural and gentle way to begin praying together. This is something each partner can take turns doing daily.
- *Pray with children*. If you have children, pray out loud with them before they retire each evening. This, too, is a good way to become comfortable praying with others.
- *Pray together during crisis times*. People often pray better when there is a strong, specific need. Families should quickly turn to God during hard times.

People who pray together may feel awkward at first but soon will discover that praying together is a powerful tool for deepening intimacy and communication as together they "look to the Lord for help."

Thought for the Day

Knit your hearts with an unslipping knot.
William Shakespeare

Great and mighty is our Lord;
his wisdom cannot be measured.
Psalm 147:5

Reverence, Don't Ignore

A farmer was tilling manure into a large field using a tractor and disk plow. The tractor moved at a turtle's pace of five miles an hour, and the man was bored—with the job, with life. He disliked farming, and he disliked working for his father.

Out of sheer boredom, the man dozed off and started to fall backward off the tractor seat. He woke up falling and, because the tractor was an old model with a throttle lever that was notched into place, the tractor just kept moving.

The man fell between the tractor and the sharp disks. As he hit the ground, he grabbed onto the tow bar. Quickly, he pulled himself up but could not pull himself up to complete safety. If he lost his grip, he would be cut into pieces by the moving disks. As the steel disks moved behind him cutting the earth, the man clung to the tow bar with both hands. His body was literally dragged through the dirt and manure.

No one could hear the young man's cries for help as the tractor kept moving, ever so slowly, toward the end of the field, up an incline, and into a tree. Although the tractor wheels kept spinning, the young man was able to let go and roll away to safety. It took a few minutes before he could stand, climb up to the tractor seat, and turn off the key.

In a sense, the man lost his life and got it back again. Although it is not known what impact that event had on his life, one can hope that it ended his boredom with life. Being given a second chance should deepen his sense of awe, wonder, and beauty. Perhaps he came to reverence, not ignore, the very gift of life itself.

Fortunately, we do not need a near-death experience to appreciate life. Our prayer and thoughts daily should be that of the psalmist: "Great and mighty is our Lord; his wisdom cannot be measured."

Prayer for the Day

Holy God and creator of all life,
As the sun rises each day,
let me be ever more aware
of the greatest of all lights,
that of your love growing in my heart.
VMP

My soul will feast and be satisfied
Psalm 63:5

The Need to Be Alone

On the occasion of his fortieth birthday, a man decided to make a week-long retreat. It was something he had thought about for several years but was unable to do. The week he spent at a Trappist monastery proved to be such a worthwhile experience that he decided to make it a yearly event. He cites the following reasons for an annual retreat:

- *The need for solitude to be whole.* A week of silence and prayer deepens commitments. A healing and unifying of the inner spirit takes place.
- *The need for silence to hear properly.* The world is a noisy, busy place. A retreat allows a brief relief from the pervasive activity and noise. It also permits the soul to open up a little more to God's voice.
- *The need for the mind to experience a rest.* All sorts of images, demands, calls, and distractions bombard us in daily life. During a week-long retreat the mind is allowed to rest and focus upon quiet, spiritual themes: a crucifix, a short passage of Scripture, a parable of Jesus, an exhortation of Paul.
- *The need to recall the basics of faith.* On a retreat one remembers that God is holy and that this same God calls all people to holy living.
- *The need to know mortality.* Away from occupations and preoccupations, one can recall that life has a termination point. This is not a depressing thought but one of hope. It renews awareness that life is a glorious gift. This thinking also permits one to review priorities, to be certain they are correct.

Of course a week-long retreat may truly be impossible for many people. However, consider a one-day retreat to nourish your soul and animate your life.

Thought for the Day

Holiness never points to itself,
but always beyond itself—
to God.
Kenneth Leech

He helps those who are in trouble;
he lifts those who have fallen.
Psalm 145:14

What Can We Make Out of What Is Left?

A little boy in kindergarten spent several class sessions working on a small ceramic dish to give to his father for Christmas. On the last day before the holidays, the boy was running down the hall and trying to put his coat on at the same time. In the process, he slipped and crushed the carefully wrapped gift he had worked on with dedication and love.

After a moment of silence, the child realized what had happened and broke into uncontrollable tears. In an effort to comfort him, the teacher said, "Don't cry. It really doesn't make any difference. You can buy something else."

Fortunately, the father, there to pick up his son, knew better. He swept the child into his arms and shed a discreet tear with him. "Let's pick up the pieces and see what we can make out of what is left," he whispered to his son. The little boy stopped crying and, with his dad, picked up the remains and went home.

This story is a parable of God in our lives. Perhaps we feel as though we have made a mess of our lives. Perhaps our lives feel as though they have been shattered by an event. God, who is like a father, comes to us, places a loving arm around our shoulders, and says, "Let's pick up the pieces and see what we can make out of what is left."

.... *Thought for the Day* ....

Trust the past to the mercy of God,
the present to his love,
and the future to his providence.

Saint Augustine of Hippo

As for me, I do what is right.
Psalm 26:11

There's Always Time to Pray

This story might prompt some revisionist thinking for those who feel they are too busy to pray. Carolyn tells of her parish church where there is a little yard between the rectory and the convent. The yard serves as a walkway leading to a simple but beautiful statue of Mary. People often stop there to pray.

One evening, Carolyn's sister, who was on the college track team, asked her to bike the four miles around the airport while she jogged; the parish church is directly across the street from the airport. Her sister runs daily each evening but is usually accompanied by a friend. That evening the friend was unavailable so Carolyn agreed to join her.

When the girl completed her run, she told Carolyn to bike on ahead saying she would catch up. Carolyn rode on but looked back once. She saw her younger sister jog into the parish walkway and kneel. "That simple action touched me," she recalls. "It made me think that if my sister found time to pray, I should be able to find time too."

There is always time to say a prayer, but we simply need to make the effort. "As for me, I do what is right," declares today's psalmist.

Thought for the Day

Is not prayer precisely of itself
peace, silence, strength,
since it is a way
of being with God.
Jacques Ellul

Proclaim with me the LORD's greatness;
let us praise his name together.
Psalm 34:3

Bearing Witness to Others

At the turn of the century a missionary doctor in China treated a man for cataracts. Before the surgery the man was practically blind; after treatment he could see quite well.

The man was ecstatic. There seemed to be no end to his gratitude toward the physician, and he freely shared his joy with other patients at the small mission clinic.

Leaving the clinic, the man made his way back to the remote village where he lived. However, he did not remain there long. Instead, he went on a tour of the villages throughout the region and after three months, made his way back to the small mission clinic where he had regained his sight.

The mission doctor was astonished to look out his window and see the man pulling a rope to which forty-eight other people held tightly. The man had guided them through the countryside to the place where he had been treated. Besides the rope, the only other thing they had in common was their blindness. The grateful man told them of the medical missionary and offered to lead them to the place where he regained his sight.

A story like that raises questions:

- Do we share our good news of God's love with others?
- Does our joy in God's goodness drive us to let other hurting people know the source of comfort and strength?
- Is our gratitude deep enough that it overflows and touches others as well?

-------- *Thought for the Day* --------

A holy clumsiness
is better than a sincere eloquence.
Saint Jerome

Would you like to enjoy life?
Do you want long life and happiness?
Then...do good.
Psalm 34:12-14

Compassion With Dignity

A man recently wrote his newspaper to describe a gracious act of compassion. He prefaced his comments by saying, "In these days when so many people are cynical and tend to be insensitive and uncaring, I witnessed something that restored my faith in humanity."

The writer was riding a city subway and sitting across from a homeless man. The homeless man's coat was tattered and torn, held together with pins and string. His trousers were in no better shape. He had holes in his shoes, and he wore no socks. He probably had not bathed in months.

"I tried not to stare, looking left, right, up and down, but I couldn't keep my eyes off him. I never saw anyone who was so down and out," he recalls.

Then, as the train came to a stop, a neatly dressed woman approached the homeless person. She handed him a dollar bill saying with great dignity, "I believe you dropped this." The startled old man reached out, took the dollar, and said, "Thank you."

"There was nothing on the floor before the woman came by—of that I am positive," the witness reports. "That vignette made me think of how wonderfully generous and kind people can be. I learned a lot about life that day."

Certainly, we can take to heart a lesson in compassion from this story, but there is more. Evidently there were two people aware of the man's plight. One, the writer, who merely observed and looked but did not act. The other, the woman, who observed, looked, and acted. A kind thought is of little value until it is acted upon.

Thought for the Day

Compassion means justice.

Meister Eckhart

Rescue me...save my life.
Psalm 35:17

Grace Can Restore Us

A decade ago the superintendent of a large Ohio school district committed suicide. He was a graduate of Harvard University and Temple University.

For over twenty-five years, this man had been an outstanding member of his community. He had an illustrious career as an educator, administrator, and civic leader.

As his leadership became subject to rising criticism, however, the man faced a time of scrutiny. Various groups called for his dismissal, while others continued to be supportive. Through that time, he became extremely depressed and despondent.

Finally, after giving a radio interview one morning, the man went to his office at the school, wrote a suicide note, and shot himself. His note declared: "Life's purpose seems to be lost."

There are times when we experience life's harsh, negative side. It can drive us to despair. Yet it is vital to recall that God's grace can restore us. We must ask for it, and we must be patient. God can help us deal with the pain. God can even terminate the pain—but we do not need to terminate our lives.

Thought for the Day

Down in the human heart, crushed by the tempter,
Feelings lie buried that grace can restore;
Touched by a loving heart, wakened by kindness
Chords that were broken will vibrate once more.

Fanny J. Crosby

You crowned him with glory and honor.
Psalm 8:5

The Importance of Self-Acceptance

An ancient legend tells of a man who lived in a small village. Due to birth defects, his body was twisted and his face severely disfigured. Village adults stared at him and children ran from him. Even the village dogs barked at his presence. Eventually, the man's hurt turned to bitterness, and he left the village of his birth to live alone deep in the forest.

Living alone in the woods brought him some peace because no one stared, teased, or ran from him. However, the pain of rejection experienced earlier lingered. One day a stranger arrived at the hermit's hut and, as they sat together, the hermit asked the visitor to offer a prayer for the meal. The visitor declined saying, "You are the master here. It is you who should offer the blessing."

And so, the hermit, nervous at first, spoke his gratitude for the beauty of the forest and the wonder of nature and the nourishment they were about to share. At the close of the prayer, the visitor said, "You have forgotten one thing. You have neglected to thank God for yourself." The hermit looked away and said nothing. The visitor continued, "You have retreated into the forest because you have despaired of your physical condition. But you have forgotten that in the eyes of God, you are far more beautiful than all the trees and all the flowers and all the birds of the forest."

The strange guest left, but the hermit did not forget his words. Eventually, he moved back to the town of his birth. Interestingly, people no longer stared, teased, or made him an object of ridicule. His heart sang with joy as he realized that he was living in the same town, with the same people, even the same dogs, but everything was transformed. It was transformed because he himself was transformed. He had learned to be self-accepting.

Today's reading is from Psalm 8, which speaks about human dignity and God's glory. It reminds us that we are all created in the image of God and that God views us with "glory and honor." God loves, respects, and values us. God gives us dignity.

Thought for the Day

If God be my friend,
I cannot be wretched.
Ovid

The protector of Israel
never dozes or sleeps.
Psalm 121:4

God Is Our Constant Protector

A California woman tells of an unforgettable experience that took place when she was five. At that time her great-grandmother lived with the family in a large Victorian house. At ninety-two, the great-grandmother was frail, virtually an invalid. She spent most of her time confined to her bedroom.

On rare occasions when she ventured out of her room, the elderly woman shuffled slowly, carefully balancing herself by holding onto the backs of chairs. The woman's bedroom was right next to the kitchen, where the five-year-old's mother usually tended a wood stove and stirred a pot of beans or soup.

One day the five-year-old was alone in the kitchen where the stove was already lit. She had often watched her mother use kerosene to start the fire, causing flames to leap up in a kaleidoscope of brilliant colors. The little girl decided to pour some kerosene herself.

She pushed a chair close to the stove and climbed up. Tilting the bottle of kerosene unsteadily with one hand, she opened the lid with the other. As she leaned over to pour the fluid, the bottom of her dress brushed the top of the stove.

Just at that moment her great-grandmother shuffled in and realized the danger her granddaughter was in. Immediately, the ninety-two-year-old pounced across the kitchen, grabbed the kerosene, and snatched the little girl off the chair.

Today's psalm reminds us that God is always on watch. Our God is a constant protector, aware of potential danger and harm even before we become aware of them. This day, let us live in gratitude for God's constant care.

Thought for the Day

Protect me, my Lord,
my boat is so small,
and your ocean so big.
A Fisherman's Prayer

I kept on believing even when I said
"I am completely crushed."
Psalm 116:10

Letting Pain Teach the Soul

Although horrifying experiences are not sent by God, they are used by God to instruct, inform, and inspire us. Cruel suffering often leads to deep learning and great insight. Novelist Eli Wiesel was transformed by horrendous suffering as a Jewish boy who barely survived the Holocaust. At age fourteen, this gentle, sensitive youth was herded up by Nazis and imprisoned. He suffered the loss of his mother, his father, and his baby sister.

While imprisoned, a gold-crowned tooth was ripped out of Wiesel's mouth. He was starved, beaten, forced into slave labor, and made to watch indescribable inhumanity. His faith in a God of mercy and justice was tested to its limits.

Yet Eli Wiesel emerged as a poetic and best-selling author who has transformed his personal witness of inhumanity into a universal condemnation of all violence, hatred, and bigotry. His writings are considered powerful literary expressions about the Holocaust. In 1986, Eli Wiesel was awarded the Nobel Peace Prize for Literature.

Across the centuries spiritual masters have known that suffering and tears have a purifying, rejuvenating, light-bearing power. In God's hands, the midnight of the soul gives way to a powerful dawn in the spirit. Today's psalm succinctly states: "I kept on believing, even when I said 'I am completely crushed.'" The writer reveals a spiritual maturity about his suffering. He knows that God is a divine alchemist. God takes our fears and the events which create them and transforms them into tools that can be used to deepen life and inform the soul.

The most compassionate and prophetic voices in a society often come from those who have suffered in great darkness. When we experience a difficult time that brings us great pain, even shame, we can take comfort with the truth: God will use our suffering for good.

Thought for the Day

It is by those who have suffered
that the world has been advanced.

Leo Tolstoy

The needy will not always be neglected.
Psalm 9:18

The Therapy of Helping

A widow, anxious about the approaching holidays, consulted her minister early in November. The festivities of the holidays always depressed her because she was alone. The pastor responded by picking up his pen and a sheet of paper. "I'm going to give you a prescription," he said.

The pastor wrote out the name and address of a very elderly couple who were poor and sick with the flu. "These people are in very difficult circumstances. Go do something for them," he urged.

Although the woman thought it was an odd response to her expression of loneliness, she went to see the elderly couple the following day. She found them in a tiny apartment, barely able to fix meals for each other, and terribly frightened that one of them would have to enter a nursing home.

The widow promised to help them. During the next several weeks, the woman cooked meals and baked cookies for them. Shortly after Christmas, she went back to see her pastor, this time with a bounce to her step and excitement in her voice. "I haven't baked or cooked much since my husband died," she explained. "But each week during the holidays, I shopped for ingredients to make good meals and bake cookies for the older couple. It proved to be the best holiday I've had in several years."

If you are like many in our society who find the holidays stressful, hectic, and depressing, think about the example of this widow. Consider bringing yourself holiday joy by helping a needy person. That way you will fulfill the statement of Scripture: "The needy will not always be neglected."

Thought for the Day

I often try to put depressed patients
in contact with someone they can help,
for there is something therapeutic
about doing another person a favor.
Dr. Alan Loy McGinnis

Give us success, O LORD!
Psalm 118:25

Learning to Say "Yes" More Often

One way of experiencing greater success and joy in living is to expand our boundaries by taking on challenges. This means learning to say "Yes" more often.

- Yes, I will give that speech.
- Yes, I will run for office.
- Yes, I will attend a social event full of strangers.
- Yes, I will try in-line skating.
- Yes, I will join an exercise class.
- Yes, I will host a dinner party.
- Yes, I will donate my time at a shelter.
- Yes, I will enroll in a class.
- Yes, I will reach out to a hurting person.
- Yes, I will look for a new position.
- Yes, I will go to the theater.
- Yes, I will compliment a stranger.
- Yes, I will lead a Bible study.
- Yes, I will learn a foreign language.
- Yes, I will do it!

This week when you would normally say "No" to a challenge, deliberately choose to say "Yes." Taking a risk is the only way to stretch your capacity for success.

Thought for the Day

Better hazard once
than always be in fear.
Thomas Fuller

You are my God and I give you thanks.
Psalm 118:28

Happiness Is a Choice

Some people make up their minds to be unhappy. Given the various emotional choices they can make, they choose to curse the darkness rather than light a candle; they choose to see darkness, not light.

For example, a woman whose income is very limited has chosen unhappiness. Because of her attitude she worsens her situation into an emotional and physical poverty. She refuses to ride a bus, visit the library, frequent a thrift shop, attend free community lectures, or walk through the park outside her apartment. She does not write letters or chat on the phone. Little by little, she made the poor choice of retreat, withdrawal, isolation, and bitterness.

On the other hand, there is a recently widowed woman who declares, "I don't have the time or energy to be depressed." Although her income is severely limited, she fills her life with positive, constructive activities. She reads good books, writes letter, goes to church, visits nursing homes, and attends a support group for the widowed. "When I feel down, I think of how lucky I am. I am surrounded by good books, good people, good experiences."

Recall these two examples and remember that happiness comes from within not without. It is always a choice that you must make.

-------- *Prayer for the Day* --------

Loving and glorious God,
Remind me again
that I am responsible for my happiness.
Remind me again
that happiness does not come from without,
but from within.
Remind me again
that happiness is a choice.
Today, help me to choose wisely.
VMP

He is not afraid of receiving bad news;
his faith is strong, and he trusts in the LORD.
Psalm 112:7

Outlook Determines Outcome

As producer of such smash films as *Fatal Attraction, Indecent Proposal,* and *The Accused,* Sherry Lansing has found success in the male-dominated Hollywood industry. Today, she is chairperson of Paramount Pictures. Lansing accredits her success to the exceptional role model of her mother.

At seventeen years of age, Lansing's mother fled from Nazi Germany and came to the United States. Here she sold dresses and learned to speak perfect English. When her father died of a heart attack, Lansing recalls seeing her mother cry and mourn and then take over his real-estate business. She vividly remembers an office manager saying, "You can't do this. You don't know anything about real estate." Lansing's mother quickly responded, "Teach me. I can do it." Throughout her own career, Lansing has used those sentences to guide, inspire, and motivate her: "Teach me. I can do it."

Our outlook determines the outcome. If we see ourselves succeeding, overcoming, completing, triumphing over a situation, we usually can do it. However, if our view is timid and hesitant, leaving large room for failure, that, too, will influence the outcome.

Today's psalm is a powerful reminder that we have good reason to be optimistic about our futures. In the presence of "bad news" and other setbacks, we need to exercise our faith and trust God to guide us safely through the dilemma.

Thought for the Day

Determine that the thing can and shall be done,
and then we shall find the way.
Abraham Lincoln

Don't hide yourself from your servant.
Psalm 69:17

God Uses "Down" Time

There are times when we painfully and powerfully feel God's absence. That is the dilemma of the psalm writer who cries: "Don't hide yourself from your servant." However, God is present in all of life's experiences, whether we sense that benevolent presence or not. In fact, God often uses "down" time to do much good work. On our part, we must continue to be faithful and patient.

A woman and her husband tell of adopting a three-year-old boy who had suffered great emotional and physical abuse. As a result, the child was filled with fear and anger, often lashing out at his adoptive parents. Although the couple believed that love could conquer all things, they quickly found themselves doubting and struggling. When the little boy was upset, the adoptive mother would gently hold and rock him. But his response was to declare: "I hate you! I want my real mommy!"

Each night when he prayed, the boy asked God for his green house; the foster home in which the boy lived was brown. His "old" home had been green. The adoptive mother's heart ached when she heard the prayer. Yet she and her husband continued to love and nurture the youth, trusting that God would bring them all together as a family.

"After a few months we had a breakthrough," the mother recalls. The boy ceased praying for his green house and began to thank God for the brown house. He also began including his new mother and father in his prayers. "That was when we knew that God was with us in our struggles and that love was paying off," she says.

When we feel God's absence let us recall this story. Let us remind ourselves that feelings are not always an accurate reflection of truth. Let us remind ourselves that God is always interested in our lives and is constantly working for us, even during "down" times.

Affirmations for the Day

I affirm your presence fills me with peace.
I affirm your presence illumines me,
and I act wisely and lovingly.
I affirm your presence dwells within me,
and I think clearly.

VMP

He guides me in the right paths.
Psalm 23:3

Following Our Inner Guide

Too often we are influenced by comments, opinions, and judgments others make of us. While we can learn from criticism, ultimately we must discover the importance of following our own inner guide and being less influenced by other voices. This pattern of minimizing the comments of others while maximizing the inner voice is common to many successful and creative people. Consider

- Lucille Ball, whose early drama teacher told her to try another profession—any profession other than acting
- Jimmy Durante, who was told his large nose would keep him out of show business
- Clint Eastwood, who was told by an executive at Universal Pictures to forget about being an actor because he spoke too slowly and his Adam's apple stuck out
- Peter Ilich Tchaikovsky, who suffered from terrible self-confidence because his teachers were very critical of him

Let us hear and heed that divine inner voice that constantly calls and guides us "in the right paths."

Prayer for the Day

Loving and gracious God,
I affirm that your guiding light
shows me where to go,
what to do,
whom to see,
when to act.
VMP

Praise him with drums and dancing.
Psalm 150:4

Cherishing Play

Psychologists note that one essential mark of maturity is the ability to play, to dance, to make music, to take delight in life. The Psalms are filled with references to singing, dancing, and being joyful.

"Praise him with drums and dancing" is today's reading. Too many of us focus upon the serious, heavy, responsible side of living. We need to balance that view with biblical joy. This may be what Jesus had in mind when he taught that the kingdom of God must be received like a child (Mark 10:15).

Let us resolve to increase our capacity for joy by following these steps:

- Do more of what you want to do and less of what you should do.
- Break a self-imposed rule from time to time. This will add variety, spice, and interest to your life.
- Eat something that tastes very good occasionally.
- Stay up late one night doing something you enjoy.
- Sleep in one morning like you did when you were younger.
- Invite your friends or children or spouse to join you in some board games one evening.

-------- *Thought for the Day* --------

Anyone who has the light to understand what I mean
and the grace to follow it
will experience, indeed,
the delight of the Lord's playfulness.
For like a father frolicking with his son,
he will hug and kiss the one
who comes to him
with a child's heart.

The Cloud of Unknowing

He leads the humble in the right way.
Psalm 25:9

Following Guidance Without Proof

Two days ago we considered the importance of following our inner guide. Often this is difficult to do because we lack exterior evidence for the inner voice.

As the season of Advent approaches, we can learn an important lesson from the Magi. According to the gospel stories, they simply started out to follow the star. They had no outer proof that a king was to be born; no outer proof that anything unusual would occur. However, something inside called and drew them. They followed their inner guide.

Actually, we share in their experience more often than we realize. Have you ever received a "leading" to follow a certain course of action? Have you ever received a "calling" to engage in a task that seemed workable and right?

Even though nothing in the visible world seems to warrant a certain action, we often feel almost a compulsion to follow an idea or course of action. If we try to explain intellectually why we feel something is right, we discover that language cannot properly convey the inner guidance.

It is often very difficult to explain such intuition through logic and language. It took faith for the Magi to follow their star. Similarly, it takes faith for us to follow our leading star. Yet it is when we move in faith that we realize our goals, dreams, and aspirations. So let us take a risk, a leap of faith, and follow guidance without external proof.

Prayer for the Day

Loving and kind God,
I affirm you are my light and my guide.
I walk confidently in the way you lead me.
I trust you to enfold, protect, support, and sustain me.
VMP

I have greater wisdom than old men.
Psalm 119:100

The Need for a Greater Wisdom

So many of our relationships with family, friends, and colleagues are warped and even poisoned by power struggles.

Too often we fight to get our way not because the I is truly important, but too certain that *we* are.

Yet we can win the immediate battle but lose in the larger arena of life. When we get to pick the movie, select the restaurant, choose the vacation spot, we often pay a costly price in pain, tension, and anxiety.

Clearly, most of us can use the greater wisdom mentioned in today's psalm. Instead of fighting, let us choose to bend a little. And, instead of resisting the wishes of others, let us choose the wisdom of exercising flexibility.

Today, let us surprise a loved one by giving in generously.

Today, let us surprise a family member by going along with his or her wishes.

Today, let us surprise a friend or colleague by going with his or her flow.

Today, let us begin to demonstrate a wisdom beyond our years.

Prayer for the Day

Loving God,
Help me respond
with knowledge and wisdom,
with intellect and spirit,
with head and heart.
Grant me your greater wisdom.
VMP

May my words and my thoughts be acceptable to you,
O Lord.
Psalm 19:14

Replacing Unhealthy Thoughts

There is great truth to the idea that we become what we think. Those who see themselves as weak, inferior to others, lacking in talent, often create their own psychological limits. On the other hand, those who see themselves as strong, talented, creative, can often make impressive achievements, personally and professionally.

If you are one who suffers from an inferiority complex, the good news is that you can replace unhealthy thoughts. It is possible to move from feeling hesitant and timid in life to feeling confident and bold. Several times a day, try reciting these affirmations:

- With God as my life companion, I can do anything.
- With God as my life companion, I can live a rich, satisfying life.
- With God as my life companion, I can manage any and every crisis.
- With God as my life companion, I can make a difference.
- With God as my life companion, I can establish and maintain healthy relationships.
- With God as my life companion, I can conquer the unconquerable.
- With God as my life companion, I can engage in work that is fulfilling.
- With God as my life companion, I can build the future that I dream about.
- With God as my life companion, I can overcome all problems.

Do not hesitate to recite these statements even in the face of evidence to the contrary. By repeating such affirmations several times daily and letting them sink deep into your subconscious, you can make your thoughts become your reality. If this exercise feels unnatural to you, begin with the psalmist's prayer, "May my words and my thoughts be acceptable to you, O Lord."

Thought for the Day

The secret of a better and more successful life
is to cast out those old dead, unhealthy thoughts.
Substitute for them new, vital, dynamic faith thoughts.
Norman Vincent Peale

Send your light and your truth.
Psalm 43:3

God's Thousand Points of Light

Shortly before the holidays in 1944 a young soldier received word he was given a three-day pass for the Christmas holidays. Since it was Christmas Eve it was too late to book passage home on a train or bus. With his duffle bag slung over his shoulder, the young man hitchhiked and was picked up by a family driving north.

As they rode, snow began to fall heavily. The one-hundred-fifty-mile trip took eight hours because conditions became severe. In the early hours of Christmas morning, the car stopped and the soldier walked the last few miles to his parents' home, the snow crunching under his feet.

Gazing toward the end of the road, he was surprised and delighted to see a small electric candle flickering in the window. Quickly, he climbed the steps on the porch. As the door opened, a delighted father peered out into the darkness. Warm embraces were followed by smiles of joy at the reunion.

Later that morning, as the father and son sat around the kitchen table enjoying breakfast, the youth asked, "Dad, why did you have the light burning when I arrived this morning? You weren't expecting me. For all you knew, I could have been shipped overseas by now."

The father responded simply, "I let it burn just in case you came home."

That story can serve as a reminder that God's light always burns to welcome us home. No matter where we have been, what we have or have not done, God's light and love always welcome us home.

Thought for the Day

God shall be my hope, my stay, my guide,
and lantern to my feet.
William Shakespeare

Sing, earth, and all who live on you!
Psalm 98:7

Practicing the Fine Art of Praise

Today, accept the challenge of asking yourself, *Who around me deserves a word of praise or affirmation or approval? my child, my spouse, my neighbor, the librarian, the postal clerk, my pastor, a teacher?*

When you identify people who could use a good word, pick up the phone, write a note, or go see them and "sing" their praises by offering a compliment. Here are some simple guidelines for practicing the fine art of praise:

- *Be sincere.* People love a compliment but can usually see through false expressions.
- *Be specific.* Complimenting someone on their appearance is nice, but saying "What a beautiful tie you are wearing!" is even nicer.
- *Be short.* Two or three sentences are plenty. Too many words can create an uncomfortable situation for everyone.
- *Be spontaneous.* Spontaneity generates freshness and enthusiasm, both of which add to the compliment.

Finally, don't be afraid to use superlatives when offering praise. Words and phrases such as "greatest," "best," "most handsome," may run a little ahead of reality but have a great impact nevertheless.

········ *Thought for the Day* ········

Christ has no body now on earth but yours;
No hands but yours; No feet but yours.
Yours are the eyes through which is to look out Christ's
compassion to the world. Yours are the feet
with which he is to go about doing good.
Yours are the hands with which he is to bless now.

Saint Teresa of Avila

When I see the wicked breaking your law,
I am filled with anger.
Psalm 119:53

Standing Up for Others

Jackie Robinson made baseball history when he joined the Brooklyn Dodgers in 1946, becoming the first black player in the major leagues. Although Robinson was an exceptional athlete, he was not easily accepted by others. He was abused verbally and physically by other ball players, and racial slurs from the spectators were common.

One day, Robinson was the victim of heightened hostility from the crowd as boos cascaded all over the stadium. Suddenly, the hostile action ceased when Pee Wee Reese, the team captain and Dodger shortstop, walked over and put his arm around Robinson. Reese remained there with his arm around Robinson until the jeering stopped. "That may have saved my career," Robinson later reflected. "Pee Wee made me feel that I belonged."

Although it is never easy, we must always stand up for those who are victimized by racism, sexism, agism. Whenever there is an injustice, we who are God's people must act courageously and redemptively. Like Pee Wee Reese, our anger over injustice should drive us to act as agents of change and transformation.

Thought for the Day

Delay in justice is injustice.

Walter Savage Landor

How good it is to give thanks to you, O LORD.
Psalm 92:1

Count Your Blessings

Everyone has heard the phrase "Count your blessings." That sentence took on new meaning and was permanently etched into the mind of a nine-year-old girl more than five decades ago. She lived on a farm in Iowa.

It was late November, the day before the American celebration of Thanksgiving Day, when the little girl was being tucked into bed. "Tomorrow will be a big day," her mother reminded her. The little girl drifted off thinking about the final preparations she and her mother had made for Thanksgiving dinner.

Her sleep ended abruptly when her father pulled her off the bed. She could see flames penetrating through her bedroom wall. Her father threw a blanket around her and held her close as he ran out the front door to place her on the snow-covered grass.

The little girl watched the snapping, fiery inferno sending bursts of sparks into the night sky. In a short time the entire house caved into a heap of smoldering ashes with terrible finality.

The next day the girl and her family, all in borrowed clothing, shared Thanksgiving dinner with relatives. As they bowed their heads for the prayer of thanks, the little girl wondered how she could be thankful. Her home and everything in it were gone.

"We've lost our home, but we're all safe and well, having Thanksgiving dinner with people we love," her mother said as if she had read the little girl's mind. "We can make a new home, but a family can't be replaced. We do have much to be thankful for," she added.

As the little girl heaped her plate with scrumptious food, her nine-year-old mind focused on the true meaning of Thanksgiving. It was no longer merely a holiday, but a time to count her blessings and give thanks.

Thought for the Day

A person who is to be happy
must actively enjoy his blessings.
Cicero

In him I trust, and I will not be afraid.
Psalm 56:11

Being an "I Will" Person

Too many people live half alive. They hold themselves back because of fear: fear of others, fear of failure, fear of their own ability and power. One way to begin moving away from being half alive toward more full living is to become an "I will" person like today's psalm writer: "In him I trust, and I will not be afraid."

The next time you face discouragement or fear, try saying:

- I will learn to be more independent.
- I will accept life's challenge and meet it.
- I will create new opportunities out of this crisis.
- I will find more meaning in my life.
- I will make some good come out of all this.
- I will celebrate what is good in my life.
- I will face every trial with faith.
- I will trust in God and not be afraid.

Affirmations for the Day

I am in charge of my thoughts and feelings.
God gives me strength to go on with my life.
I am accepting what cannot be changed.
God gives me all I need to overcome.

VMP

Don't be worried on account of the wicked.
Psalm 37:1

Face and Erase Worry

Worry plagues all of us at one time or another. Worry over a hostile person was very real to the psalm writer who managed to overcome it and advise others "Don't be worried on account of the wicked."

Whether our worry results from someone who is hostile toward us or some impersonal fear, there are three steps we can take to face and erase worry whenever it manifests itself: realize, redirect, and replace.

- *Realize* that worry is a misuse of the mind. When we worry, we play a mental movie that is usually catastrophic. Seldom do the things we worry about take place.
- *Redirect* the mind. Take the mental movie and push it beyond the dreaded event. When we see the worst that could happen, we can envision ourselves rising to the challenge, coping successfully, and overcoming fear.
- *Replace* worry thoughts with those of confidence. Thinking positive thoughts and seeing ourselves as triumphant survivors is a healthy way to expend mental energy.

Doing this opens the path to growth whereas worry merely takes us on the path to setback.

-------- *Affirmations for the Day* --------

God gives me strength for every trial.
God gives me grace to bear every difficulty.
God gives me power to transform every adversity.
VMP

Have faith, do not despair.
Psalm 27:14

Trust Your Hopes, Not Your Fears

The humorous story is told of a father whose son purchased his first eighteen-speed bicycle out of his own earnings. Shortly after he bought the bike, the young man learned that an all-state professional race was to take place in his town.

The young man decided to enter the race. His father tried to discourage his son, telling him that bike racing was a very sophisticated sport and that he had not done the proper training to compete. The young man told his father that no matter how it ended, the experience would be good. Disregarding his father's advice, the youth paid the fee and registered as a racer.

After the race the young man returned home beaming with pride. He came in first and was awarded the large, first-place cup. Of course, the father was surprised and astounded. When he asked his son how he managed to beat so many experienced racers, the young man replied, "When I arrived at the race, I overheard people talking about timing, pacing, and making your move at the right time. I realized then that I didn't know much about racing so when the race began, I just peddled as fast as I could and no one ever passed me."

The moral of the story? We must learn to trust our hopes, not our fears. The young man was motivated by the excitement and opportunity of racing. He was not held back by the fear of losing. He emerged the winner because he trusted his hopes and not his fears.

"Have faith, do not despair" is the advice of today's psalm writer.

-------- *Thought for the Day* --------

Hope is faith
holding out its hands in the dark.

George Iles

You, Lord, are all I have,
and you give me all I need.
Psalm 16:5

God Comes Through in Surprising Ways

A man was stricken with shock and grief when his young wife was tragically killed in an automobile accident. When the grief did not diminish, the man's physician suggested a trip abroad to take his mind off his pain.

The man arranged for a trip to Italy. However, the travel and change of scenery did not provide him with any relief. So one day he climbed up a mountain with a single thought in mind: *I will commit suicide and end my pain.*

After a long climb, the man found a place where he could end his life by jumping off the mountain. As he stood at the edge of the precipice, ready to make the plunge, he suddenly heard music. Looking around, he saw a barefoot youth who playing a harmonica.

As the man listened to the music, he was moved to tears. "I was completely despondent and consumed by my grief," he later told a friend. "But that music, so pure and so simple and so unexpected, affected me profoundly." He went on to explain that the music made him realize how much beauty and goodness life still had to offer in spite of his loss. It also made him see how self-absorbed he had become in his own pain.

This is a wonderful story that shows how God can come through for us in amazing ways. We must never underestimate God's creativity in breaking through to us.

Thought for the Day

God works powerfully,
but for the most part
gently and gradually.
John Newton

The Lord *sets prisoners free*
and gives sight to the blind.
Psalm 146:7-8

Cultivating Hopeful Thoughts

When a crisis emerges most people experience an array of negative emotions and thoughts ranging from guilt, anger, remorse, and self-blame to hostility, fear, lack of confidence, despair, and despondency.

The best antidote for depressing, immobilizing thoughts is to fight back with truer, more balanced, more hopeful thoughts. When hopelessness strikes, say to yourself:

- *Even though I have no control over what happened, I do have control over how I will react to it.* Psychologists say that how we respond to a crisis event is crucial. It can make the difference between coping successfully or failing.
- *I will take small steps toward healing, recovery, overcoming.* Progress is made by taking one step at a time. Don't try to fix everything. Just do what you can when you can, and give yourself time to recover and heal.
- *This, too, shall pass.* This phrase has a biblical ring to it. It means that new stability emerges from chaos and that crisis does subside. No pain or heartache lasts forever.
- My *future can be better than my past.* Rather than presuppose a negative future, remind yourself that things could actually turn out better than they were.
- *I will live in the present tense.* There is a simple but useful philosophy to live by which states that the past is finished, the future is uncertain, and all we have is the present. Therefore, shape the present into something comfortable, beautiful, useful, noble. Live today without worry or fear about the future.

During a crisis, recite biblical affirmations of faith such as today's psalm: "The Lord sets prisoners free and gives sight to the blind." Reciting such biblical affirmations deepens faith while building confidence.

Thought for the Day

A single event can awaken within us a stranger totally unknown to us. To live is to be slowly born.

Antoine de Saint-Exupery

Light shines in the darkness for good men.
Psalm 112:4

Poking Holes in the Darkness

Near the end of the nineteenth century, a boy from the country was visiting his relatives in the city of London. It was his first trip to that great urban center.

As the sun set on his first evening, the boy sat on the front porch of the house and gazed in amazement at the beautiful sights of the city. As he looked down the street, he saw a man making his way toward him. At each corner the man stopped beside a lamp post, and a round globe of light would burst forth through the darkness. As the boy watched in wonderment, the street gradually changed from darkness to light.

The young boy became so excited by what he saw that he ran into the house and exclaimed, "There's a man outside poking holes in the darkness."

That phrase is an appropriate image for every Christian. We are to be the people of God, women and men who "poke holes in the darkness."

- Wherever there is injury, we are to be healers.
- Wherever there is hate, we are to be living expressions of God's love.
- Wherever there is cruelty, we are to be kind, compassionate, loving.

By living as the people of God, we "poke holes in the darkness" which surrounds so many people.

Prayer for the Day

Loving God,
Remind me often
that you have not asked me
to be the light of the world,
nor do I have to light the whole world.
But I do have to light my part.
VMP

I will praise God with a song;
I will proclaim his greatness by giving him thanks.
Psalm 69:30

A Living Gift or a Memorial Gift

In 1969 a young American was killed in Vietnam. After his parents grieved, they felt compelled to make a sizable memorial gift in memory of their son. At Thanksgiving, they spoke with their pastor and explained that they wanted the gift to be given quietly and privately. They did not want to be personally acknowledged in any way and said that the memorial was their way of expressing gratitude to God for the gift of their son whom they enjoyed for twenty years.

The pastor persuaded the parents to go public saying that their gift would sharpen the meaning of Thanksgiving for everyone who was present in worship that year. Reluctantly, the parents agreed to the suggestion, and on Thanksgiving, the pastor publicly accepted the memorial check from the parents. He explained to the congregation how it came to be given and how it would be used in the church.

That presentation had an impact on several families in the congregation. A few weeks later these families offered a gift to the church and explained that theirs was a "living" gift rather than a memorial gift. "Our sons did not die in the war and we want to publicly express gratitude to God," they told the surprised pastor.

These families make an excellent point. So often we give memorial gifts after a death but seldom offer a living gift that expresses gratitude to God for the gifts of life, health, happiness, security, success.

Thought for the Day

Loving God,
It is with a grateful heart
that I thank you
for all the benefits
you have given
and for all the blessings
that you cause to flow over me.
VMP

You will make me greater than ever.
Psalm 71:21

Using Growth Sentences

The person who wrote today's psalm is clearly a survivor. Survivors use growth sentences: "You will make me greater than ever." Victims resort to the language of loss and limitation: "I'll never get over this."

The words you use to describe your crisis can make a difference in how you move through the crisis because words do more than describe your feelings; they shape your thoughts and actions. Whenever a crisis looms, follow the example of today's psalm writer and use growth sentences such as

- I am discovering strengths I never knew I possessed.
- I am learning to take care of myself.
- I am developing new relationships.
- I am acquiring new, important skills.
- I am gaining a greater appreciation of life.
- I am finding that I can cope with adversity, change, termination, chaos.
- I am broadening my awareness of kindness and compassion.
- I am infinitely more grateful than I was before.
- I am deepening my faith in God.

Victims use language that leads to a dead end. Survivors use language that opens doors to growth and opportunity.

Affirmations for the Day

God cares about me.
God is helping me survive and grow.
God empowers me to adapt creatively.
VMP

Give me wisdom....
Psalm 119:66

Responding With Wisdom

From several centuries ago comes a story of an Eastern Orthodox priest named Father Demetrius. He was an exceptional priest with great pastoral gifts. One day a riot broke out in his city causing great loss of life and much property damage.

One family in his parish lost everything they owned: their home, all their possessions, and their family business. Among the first offering assistance was Father Demetrius. When he offered to take the youngest daughter shopping for new clothing, he sensed that the little girl was not only frightened by what took place but was feeling extremely vulnerable.

Together the two went to the market where the little girl selected a new wardrobe. When that task was complete to the little girl's satisfaction, Father Demetrius took her to a jeweler where she was allowed to select a ring that he paid for.

When the people of the community heard about the purchase of a ring, they became privately critical of Father Demetrius. Some said it was a foolish extravagance. Others shook their heads in disbelief saying the priest was naive and had no business sense whatsoever.

One day Father Demetrius happened to overhear the criticisms and quietly responded, "I just wanted to give the little girl something that would help her know she is loved and valued."

The priest exhibited great wisdom. The ring he purchased after the riot would indeed become a lifelong symbol of love, value, caring, compassion, and kindness from a time and place where there had been hatred and destruction.

When we see a need, let us first ask God how we can respond with wisdom, thus giving greater meaning to our response.

Prayer for the Day

Loving and glorious God,
Grant me wisdom in my daily interactions with others
that I may be a true friend to the lonely,
a source of hope for the sick,
a point of light for those in darkness.

VMP

Make your way plain for me to follow.
Psalm 5:8

Using Adversity as Energy

Darrell Waltrip is a world-class champion stock car driver who has twice won the Grand National Winston Cup. When he was six years old, his grandparents would take him to the dirt track races where he grew to love the cars, the noise, and the commotion. "Racing is all I ever wanted to do since then," he said in a *New York Times* interview.

But when Waltrip began racing full time in 1973, he found it difficult. He had few sponsors and very little money. Waltrip and his wife, Stevie, slept in a truck, ate from canned goods, and were constantly borrowing money from family and friends just to keep him racing.

Interestingly but not surprisingly, Waltrip values that time. "We were on the bottom, but I think that you have to be on the bottom once to be able to succeed," he explained. "It spurs you on. It gives you the determination and desire to make it to the top."

Waltrip is a good example of someone who could take adversity and let it drive him forward. Rather than be defeated by his circumstances, he chose to let it become the energy and fuel that propelled him onward toward his goals and dreams.

That ability is something given to all of us by God. We can look at adversity and give up, or we can shape our thoughts and direct our wills so that the circumstances drive us to change things. As you move toward your goals, keep in mind the psalmist's statement: You "are guided and protected by the Lord."

-------- *Thought for the Day* --------

Do not wish to be anything but what you are,
and try to be that perfectly.
Saint Francis de Sales

With God on our side we will win.
Psalm 60:12

Power for Life's Journey

A television documentary on the majestic American eagle described how these birds nurture their young in nests built on cliffs at high altitudes. The camera caught shots of a little eagle standing on the edge of a nest looking down into the great expanse below. The small eagle was ready to take off on its first flight.

Of course, one cannot know what is in the mind of an eagle, but could that small creature have been thinking *How can my wings ever make it? Where will I get the strength? How will I accomplish this feat?*

Yet when that little eagle made the great leap from the safety of the nest into the unknown skies, he discovered that the air itself supported him and his wings. The air and the winds undergirded him and lifted him up higher and higher.

That is a parable of our own living. There are times when we cannot depend merely on our own resources, our own power. Yet the power we need is available to us always.

The psalmist reminds us that we can trust unconditionally the power of God to undergird and support us through life's journey.

Thought for the Day

In God's faithfulness lies eternal security.

Corrie Ten Boom

The LORD has been good to me.
Psalm 116:7

Symbols of Gratitude

Every Christmas for several decades, Johnny Horan and his wife carefully have placed two refrigerator racks underneath their Christmas tree. Those refrigerator racks are symbols of their deep gratitude to God for safety from certain death.

The saving event took place in December 1955. That year the couple had completed a military tour of duty in Japan. Johnny's wife was sailing from Japan to Seattle, and Johnny was flying from Fort Bragg, North Carolina, to Seattle, Washington, where they were to be reunited. Somewhere over the Cascade Mountains, the plane, a C-45 transport, began to spin out of control. At ten thousand feet, the pilot ordered his passenger to parachute out to safety. Ironically, the plane landed safely leaving Johnny Horan to find his way down the mountains.

After trudging all night Johnny found a cabin. He tried to make snowshoes out of shingles from the roof, but they fell apart when he walked on them. The next morning Johnny's feet were so swollen from the cold that he couldn't put on his boots. Four days later, on December 22, Johnny was out of ideas. He slumped into the corner of the cabin desperately analyzing every item in sight.

Then, something told him to open the refrigerator again, although he knew it was empty. When he opened the refrigerator door, his spirits soared: a rack! He found a second refrigerator rack under a bed. Using strips of material cut from his parachute, Johnny strapped the racks to his feet and set out in the deep snow.

At 4 p.m. the next day, Johnny staggered onto a road where two men recognized him as the lost parachutist. Although doctors had to amputate all his toes, Johnny Horan survived and was reunited with his wife. Since that Christmas, the Horans have carefully set out the refrigerator racks as symbols of gratitude.

As the Christmas season begins, consider the symbols of gratitude you might place under your tree.

Prayer for the Day

Loving and gracious God,
Do not let me be the kind of person
who takes things for granted.
May I be a person
who receives all of your blessings
with sincere gratitude.
VMP

Be glad and rejoice
because of what the LORD has done.
Psalm 32:11

Finding the Christmas Spirit

The signs of Christmas are appearing everywhere. Shopping centers are decorated and stores play Christmas music. But how do you catch the spirit of Christmas? Here are some ways to capture the true pleasures of this season.

- *Sight.* A simple string of lights dangling over the door of a homeless shelter can remind you of what the season is all about. Be reminded that God is the light of the world.
- *Sound.* Community and church choirs are reminders of the coming of Christ. Be reminded that God is the hope of the world.
- *Speech.* Churches have additional services this time of year where you can hear Bible readings and sermons tell of Christ's birth. Be reminded that God is love.
- *Smell.* People do more baking this time of year, often sharing their cookies, cakes, pies, and breads with family, friends, and neighbors. Be reminded that God's compassion is contagious.

As the pace of this season picks up, allow your senses to capture the spirit of Christmas. Then, once you find it, share it with your family, friends, neighbors, and colleagues.

Thought for the Day

How many observe Christ's birthday!
How few, his precepts!
O! 'Tis easier to keep holidays
than commandments.

Ben Franklin

Redeem me and be merciful to me.
Psalm 26:11
(New International Version)

The Power of God to Save Us

Distinguished German pastor and educator Helmut Thielicke said he had an old photograph that he always kept near his desk: a snapshot of a nativity pageant. The photograph captures a group of rough looking men wearing white robes and holding candles while another group of men kneel before them, feigning terror. It is clear that the rough-looking men are angels speaking to the frightened shepherds.

Why does Dr. Thielicke keep this snapshot within eyesight on his desk? He explains that the photograph was taken at a nearby prison. The men in the snapshot are all convicted felons, hardened criminals whose lives were truly transformed by Christ. In his memorable photograph, convicted murderers and thieves are dressed like angels and humble shepherds of faith.

For Dr. Thielicke, the snapshot is a beautiful parable of God's power to redeem all of us. The picture is a visible reminder of God's power to overcome human depravity, thoroughly changing us.

Thought for the Day

Whenever Jesus Christ is accepted as Lord,
men have the chance
to make a new beginning in their life,
and they face possibilities
that no world could ever offer of itself.
Helmut Thielicke

Reach down from above,
pull me out of the deep water.
Psalm 144:7

Human Extremity Is God's Opportunity

In a remarkable article published in the *New York Times Magazine*, titled "Returning to Church," novelist Dan Wakefield movingly described his turn to God. He told of a torturous time in his life when a long-standing relationship with a woman friend dissolved. Within a span of a few months, he buried both of his parents, became financially destitute, realized tremendous dissatisfaction with his work, and lost this valued relationship. To numb his pain, Wakefield turned to liquor and drugs, always a self-destructive action.

Wakefield then had a chance conversation with a house painter who was looking for a place to attend Mass on Christmas Eve. That encounter stimulated Wakefield's spirit. He decided to attend a Christmas candlelight service which then led him to participate in other worship services as well as Bible study. Soon he was developing his spiritual life.

As Wakefield's religious involvement increased, he experienced a growing freedom from his sense of purposelessness. He no longer felt as though he was drifting randomly. Rather, his life felt like it was moving in a healthy direction. Of his life change he wrote, "The only concept I know to describe such experience is that of 'grace,' and the accompanying adjective 'amazing' comes to mind along with it."

Often our extreme situations become the door that permits God to enter our lives. We need to remember that God is always seeking ways to enter our lives not only to "pull us out of the deep water" but to fill us with love, joy, peace, power, security, stability, wisdom, and many other blessings.

Thought for the Day

God is never found accidentally.

A. W. Tozer

Come, praise the LORD.
Psalm 134:1

Capturing the Joy of Advent

A great many people express increased frustration during the Christmas season. The complaints usually are twofold: financial ("I spend large amounts of money on gifts that nobody really needs") and emotional ("I dread this time of year because I am forced to spend time with people I do not enjoy being with"). Consequently, Advent is not a time to "Come, praise the Lord."

However, with a little creativity and change of attitude, Advent can be a season of joy. Here are some simple suggestions:

- *Focus on the spiritual aspects of Advent*. Read biblical accounts of Christ's birth. Take time to worship each week, perhaps more than once. Buy an inspirational book about Christmas, and read it from cover to cover.
- *Offer gifts that build relationships*. Take a valued friend out for lunch as a Christmas gift. Invite a special friend for dinner.
- *Give something of lasting value*. A good friend of mine was a POW in Vietnam for nearly six years. A talented artist, he gave me one of his sketches depicting life as a POW. It hangs on the wall of my writing studio year round and will be there for many, many years. Every time I see his sketch, I think of him and thank God for his friendship.
- *Create a tradition*. Identify something you can do every year to make Advent unique. This may include adopting a needy family and providing them with Christmas gifts, baking special desserts as surprise gifts to people who would not expect a gift from you, treating a group of children to an afternoon of skating.
- *Donate to a charity*. Rather than buying many presents, cut back and donate what is saved to a worthwhile charity. In September one family sent a letter to scattered uncles, aunts, nieces, nephews, and cousins asking they not send gifts at Christmas and that the equivalent amount be given to a local charity.

Thought for the Day

It is Christmas every time you let God
love others through you.

Mother Teresa of Calcutta

Teach us to number our days aright.
Psalm 90:12
(New International Version)

Evaluating the Use of Time

The story is told of a man who took great pride in being on time and adhering tightly to his schedule. His daily routine was precise and he followed it rigidly. If one part of his daily agenda was mistimed or late, it would throw his schedule off and the entire day's planned events would crumble.

Alas, one morning his alarm failed to go off, and the man slept fifteen minutes later than his scheduled time. When he did awake, he was panic stricken. Realizing he might be late for work, the man raced through each part of his morning schedule. As a result, he cut himself while shaving, burned his mouth on the coffee, tripped and fell on his way out the door. As he rushed to the ferry which would take him to work, he saw the boat fifteen feet from shore.

"I think I can make it," he convinced himself. Running toward the dock at full speed, the man made an enormous leap out into the water and, miraculously, landed with a heavy thud on the deck of the ferry. The captain rushed down to make sure the man was not injured. "Man, that was a tremendous jump," the captain said. "But if you would have waited just another minute, we would have been at the dock!"

In December, the pace of life picks up considerably for most of us. There are gifts to purchase, parties to attend, additional worship services and related religious activities, special school programs involving children, and so forth. Thus December provides an ideal opportunity for evaluating the use of our time. Here are some questions to prayerfully ask yourself:

- What is central and what is peripheral?
- What is important and what is not important?
- Is my schedule so crowded that I am not allowing time for prayer, meditation, spiritual reading?
- Are my relationships with people being short-changed because I am so busy?

-------- *Prayer for the Day* --------

Eternal God,
In my earthly pilgrimage help me
use my time wisely, compassionately, lovingly.
VMP

Practice good...pursue it.
Psalm 34:14
(Jerusalem Bible)

Doing an Unexpected Christmas Kindness

In addition to sharing kindness with family, friends, and colleagues, consider doing an unexpected kindness for someone beyond your normal circle of relationships. There is great power in such an unexpected kindness.

One man wrote a letter to the editor of his community newspaper telling of the delight he experienced when a stranger treated him with a very kind act. It was Christmas night and he was driving his eighty-four-year-old grandmother home after a day of festivity. As they reached the highway toll booth, the man extended his hand to pay the attendant. She refused his money saying, "You do not have to pay the toll. The person ahead of you has paid it for you. And he asked me to wish you a Merry Christmas."

The recipient of that kind act was astonished. Pondering that unexpected kindness from a stranger, the man stated that Christmas night will "shine like a diamond" in his memory. He went on to say that when he shared that experience with other family members, they too were profoundly affected by the stranger's kindness.

This Christmas, as you shop and buy, give and receive, remember to do a spontaneous act of kindness for someone who would not expect it from you. Join with the stranger on the toll road in making Christmas more memorable for someone else.

Prayer for the Day

Eternal and glorious God,
Enlighten my living
and give me wisdom in my actions,
purity in my motives,
love in my thoughts,
so that I may be your faithful witness.
VMP

God will put his angels in charge of you
to protect you wherever you go.
Psalm 91:11

God's Protective Angels

Angels figured prominently at the time of Jesus' birth. They brought comforting, good news to Mary, Joseph, and the shepherds. These special emissaries of God continue to do their good work today.

A man identifying himself only as "a firm believer in North Carolina" wrote an advice columnist to tell of his supernatural encounter with an angel. He had been working the third shift and had a thirty-minute drive home after getting off work at 8 a.m. One morning he was completely exhausted and fell asleep at the wheel.

Suddenly, he was awakened by a strong male voice calling out his name. "Firm believer" opened his eyes to see he had crossed the center line and was face to face with an eighteen-wheeler. There was no way for him to avoid a collision yet, in a split second, he was able to get back on the right side of the highway.

"I know my guardian angel was watching over me that day and God called my name," he said.

The presence of God's protective angels is just another reminder that we have not been left alone in the world; that God is vitally interested in our well-being and can act decisively when danger lurks.

Thought for the Day

Christians should never fail
to sense the operation
of angelic glory.
It forever eclipses
the world of demonic powers,
as the sun does a candle's light.
Billy Graham

The good man is generous with his gifts.
Psalm 37:21

Be an Angel for Christmas

Diane recalls how difficult it was to capture the spirit of Christmas for herself and her family during one Advent season. The mortgage payment was overdue, and the electricity was scheduled to be shut off. Employment had slowed down, and the family had very little income and no savings.

Rummaging through an old box of childhood memorabilia, Diane came across her collection of Beatles cards from the early sixties. Pawning those cards would bring in some money to purchase gifts for her children. She sold one hundred cards for seventeen cents each. As she passed a card and gift shop on the way home, she became mesmerized by a collection of carved wooden ornaments on display in the window. Going inside she purchased three, spending nine dollars of her gift money.

Arriving home, Diane hung the delicate ornaments on the tree, but her joy quickly turned to guilt. The money spent for the ornaments meant fewer gifts for her children. The next day she took the ornaments back to see if she could get a refund. Speaking with the manager in a small room in the back of the store, Diane tearfully explained her predicament. The manager listened carefully, took Diane to the cash register, and promptly handed her nine dollars. When Diane handed him the ornaments, he refused to take them. "Take those ornaments home and hang them on your tree. Use the money as you see fit." The manager then gave his tearful customer some stuffed animals and candy canes, instructing her to place them in her children's stockings. "I will never forget this man who was an angel to me one Christmas when times were tough," Diane concludes with a smile.

This December consider being an angel. Reach out to those in need. Brighten their day by lifting their burden.

Prayer for the Day

Eternal and glorious God,
Let my life abound in actions of mercy,
kindness, compassion, and love.
Let me be an angel this Christmas.
VMP

You welcome me as an honored guest.
Psalm 23:5

Treat Yourself With Tenderness

In this season which highlights the virtues of kindness, compassion, and mercy, we must remember to treat ourselves with tenderness as well. When we are tempted to be harsh with ourselves, let us recall the psalmist's reminder that God treats us as an "honored guest."

This December let us

- speak nicely to ourselves
- see our weakness through loving eyes
- treat ourselves with respect and courtesy
- make a sincere effort to affirm our lives
- identify our many God-given virtues and talents
- appreciate our capacity to give and receive love
- quiet the harsh inner voice that reviews our behavior

This December let us catch and stop ourselves when we begin to refer to ourselves in derogatory terms like fat, boring, sloppy, ugly, unpleasant. Let us remind ourselves that such language is no way to talk to a friend.

This December let us attach the same high value to ourselves as God does.

Thought for the Day

Our humanity were a poor thing
were it not for the divinity
that stirs within us.

Francis Bacon

Those who obey him have all they need.
Psalm 34:9

Holding On to What Really Counts

While making a routine flight from Portland, Maine, to Boston, Massachusetts, pilot Henry Dempsey heard an unusual noise near the rear of his small commuter aircraft. He turned the controls over to the copilot and went back to investigate.

As he reached the tail section, the plane hit an air pocket and Henry was thrust against the rear door. In a split second he discovered the source of the mysterious noise: the rear door had not been properly latched prior to take off. As the weight of Henry's body fell against the unlocked door, it flew open, sucking the unsuspecting pilot out of the jet.

When the red warning light flashed in the cockpit, the copilot nervously radioed the nearest control tower. Trying to stay composed, he reported his colleague had accidentally fallen out of the plane and requested permission to land. He also requested that a rescue helicopter be dispatched to search the ocean for the lost pilot.

Miraculously, Dempsey had not fallen into the Atlantic but had managed to grab hold of the outdoor ladder at the rear of the plane. There he clung by his bare hands, four thousand feet in the air. The aircraft continued flying at two hundred miles per hour for another ten minutes until the copilot was able to land. As the plane touched down, Dempsey's head was a mere twelve inches above the runway. Henry Dempsey survived with only minor scrapes to his body, but it took airport personnel several minutes to pry his hands loose from the ladder.

As we celebrate Advent, this is a good time to ask ourselves *What am I holding on to that tightly?* All of us have "ladders" to which we cling tenaciously: the ladder of success, wealth, prestige, material things. Like Henry Dempsey, we need to keep holding on to what really counts, remembering the psalmist's words: "Those who obey him have all they need."

Prayer for the Day

Loving and glorious God,
Guide my thinking and my living,
by your higher love and wisdom.

VMP

Have faith, do not despair.
Trust in the LORD.
Psalm 27:14

Becoming Better, Not Bitter

Art Buchwald is a popular syndicated humor columnist. When he is asked, "How do you become a humorist?" he offers this standard answer, "Well, first you have to become a foster child."

In his autobiography, *Leaving Home: A Memoir,* Buchwald tells of the desperate circumstances which plagued his family and his childhood. He never met his mother, though she lived until he was in his thirties. Afflicted with depression, she spent most of her life in mental institutions. When Buchwald was a child, his family did not let him visit her. When he was an adult, he chose not to, preferring the "mother" of his imagination.

Buchwald's father, a drapery installer, tried to support Buchwald and his three older sisters, but the Depression kept the father completely destitute. He appealed to the state, asking that his children be placed in the Hebrew Orphan Asylum. From 1931, when he was six, until he was fifteen, Buchwald lived in the orphanage or various foster homes. It was a difficult, lonely, confusing, and emotionally painful childhood.

Because of his own unfortunate and unhappy life, Buchwald decided to become a humorist. His one and only goal was to make people laugh—and he has succeeded. He has risen above and beyond his tragic circumstances.

Art Buchwald is an example of the truth that God has created us to emerge victorious over life's crises and pains. When difficulties, large and small, come our way, we must learn to tap our God-given inner strengths, abilities, and talents. We can lean on God and follow the psalmist's advice: "Trust in the Lord. Have faith, do not despair."

Affirmations for the Day

I freely confide in God.
I fully trust God to guide me.
I faithfully wait for God to provide
this day and every day.

VMP

Let us sing for joy to God.
Psalm 95:1

Christmas Is Worth the Effort

Most people experience this time of year as extremely hectic. Sometimes we wonder whether or not it is worth the effort. Perhaps this story of an African youth and his missionary teacher can guide us.

One Christmas, the youth, whose family was very poor, wanted to show his appreciation for his missionary teacher by offering her a special Christmas gift. He decided to bring her a unique and beautiful seashell. Since he lived inland, it meant a long, long walk of several hours for him to go to the seashore. It also meant a walk over rough terrain to the only place on the coast where these particular shells could be found.

After the youth found just the seashell he felt would be the most appropriate, he made the long journey back to his village and presented the teacher with his gift. The teacher was deeply touched. "You've traveled so far to bring me such a wonderful present."

The boy looked puzzled, then his eyes widened with excitement and he responded, "Oh, Teacher," he explained, "the long walk is part of the gift."

The next time you feel frazzled and hassled by the crowds, the hectic pace, the late-night wrapping, remind yourself that bringing Christmas joy is worth the effort. Say to yourself, *The long walk is part of the gift.*

This Christmas let us truly "sing for joy to God."

Thought for the Day

Try to fulfill each day's task
steadily and cheerfully.
Be merry, really merry.
The life of a true Christian
should be a perpetual jubilee,
a prelude to the festivals of eternity.

Theophane Venard

I sing a hymn of thanksgiving
and tell all of your wonderful deeds.
Psalm 26:7

Living With Joy Day by Day

This is the season of joy. We can heighten our joy as well as that of others by generating love and goodwill. Each day from now until Christmas look for an opportunity to generate joy by

- ending a quarrel
- keeping a promise
- letting go of an old hurt
- standing up against injustice
- replacing fear with faith
- transforming suspicion into trust
- encouraging a child
- complimenting a stranger
- maintaining contact with an old friend
- working on behalf of the less fortunate
- promoting harmony between opposing individuals
- dreaming a great dream
- acting on your dream
- singing a cheerful song or hymn
- praying for an enemy

By taking these types of redemptive actions we will live with joy day by day. Not only will our lives have a better and brighter tone, but those around us will be blessed by our acts.

Thought for the Day

Never lose an opportunity for seeing anything that is beautiful;
for beauty is God's handwriting—a wayside sacrament.
Welcome it in every fair face, in every fair sky,
in every fair flower, and thank God,
for it is a cup of blessing.

Ralph Waldo Emerson

You protect me from the power of death.
Psalm 16:10

Our Invisible Means of Support

Some individuals dramatically experience the protecting power of God. One woman tells of driving home after visiting her family at Christmas. Traffic on the two-lane road was slow but steady. As the temperatures dropped, the highway became slippery.

Suddenly, her wheels skidded and the brakes locked. Her car was careening off the road into a guardrail. "God, help me!" she cried out. The impact of the crash threw her over the seat and she blacked out. When she became conscious, the woman was on the floor in the back seat. A man and a young boy were bent over her. "You hit a patch of ice," the man explained. "A policeman saw the whole thing. He's radioing for help."

Peering out the window, the woman realized her car had been moved to the opposite side of the highway and parked safely on the grass off the shoulder. *How in the world did I get over here?* she wondered. Shortly the policeman came over and asked, "What happened to your companion?"

Puzzled, the woman responded, "What companion?"

"He drove the car to this spot," the officer said. "I saw him drive." The father of the boy added, "I saw him too. He crossed the lane of oncoming traffic and parked right here. But no one got out. In fact, we had to break a window to get in."

Silently and profoundly, the woman realized that no one had been in the car with her. Yet someone had been with her and had driven the car to safety.

Although not all of us will have such a dramatic encounter with God's protecting power, we should always remember that there is an invisible means of support for us.

Thought for the Day

God's calling the shots.
He's running the show.
Either he's in full control
or he's off his throne.
Charles S. Swindoll

He is good to everyone.
Psalm 145:9

Expanding and Extending Our Love

Diane and Ken tell of meeting a new couple at church one Sunday. As they visited together during the coffee hour following the service, Diane and Ken described the friendly neighborhood they lived in. Sympathetically, they listened to the other couple lament the fact that their neighborhood was just the opposite: cold and unfriendly.

After saying good-bye, the two couples got into their respective cars and drove home. As Ken and Diane approached their house, they were extremely embarrassed to see that their newfound friends were pulling into the driveway next to their own.

In this season of joy and goodwill, let us ask ourselves if we are truly friendly people. Are we people who embrace people who are new to the community? Are we people who welcome the stranger in our presence? Are we people whose love is wide enough to include the outsider? Are we people who are ready to extend our love beyond our immediate family? Are we people who are constantly expanding our circle of friends?

In today's reading the psalmist praises God because "he is good to everyone." Let us accurately mirror God's compassion and love by being "good to everyone" we encounter.

-------- Prayer for the Day --------

O God,
Where there are only strangers,
let me bring friendship and hospitality;
where there is indifference,
let me bring caring and concern.
O God,
In the midst of darkness and despair,
discouragement and defeat,
let me bring light and hope,
joy and victory.
VMP

The righteous are guided...by the L*ORD.*
Psalm 1:6

Responding to Need Immediately

A pastor regretfully recalls a bitter cold Christmas Eve several years ago when a black youth, without gloves, scarf, or hat, asked if he could shovel snow from his driveway. After turning the youth away, the pastor immediately felt remorse.

Upon opening the door again, the pastor found the youth was gone; there was no sign of him. He got into his car and drove up and down the neighborhood streets, but never found him.

There is this important series of lessons from such an experience:

- We need to ask for God's help to truly see and respond to people in need.
- We need to be grateful to God for our blessings and share our abundance with others who are less fortunate.
- We need to respond immediately and boldly when God provides us with opportunities to help—"The righteous are guided...by the Lord."
- We need to exhibit the love and the light of compassion, mercy, and kindness to others.

Thought for the Day

So many gods, so many creeds,
So many paths that wind and wind,
When just the art of being kind
is all this sad world needs.
Ella Wheeler Wilcox

They do not speak peaceably.
Psalm 35:20
(New International Version)

Being Channels of Peace on Earth

In this season of peace and goodwill, let us briefly conduct an examination of conscience to be certain that we are being channels of peace on earth.

- When I witness hatred, am I quick to bring acceptance and love?
- Where there is wrong, do I bring the spirit of forgiveness?
- When I experience discord around me, do I act in ways to create harmony?
- Where there is fear and doubt, do I live in faith and hope?
- When others experience despair and darkness, am I a source of consolation and light?
- Where there are heavy loads being carried, am I the one who lightens the burden?
- When others experience shadows and sadness, do I provide illumination and joy?

-------- *Prayer for the Day* --------

Loving and holy God,
Let me be a channel of peace on earth.
Day by day may my life reflect
your love, peace, joy, light, hope,
forgiveness, harmony, wisdom.
Let there be peace on our earth
and let it begin with me.
VMP

I will be glad and rejoice
because of your constant love.
Psalm 31:7

A Christmas Reflection on God's Love

This Christmas, let us all remember the reason for the season is God's love as revealed through Jesus Christ.

- God loves people even though they live and walk in darkness so he sent Jesus to be the light of the world.
- God loves families so he sent Jesus, not only to be in the family of Mary and Joseph but also to make all of us a part of the family of God.
- God loves needy, hurting, suffering people so he sent Jesus to comfort, encourage, heal.
- God loves people with abilities, talents, and resources so he sent Jesus to challenge them to use those things to build a better world.
- God loves people who suffered under injustice, oppression, cruelty so he sent Jesus to break chains and set prisoners free.
- God loves people whose vision is impaired and limited so he sent Jesus to build hopes and aspirations.
- God loves people who are marginalized, neglected, and rejected so he sent Jesus to love outcasts, untouchables and other social lepers.

Thought for the Day

It is Christmas
every time you let God
love others through you...
yes, it is Christmas
every time you smile at your brother
and offer him your hand.

Mother Teresa of Calcutta

I know that your goodness
and love will be with me all my life.
Psalm 23:6

Home Alone on Christmas Day

While most people will be with family and friends on Christmas day, many will be alone by choice or by circumstances. If that includes you (or someone you know), here are some creative ways to spend Christmas alone and cut down the feelings of loneliness:

- Read a special Christmas passage from the Bible or other inspirational book.
- Open any presents which have come your way.
- Plan now for a special Christmas meal. You can either prepare it yourself on Christmas day or look over the newspaper to see what restaurants will be open.
- Take a plate of food to someone who is also alone but unable to cook or get out of the house.
- Take time on Christmas day to write thank-you letters for gifts received, for favors given, or just to encourage someone who needs a lift.
- Telephone family and friends to wish them a merry Christmas. Be cheerful, optimist, and upbeat.
- Use the day to think about your life, review the past, and look at ways to revamp the future as a new year emerges.
- Spend time in prayer. Be sure to thank God for the many blessings received, not only in this season but in the previous eleven months as well.
- Reflect on today's psalm as it applies to your life, past, present, and into the future: "I know that your goodness and love will be with me all my life."

-------- *Affirmations for the Day* --------

God is so good.
God's goodness flows abundantly into my life.
I gladly accept God's goodness and blessings.
VMP

I can hardly see;
my eyes are so swollen from weeping.
Psalm 6:7

Banish the Blues

People who believe in God get the blues just like anyone else. Today's psalm writer is clearly depressed: "I can hardly see; my eyes are so swollen from weeping." Even though we know God loves us, we can experience depression. Here are some suggestions to help banish the blues:

- *Take a blessing inventory.* Make a list of all your assets: money, talent, friends, the love of family, meaningful work. You may be surprised how much you really have. Then take a moment to thank God.
- *List what is depressing you.* Write everything that is causing you to feel blue. If you have said or done something, make amends and seek forgiveness. If you have been hurt, privately forgive and begin to let it go.
- *Pamper yourself.* All of us need a little tender loving care once in a while. Do something that will make you happy today.
- *Improve your environment.* Maybe looking at the same four walls contributes to depression. Brighten things up with a new plant, curtains, or a piece of furniture.
- *Boost your health.* Your diet may be a contributing factor. Try to reduce or eliminate some items such as salt, caffeine, sugar. Replace them with healthy, natural foods, such as fruits and vegetables.
- *Pray about your feelings.* Ask God to guide you, help you, lift your spirits.

Affirmations for the Day

God is showing me the way now.
God is love and loves me completely.
God brings joy, energy, and vitality to me.
VMP

Why must I go on suffering....
Psalm 43:2

Letting Go of Hostility

This is a perfect time of year for letting go of anger, hostility, and past hurts. One woman, writing to an advice columnist, said that members of her family did that and experienced the most joyous holiday season ever. "I want to shout from the rooftops," she declared.

She explained that the couple had six children. The parents divorced and then fifteen years later they got married again—to other people. Over the years there was great division, hostility, and anger over the divorce and remarriages. Much of that anger was directed toward the father and his second wife.

Then when the father had a heart attack and nearly died, the entire family was shocked into thinking differently. On Thanksgiving of that year, the father and his second wife invited all the children, their spouses, the grandchildren *and* his first wife and her husband to their home for Thanksgiving dinner.

The time together was so pleasant and healing that, in turn, the mother and her second husband invited everyone to join them at their home for Christmas.

"What a wonderful time we had. No one was uncomfortable, no angry words were exchanged—just lots of love. The feeling was indescribable," the woman reported. Now, the entire family is looking forward to continuing a new holiday tradition.

Perhaps this is the time for all of us to consider letting go of past hurts, angers, and hostilities. This may be the time to open up our hearts to peace, harmony, and goodwill. "Why must I go on suffering?" cries the psalmist.

Thought for the Day

Reconciliation is not weakness or cowardice.
It demands courage, nobility, generosity,
sometimes heroism,
an overcoming of oneself
rather than one's adversary.
Pope Paul VI

He...fills the hungry with good things.
Psalm 107:9

Fasting Is Not Just for Monks

Many Christians feel that fasting is only for monks and other spiritual leaders. Yet Scripture recommends that all of us skip a meal or several meals from time to time. It is worth noting that Jesus said "When (not if) you fast..." (Matthew 6:16). So, fasting is not just for monks. The holidays, when most people tend to overeat, are a good time to think about these benefits of fasting:

- *Fasting is healthy*. Being overweight is a major medical concern in North America. Fasting is one way to reduce caloric intake for a day. By starting during the holidays, perhaps we can eventually practice a fast day once a week.
- *Fasting is good for self-discipline*. We deny ourselves very little. It is a good spiritual discipline to skip a meal using that time for prayer or some good work.
- *Fasting makes us more appreciative of food and drink*. When we don't eat for a day or two or three, the next meal becomes absolutely delightful and delicious.
- *Fasting sensitizes us to world hunger*. Eating only one meal a day will make us hungry, tired, perhaps irritable. Use a fast day to consider what it must feel like to live in a place where there is no regular food supply and where people go days, even weeks, without a meal.
- *Fasting is good for the soul*. Mystics of all ages have recommended fasting as an aid for spiritual experiences. God honors serious self-denial. Today's psalm reminds us that God "fills the hungry with good things."

-------- *Thought for the Day* --------

It is almost certain
that excess in eating
is the cause of almost all the diseases
of the body,
but its effects on the soul
are even more disastrous.
Saint Alphonsus Liguori

The LORD protects the helpless.
Psalm 116:6

Organizing to Make a Difference

Life changed dramatically and rapidly for one family when the thirty-nine-year-old father died of pneumonia. His wife and four small children faced a large mortgage and no insurance.

Fortunately, the bank officials were compassionate. They told the woman that the bank would not foreclose if she could pay the interest on the loan. However, even the monthly interest was more than the woman could handle. The very real prospect of being homeless with four children brought terror into the mother's heart.

Learning of her problem, a man shared the information with others in his small Catholic parish. They organized and began raising the necessary money through bake sales, raffles, and contributions. Each month someone from the parish would quietly press the precise amount of interest money into the mother's hands. After taking it to the bank, the woman and her children would breathe a sigh of relief because they were secure for another month.

The parishioners continued to meet the interest payments for four years until the widow's youngest child began school, allowing the mother to work during the day. In the following years, the mother, who kept track of the contributions, voluntarily repaid the debt to the parish.

Sometimes one person can't do it all. But just because we can't do it alone does not preclude some compassionate response. There are times when many hands are necessary to meet a need. When people band together they can accomplish a large task. In the process, they make real the words of the psalmist, "The Lord protects the helpless."

Thought for the Day

We are never more like God
than when we give.
Charles Swindoll

Set me free from my distress.
Psalm 142:7

Being God's Agents of Help

Today's psalm reading is a prayer asking God to "set me free from my distress." Divine intervention often comes through human response.

On Christmas Eve morning, 1991, Bishop Ricardo Ramirez, of the Roman Catholic Diocese of Las Cruces, New Mexico, had just completed a hospital visit. As he was leaving the hospital, the bishop saw a couple and a child hobbling along the road. It was very cold and the man looked sick.

The family asked Bishop Ramirez how far it was to El Paso, Texas. The bishop told them it was thirty miles. The family had no transportation and did not know anyone in the area, so they began walking. Although Bishop Ramirez was headed in the opposite direction, he could not let the family walk thirty miles so he offered to drive them.

On the drive, the bishop learned that the family had recently arrived in the United States from Mexico and were not prepared for the cold winter months. They had no warm clothing and their "home" was an old RV camper: tiny, with one room, one small bed, a very small stove, and no bathroom.

The bishop knew the family had no money so he gave them all he had in his wallet: twenty-five dollars. He promised to return the next day, Christmas, with additional gifts. Returning to his residence, the bishop collected items that had been given to him as Christmas gifts, including a poinsettia, some blankets, and food. On Christmas day he delivered them to this "holy family" and returned home. Upon arrival he saw that a gift had been delivered for him. He opened it and found himself holding a check for twenty-five dollars.

As we experience the season of Advent, let us be sensitive and open to others who may be praying, "Set me free from my distress." Like the bishop, let us be God's answer to their prayer.

Thought for the Day

Let your love be strong and constant,
neither giving in to fear
nor cowering at hard work.
Let us love affectionately,
discreetly,
intensely.

Saint Bernard of Clairvaux

I praise the LORD, because he guides me.
Psalm 16:7

Responding to God's Guidance

A woman tells of being stranded in the Kansas City airport on Christmas Eve. Due to a severe ice and snowstorm, flight after flight had been canceled. Even though she had her name on several standby lists, she knew there was no chance of leaving Kansas City that day. Disappointment filled her heart.

All around her passengers were frustrated and angry. A young couple holding their bags stared straight ahead without speaking to each other. An older couple argued. Several children cried. Even though it was Christmas Eve, no one seemed happy.

As she looked around, the woman saw a box filled with cookies she made the day before. She opened it and ate one. Then the woman offered a cookie to the stranger beside her. He took one and thanked her sincerely. Inspired by his response, the woman kept offering her cookies to various men, women, and children in the airport waiting area. When the box was empty, she returned to her seat. Soon a young girl, about six years old, handed her a small package wrapped in gold and red paper. "Thank you for the cookies. This is a gift for you," she said and ran back to her parents. Slipping the wrap off the box and lifting the lid, the woman saw that her gift was a delicate silver necklace with a small quartz crystal hanging in the center. She put it on and waved a "thank you" to the family. Moments later they left on one of the few flights departing.

Within minutes there was a complete transformation in the airport waiting area. Children who were crying started playing, couples began to smile at each other, and strangers started speaking with one another. The world warmed because a woman let herself respond to God's gentle guidance.

The next time you're in an awkward or difficult situation, ask yourself, *What does God want me to do?* And then, like the woman stranded in an airport, respond to God's guidance.

Thought for the Day

I wake up in the morning
and whichever way God turns my feet, I go.
Pearl Bailey

Let us be happy, let us celebrate!
Psalm 118:24

The Reason for the Season

Although Advent is a joyous season for most people, one December was an ominous month for Debbie, a young mother and wife. She and her husband walked out of a neurologist's office shaken and saddened. For three months she had suffered from perplexing symptoms. An MRI scan of her brain revealed that Debbie had a tumor. The splendor of December was shattered by that information.

On the way home Debbie and her husband picked up their three-year-old daughter at a neighbor's house. Debbie shared the diagnosis with her neighbor, Lauren. Other family and friends were anxiously awaiting the test results so Debbie and her husband spent the afternoon making phone calls.

Meanwhile, her neighbor, Lauren, was busy organizing a "task force" of six women from the neighborhood. Quietly and steadily, the needs of Debbie's family were met: meals were brought in, laundry was done, childcare was provided, housekeeping was accomplished, family Christmas gifts were wrapped, hospitality was extended to out-of-town family flying in for the surgery. Most importantly, a prayer vigil was held the night before Debbie's operation.

Looking back, Debbie says that her neighbors' gifts of caring, love, and prayerful support were the most treasured of all the gifts received that Christmas.

The reason for the season is to show our love and to get closer to God. When that happens we fulfill the psalmist's words: "Let us be happy, let us celebrate!"

Thought for the Day

Be kind because,
although kindness is not by a long shot
the same thing as holiness,
kindness is one of the doors
that holiness enters the world through,
enters us through—not just gently
kind but sometimes fiercely kind.

Frederick Buechner

You are my king and my God;
you give victory to your people.
Psalm 44:4

Exercising Confidence in God

The story is told of a man migrating on foot west across the United States in the dead of winter. When he came to the bank of the Mississippi River, the man was afraid to cross on the ice because he did not know how thick it was.

However, night was beginning to fall and he had to reach the other side. So he dropped down on his hands and knees and began to crawl carefully across the ice with his weight widely distributed.

As he reached the middle of the river, he suddenly heard singing behind him in the gathering dusk. He turned his head and saw four horses pulling a wagon loaded with coal. The driver was rapidly moving across the ice with that heavy load. He was singing his heart out because he knew that the ice was still two feet thick.

Some people crawl through life on their hands and knees in fear and trembling. Others carry heavy loads and still sing in the dark. The difference between the two is confidence in God. Those whose faith in God is deep and abiding can carry heavy loads and sing in the dark.

Thought for the Day

God wants us to be victors, not victims;
to grow, not grovel;
to soar, not sink;
to overcome, not be overwhelmed.
William Arthur Ward

Leave your troubles with the LORD,
and he will defend you.
Psalm 55:22

Overcoming Suffering

Although the world is filled with suffering, it is also filled with people who have overcome their suffering. Comedian Tom Dreesen is one example.

Tom was born into a family of nine children on Chicago's south side. The family lived in poverty. "Five of us slept in one bed," Dreesen recalls. "We had no bathtub, no shower, no hot water, in a rat-infested, roach-infested hut. That's not some Charles Dickens story; it's the truth," he declares.

In addition, Tom's father was an alcoholic and his mother worked at minimum wage in a nearby bar. The children went to school with holes in their shoes and wearing worn-out, used clothing. "My sister wore the same dress every day, washing it out, drying it out, over and over. It was tough," he says.

In spite of such a harsh background filled with poverty and suffering, Tom has emerged as a popular and highly acclaimed comic. The reality of poverty and suffering gave way to a greater reality: the power given all of us by God to overcome our circumstances. So let us act on the advice of the psalm: "Leave your troubles with the Lord and he will defend you."

Affirmations for the Day

I am peaceful and strong
for I know God's presence abides within me.
I am joyful and secure
for I know God's purpose is working in my life.
I am revitalized and triumphant
for I know God's power flows through me.
VMP

The LORD Almighty is with us.
Psalm 46:11

Transforming Pain Into Power

It was 1818, in France, and Louis, a boy of nine, sat in his father's workshop. The father was a harness-maker, and Louis loved to watch him work with the leather. "Someday, Father," said Louis, "I want to be a harness-maker just like you."

"Why not start now?" suggested the father. He took a piece of leather, drew a design on it, and said, "Now, my Son, take the hole puncher and a hammer and follow this design but be careful you don't hit your hand."

Excited, the boy began to work, but when he hit the hole puncher, it flew out of his hand and pierced his eye. He lost sight in the eye immediately. Later, the sight in his remaining eye failed as well, and Louis became totally blind.

A few years later, Louis was sitting in the yard when a friend handed him a pine cone. As he ran his sensitive fingers over the cone, an idea came to him. Louis became intrigued with the idea of developing an alphabet of raised dots on paper so that the blind could feel (read) and interpret what was written.

In this way Louis Braille opened up a whole new world for the blind. He is one example of an individual who transformed his pain into power. Perhaps you can be another who transforms pain into power and opens doors of opportunity to others.

Affirmations for the Day

The God who dwells within
makes me creative
and increases my ability
to face challenges.
The God who dwells within
helps me rise above doubt and indecision.
The God who dwells within
blesses me
as I allow this love
to flow freely within me.
VMP

Guide me in the everlasting way.
Psalm 139:24

The Fool's Gold in Our Lives

The story is told about the discovery of a skeleton in the Yukon, a Canadian territory. Found beside a dirt road, it is believed that the skeleton is that of a gold-rush miner.

Clutched in his hand was a large leather bag filled with gold. Evidently he was headed back to town after striking it rich. The gold in the bag was assayed and found to be chalcopyrite, commonly known as fool's gold. What a great disappointment for that miner had he lived!

What fools' gold are we clinging to?

- Is our fool's gold the desire for great wealth?
- Is our fool's gold the desire for fame?
- Is our fool's gold the desire for success?

Of course, there is nothing wrong with wealth, fame, and great success. We err, however, in letting those things define us. Let us exercise caution in our living and be certain we are not clinging to fool's gold.

Thought for the Day

The most important thing in life
is to live your life
for something more important
than your life.
William James

I thank you, L*ORD*, *with all my heart.*
Psalm 138:1

Banish the Winter Blues

Many people experience a letdown—seasonal depression—after Christmas. Here are some practical suggestions for banishing the winter blues and adding a little sunshine to daily life.

- *Catch up on correspondence.* Use a winter morning or afternoon to write all those letters you have been intending to write. Be sure to state something encouraging. The receiver will be delighted and your spirits will be lifted for expressing positive thoughts.
- *Complete a project.* Winter is an ideal time to start and finish a project that has been neglected. Polish your silverware, clean the basement, reorganize your chest of drawers.
- *Spruce up your daily menu.* If you are getting tired of eating the same foods, visit a library and check out a few cookbooks. Read them carefully selecting some new recipes. Try them out.
- *Telephone a friend or relative.* Once a year and always in the winter, I phone a friend with whom I attended university over twenty years ago. We have not seen each other since school days. Yet our yearly phone conversation brightens my day considerably.
- *Visit a nursery.* Whether you like indoor or outdoor plants, a visit to a nursery in the winter is bound to lift spirits. Being surrounded by colorful, living plants is a good remedy for feeling blue. Buy a new houseplant or select some seeds to plant in the spring.
- *Reflect on God's goodness.* Reflect on the last few months, and recall the many blessings that have come your way. Like the psalmist, take a moment to praise God for each blessing saying, "I thank you, Lord, with all my heart."

-------- Thought for the Day --------

We ought to praise God
even when we do not feel like it.
Praising him
takes away the blues
and restores us to normal.
Harold Lindsell

I have not disobeyed your commands.
Psalm 119:110

What Rules Do I Live By?

The ending of one year and the emergence of a new one is an ideal time to conduct an examination of conscience. Ask yourself, *What rules did I live by this past year?*

- Did I live by the golden rule: do unto others as I would have them do unto me?
- Did I live by the silver rule: do not do unto others what I would not have them do unto me?
- Did I live by the bronze rule: repay kindness with kindness or an eye for an eye?
- Did I live by the iron rule: do unto others as I like before they do it to me?
- Did I live by the tin rule: show favoritism to those who are socially higher and more important but intimidate and abuse those who are socially lower and less important?

If you feel you have come up short, quickly and quietly ask for God's forgiveness and the strength to do better in the new year. If you feel you did well during the previous year, ask for God's guidance and strength to continue growing in that pattern throughout a new year.

Thought for the Day

We have committed the golden rule to memory;
let us now commit it to life.
Edwin Markham

About the Author

Victor M. Parachin studied at the University of Toronto School of Theology where he received a Master of Divinity degree. He worked as a reporter, feature writer, and editor at *The Catholic Register* (Toronto). Currently, he is a freelance writer and author of *The Lord Is My Shepherd: A Psalm for the Grieving; Our Father: A Prayer for the Grieving; Daily Strength for Daily Needs: One Year of Biblical Inspiration*. Parachin is married and has three children.